How To Analyze People, Emotional Intelligence (EQ)
& Manipulation Protection
(2 in 1)

The Truth About Dark Psychology + Speed Reading, Body Language, NLP & Persuasion Strategies

Written By:
U.P.P

Unlimited Potential Publications

Manipulation & Dark Psychology Protection Blueprint:

The Truth About Dark Persuasion, NLP, Body Language & How To Analyze People Techniques & How You Can Protect Against Them

Written By:
U.P.P.

Unlimited Potential Publications

TABLE of CONTENTS

Introduction

Have you ever walked out of a shop with something you didn't really want? Maybe you only realized it later, but still... Have you ever looked back on a vote you cast, even years later and thought, "That wasn't really wise at all!" Or have you ever done something, at work for example, that turned out to be against your own interests? Well, you are not alone!

More and more, especially with the advent of social media, people are finding out far too late that they are being manipulated constantly. The Cambridge Analytica case is a flagrant example of how it is possible to change enough people's minds long enough (two days before the voting in this case) to get the election results you want. Whichever side you are on the vote in question, what interests us is the idea, now proven, that manipulation exists, it is being used, and we need to defend ourselves from it.

In fact, manipulation is one of the oldest psychological practices in the world. You see, while Sigmund Freud was creating that basis of psychoanalysis, and tried to free people from mental problems, at that very time someone else, Pavlov, was teaching the world that *mind manipulation and conditioning is real, easy, and feasible!*

How many ads have you seen in your life? Well, I'll leave the exact math to you, but only on TV, we are exposed to 40,000 ads a year! This is according to data found by the *Pediatrics*, Dec. 2006, in a study called 'Children, Adolescents, and Advertising' written by the American Academy of Pediatrics. And this is for children, adults may well be exposed to more!

Advertising is a $250 billion a year industry; surely they would not spend this money year on year if they didn't get something in return... And they do! On average, they get almost 10 times as much back...

"But what is advertising, and where does advertising end," you may ask? Good question... Now experts talk of *"marketing"* and *"targeting"*. I personally feel insulted at least, threatened even to know that for business I am a "target". But your question goes deeper, doesn't it?

The line between what is at least "explicit" advertising and "covert" advertising has been blurred for decades now. A star wearing a particular brand of sneakers is most likely advertising. Have you not noticed how rappers and R&B always put their sneakers in clear view? Was James Dean publicizing cigarette smoking? Did Chanel make money out of Marilyn Monroe's famous statement that she only wore #5 in bed?

Sometimes these people don't even know that they are conditioning your mind, selling a product. For example, I suspect James Dean was unaware of the fact that he made cigarettes so cool that a whole generation felt "nerdy" or "uncool" unless they smoked... And surely, he was not "the only part of the mind conditioning machine". Even medical doctors were fooled into promoting what is in fact "rolled up poison" ... But this again shows how it is possible to condition a whole generation.

But once we go past the explicit/covert line, is there more? I bet there is. Secret services have been working mind conditioning for decades. The famous case of MK Ultra, the officially acknowledged mind control program of the CIA experimented on citizens from 1953 to 1973 (officially...) In this time, they managed to experiment all sorts of mind control techniques, including using heavy drugs, and they did it on unwitting US and Canadian citizens... Yes, they experimented on people without them even knowing about it (which is very unethical).

In serious cases, **mind manipulation leads to becoming dysfunctional or totally nonfunctional in society.** People who have been serious victims often lose their job, social standing, even friends! Now, these are critical cases, but to a small extent, any level of mind manipulation interferes with your proficiency at work, with your social life, and even with your relationships.

Ok, now I see you are getting worried. I just wanted to show you how *real, widespread, multifaceted, and well documented mind manipulation is,* and that it has many levels. But of course, **I am here to give you a solution to mind manipulation!**

Let me tell you: everybody is under *some level of mind manipulation.* And in my professional life, I have even had to work on freeing people from mind conditioning. Mind conditioning is a more serious case than mind manipulation. It too happens at many levels and in many forms, but it's like addiction. You have to do something, but you don't understand why.

The good news is that **stopping mind control on you means taking control of your life.** And it is even more effective if you take family and/or friends with you on this liberating journey!

But for most readers, I suppose the main worry will be a low to medium level of mind manipulation. That is very common nowadays. But how can you get out of it?

Well, first of all you need to **know and recognize mind manipulation channels and techniques.** And you will! Just read on and in the very first few chapters of this book you will find an in-depth, detailed but easily explained analysis of all these. We will also do it in a practical way, with exercises. And I apologize in advance if, even at the early stages of "analysis" I won't resist giving some solutions.

We will of course also look at many **techniques to protect yourself from mind manipulation, and even to deprogram your mind.** The mind, you see, can be wired or unwired to a certain response. Put in the simplest possible way, mind manipulation wires your mind so that it gives a specific response. A whole mental disorder has been "invented and inflicted on people" *compulsive buying disorder,* which is how psychologists refer to "shopaholics".

In the same way as you can unwire your mind from seeking a solution in alcohol or drugs, so can you for other manipulations. But of course, it also means changing your life habits... You won't cure an alcoholic by getting him or her to work in a wine bar (even worse a wine cellar).

I know that changing habits is always met with, "Mmmm, not sure I want to change my life; I'm quite comfortable with it..." But I promise you that it will actually be fun. Most of the mind manipulation channels, activities and outlets are actually boring, and you can replace them with something far better. We will look at that too.

And we will even look at serious cases, of course. But in all this, I promise you that we will keep the tone light, but I will always be professional. And we will go through many concepts and solutions, and quick tricks to protect yourself and also many easy, short but when possible fun exercises too.

So, think about it for a second. Do you really want to continue being a victim of manipulation? Every day under mind manipulation is a day you miss out on freedom and real life. And trust me, life is so much better without it! In fact, **taking action against low-level and high-level mind manipulation means taking back control over your life!**

The sooner you start, the sooner you will actually be free. And – trust me – your social, personal, romantic, and professional life will be so much better! You will even *sleep better!*

And let me tell you what the first step to fight mind manipulation is: decide to get out of it… So now you do have the choice: you can choose to read on and soon be free… Will you?

If you now feel like a cog in an inhumane machine, reading this book is like opening a door to a garden of freedom, the garden of your real self and real potential… And I'd like to show you how to open this door, get rid of the old manipulated "cog life" and bloom as you are meant to…

Shall we start now?

Chapter 1 – Mind Control Through the Ages

I want to tell you a story. A story that is not told. Actually, it is the same story you learn at school, but from another perspective... Let me take it from an artistic point of view – why not? Maybe at school you studied art history, or you just like visiting art galleries, museums, and beautiful architectural buildings like churches...

Mind Manipulation in Rome (Classical and Later)

Walk into an old church, like those you find at every street corner in Europe. Ok, what do you see? You will say, "I can see beautiful columns, a great decorative altar, and lots of statues, paintings and art on the walls." I agree, that's what you see, but you can see more... Look at those paintings, why do you think so much time, effort, talent, and money was spent on them? They are not just there to decorate the place...

They are there to tell stories to people. Often people who could not read, and often stories they could not fully understand. True, our culture has changed and things that were clear once, are now harder to understand. But the deep meaning of many paintings, like Michelangelo's fresco on the Sistine Chapel's ceiling, in the Vatican, Rome is still debated by top academics and art historians all over the world. Do you think the average farmer would really understand the deep meanings of such art?

But did it matter though that the peasant understood the narrative and deeper meaning of those stories? No, it didn't. Exactly like it does not matter if you follow an ad on TV or you turn to something else... **It's the impression that matters.**

Some architectural styles like Baroque were literally invented to manipulate the minds of common people. It was literally devised to give an impression of grandeur, opulence, but also of strength and control, over nature and over society. So, if you lived in Rome or Sicily in the Seventeenth Century, it did not matter if you understood all the symbolism etc. of those impressive buildings... What mattered was that you walked away convinced that the Roman Catholic Church, not the reformed church, was in charge, over you and over nature.

Think about it, most of what remains in history is the product of mind manipulation attempts. The Colosseum, not to go too far, but to step 15 centuries back in history, was a colossal (excuse me the pun) but **very conscious attempt at controlling people's minds and behavior.**

It is well known that the Roman elite paid for and offered grueling and violent shows to "the people" (by which we mean everybody, not just citizens) in order to control them. You see, if you are angry and you project your anger against a gladiator, or someone being mauled and eaten alive by lions, well, then you walk away "satisfied" – *and you won't release that anger against the "government", the emperor, and the imperial institutions.*

This was done with purpose and very consciously, both by the Pope (in the first case) and by all emperors and the aristocracy (the ruling class) of Rome. And we can already get one key point: *mind manipulation has been consistently and regularly used throughout history, even on a massive scale.*

"When did mind manipulation start," is a common question. The answer is that we don't know exactly, but we can see traces of it in ancient civilizations. Kings being depicted as superior, even "superhumans" is a sign of it. For sure by the Golden Age of Rome, it was in full swing, and used on a colossal scale.

The Birth of Scientific Mind Manipulation in the Nineteenth Century

However, *mind manipulation in ancient times was rational, effective, and even well designed but not "scientific".* The Romans understood human behavior, and they acted upon it to get the desired reaction from people. In their history, causing wars, prompting the enemy to attack first etc. were common and well devised tactics. In fact, even nowadays we use the Latin (Roman) phrase *"casus belli"* (a reason for war); they caused the reason, then blamed their enemies for starting the war... And we still do it!

But what I was saying is that we cannot call it "scientific" for two reasons: at the time science as we know it technically did not exist; it was not so much based on data and analysis, more on "reason and intuition". At least as far as we know. *Modern mind manipulation instead is scientific.* And that makes it even worse because:

- *It is more effective (powerful).*

- *It is more hidden, less detectable and more "obscure".*

It is, in a few words, much more subtle, but also much more pervasive... We will see very soon how it works... You need to know it to avoid it, of course. But when did it become scientific then?

It was somewhere towards the end of the Nineteenth Century that the full scientific grounds of mind manipulation were laid. But, like with all scientific advancements, or at least most, there was "something in the air already" before the actual breakthrough was made.

In our case, what was "in the air was smog" ... Are you puzzled? I am trying to... You see, during the Industrial Revolution, mass production was invented and developed in England and the UK. London is filled with smog, but the market is filled with products...

Unlike what was happening before, these products had to be placed. In a society where little changes for generations, like a typical pre-industrial society, people know what they need, and they buy what they have known to work for them.

But if you are producing more, and new things, you need to find a way to convince them that they need your product. You see the problem? So, Victorian England saw the birth of advertising...

Advertising is, at its most honest and explicit level, quite acceptable. It can be seen as "information". But look at where it has gone, and in many cases the only actual information you get is the name of the product and, in some cases, that quick sentence at the end warning you about side effects!

Like with many things we will see in this book, **the line between "explicit and honest" to "hidden and dishonest"** gets blurred and then problems start. At first, advertisements were basic drawings of the product with name and price. Then the motto came, and then more and more sophisticated ways of "convincing you to buy" came about…

In Victorian times, from what I have studied, advertising remained mostly honest, if at times pushy. It was still on the side of "informing and trying to convince" rather than "manipulating". But soon things changed.

It was in fact towards the end of the Victorian Era (1837 – 1901) that two "scientists of the mind" were making great discoveries… And we have met them already: the Austrian **Sigmund Freud**, the "Father of Psychoanalysis" as everybody calls him and the Russian **Ivan Pavlov**, the "Father of Behaviorism", as he is called, but also the "father of mind control" as he is called behind closed doors.

We will come back to Freud in more detail in the next chapter because it is thanks to some of his studies, especially on **the subconscious** that on the one hand, mind control and manipulation have become more effective and powerful, on the other hand, **understanding how the subconscious works leads us to the solution to mind manipulation and control.**

Behaviorism – The Scientific Basis of Mind Manipulation

As for **Behaviorism**, we need to talk about it right now. **Behaviorism is at the core of all mind manipulation and mind control techniques.** Pavlov was a psychologist and he even won the Nobel Prize for his work. He did research in involuntary reflex actions but especially in **conditioning**.

Famous is his experiment of the dog and the bell. He would ring a bell every time he would give the dog some food. When we say, "Pavlov's dog," however, we mean "dogs" because he used more than 40, Bierka, Beck, Ika, Joy – ok, I'm not going to list them all… The dogs would salivate every time they saw the food. And they ended up associating the bell with food. Pavlov then stopped giving them food, and you know what? The dogs kept salivating every time they heard the bell even without food.

This method is at the basis of modern dog training, but also of much education for Humans, where we associate academic success with pleasure and failure with pain (emotional, but in the past physical too…) and it is also behind much of our behavior even when at work…

Watson and Rayner: The Development of Mind Conditioning – A Tribute to Little Albert

To be honest, it was **John B. Watson, another behaviorist who discovered the full power of fear in mind conditioning.** The experiments he carried out with his graduate student **Rosalie Rayner** just before 1920 were cruel to start with. He used a child, a baby, whose name will go down in history as the first Human martyr of mind conditioning: **Little Albert.**

They gave Little Albert some things he had never seen, like a rat, a monkey, a mask etc. They called these **stimuli** (mark this word, we'll use it a lot). The baby was fine with all of them. Then, every time poor

Little Albert touched the rat, they produced a very scary and upsetting noise. No need to say that when they showed the rat, even without the noise, to Little Albert again, he was frightened... Basically they caused a phobia in a child in the name of science...

The fact is that this system then became the core of education all over the world, and physical punishment, which already was in use, now had a "scientific justification". Ok, one of the sinister consequences of the "Little Albert Experiment" was many aching knuckles and even buttocks...

The other, however, is that *mind conditioning and mind manipulation started to refine the use of reward and punishment associated with a stimulus to become more and more powerful and effective.* If you have seen *Clockwise Orange* by Stanley Kubrick, you may think that it was all fiction...

No... What you see in the film is actually very mild compared to what mind control experiments would become in about three to four decades from where we left our story, and we'll get there soon... in 1920 Watson and Rayner published their study...

Mind Manipulation of the Masses: Mussolini and Hitler

In 1922 another event showed the power of mind control, not on a baby, not on an individual, but on a whole country: Mussolini rose to power. What? Mussolini? Yes, Mussolini is arguably the most dangerous and imitated dictator in modern times, more than Hitler in some respects. He was not as cruel, but he worked out one thing: *control the most modern means of communication and you can get a whole country to do as you wish.*

This happened near the time of the peak of technological progress (1930 ca. it has been slowing down ever since), and this is the formula all dictators and wannabe tyrants have used since. Mussolini, thanks to Marconi, understood the power of the radio, took control of it, and used it to:

- *Convince enough people to back him up on the way to power.*

- *Stop any form of dissent and create a false perception of reality once in power.*

Eleven years later Hitler did exactly the same, just with a more modern communication system: the television...

So, we went into World War II, the most horrible conflict in the history of the whole world because two people, very keen on behaviorism – both of them – managed to control the instruments necessary to manipulate the minds of entire populations...

Mind Manipulation Experiments in Nazi Concentration Camps

During this horrible war, the Nazis carried out mind control experiments in Auschwitz and Dachau concentration camps. The experiments were first realized in Auschwitz then repeated for confirmation in Dachau. No need to say that they were horrible and unethical; the idea was to reduce people to animals, machines, or slaves.

They used drugs, in particular peyote, and of course, they did not go down the "positive conditioning" route, but the negative one, using fear and torture to control people's minds and bend (actually annihilate) their will. Luckily their experiments concluded that "mescaline was too unreliable" for mind control.

What happened, however, as Professor David Salinas Flores presents in *SM Physical Medicine and Rehabilitation,* Dec 28, 2018, 'Mind Control: from Nazis to DAPRA', a review of how a particular time in the history of mind control, where the transition from Nazi to CIA led experiments took place – what happened, I was saying, is that the CIA got hold of the papers written by Dr Kurt Plönter, the SS physician that led the experiments.

And no, they did not sleep on them. But we will come to the CIA in a minute, as they are the "big experimenters" when it comes to the (at the time) hidden history of mind control and manipulation, I mean, the one they really tried to conceal...

The 1950s: Hollywood and Manipulative Commercials

But there is the other thread in our story: that mind control which occurs under everybody's eyes... So, what happened after WWII? So far, we have seen that first it was paintings and maybe hymns, then the radio, then television. In the 50s the big medium of communication was the "moving pictures" or the cinema.

During the 1950s we saw Hollywood rise to its maximum splendor, promoting, on the one side, the great Hollywood stars we remember with fondness still nowadays. On the other, it also promoted a world view; it was, quite clearly, trying to manipulate the masses.

The idea that you need to fight a faraway enemy, the American dream, the idea that the middle-class household and life was the only possible pursuit for average people... All these were promoted... You see, selling a dream and selling a nightmare at the same time is a way of manipulating minds. So, Hollywood told us that "out there" there was a horrible and cruel enemy, and when that enemy disappeared (the end of the USSR), they just replaced it with others.

They also depicted "internal enemies": Native Americans in Western movies and then – well how many Black villains can you see in movies? Far too many.

On the other side, the happy family, mostly rural or suburban, with traditional values, with a severe but benign father who goes out to work and a mother who stays at home and whose only ambition is to clean the kitchen was presented as a dream...

They do adapt dreams and nightmares, don't worry. But they will still keep you in this *"punishment / reward" pattern, which is at the core of Behaviorism and mind control.* You see, movies, radio programs, tv shows etc., are all *stimuli*.

As are advertisements! Look at the now classical ads of the 1950s and you will see that they too are telling this Hollywood story, but they add an element: you need to *buy* to be happy. So, the wife is not so happy about cleaning the kitchen, but "having the new vacuum cleaner to clean it" ...
A massive operation of mind manipulation started in the 1950s: it was aimed to turn people into consumers, and they succeeded, giving birth to that phenomenon that is consumerism, and we now are at a pathological stage of this "collective syndrome".

You see how it took time, yes, but with insistence, while before you would look for happiness in peace, relationships, etc., we now look for it primarily in gadgets and social media interactions. Not only, in most cases (in quite a few yes, however), but in the vast majority of people far too much anyway. That all started in the 50s

There is a famous and interesting episode here. That was the time when the USA was becoming "urban and modern" and ready-made products were starting to flood the market. You see, before that time, you would cook everything from the base ingredients. Betty Crocker Cake Mixes came on the market. It was perfect: you just needed to mix it and the dough was ready... But no one liked it. It was meant to be a great success... But it wasn't.

So, what was the problem? They did what was at those times a very modern market research and they found out that women wanted to have modern conveniences, but they still wanted to see themselves as "angels of the hearth", as "traditional" and capable of cooking... So, they just added a hand with two eggs to the commercial, and the slogan "Betty Crocker Cake Mixes bring you that Special Homemade Goodness" and "Because you add the eggs yourself." And it was a huge success.

Thing is, they found a weak spot in the psychology of a group of people which is that they wanted to fool themselves, because the whole story that you buy a mix and then buy eggs and that it's a "homemade" cake is hardly believable, is it? But this shows how subtle mind control was becoming...

The CIA's Declassified Mind Control Program: Project Bluebird and MKUltra

But the 50s did not hold back on the occult experiments on mind control either. Actually, they reached a peak. In this decade the CIA launched Project *Bluebird* in 1951, and the already mentioned *MKUltra* in 1953. Do you remember the SS Doctor who experimented in concentration camps? Well apparently, he even received help from the West, yes, from their sworn enemies, and his studies ended up becoming the groundwork for MKUltra.

And if what they did does not make good and easy reading: they experimented *hallucinogenic drugs like LSD on behavior modification* (which is an established byword for mind manipulation). And the numbers read are frightening:

- Scientists from 80 worldwide renowned institution
- 12 hospitals
- 44 schools
- 149 sub-projects

All these were being hidden from the people and were studying various aspects of mind control techniques. And these included:

- **Controlling brain activity;** they studied how you can "wire and rewire" the brain by promoting and discouraging the formation of neurons with positive and negative stimuli.

- **Mind torture;** they exposed people to horrible stimuli, in order to break their mind, when under the effects of LSD. They caused permanent damage to people's minds, and in 1963 they also used LSD on children (!!!) with mental problems, at times keeping them under the effects of LSD for months! This is a clear crime against Humanity, but it shows how far they were ready to go to pursue mind manipulation.

- **Extortion;** they used mapping of the brain with nanobots and managed to extract information that patients were keeping to themselves, and then forced them to do what they ordered them to do under blackmail.

As you can see, they used very advanced technology, like implants, nanobots, microchips and what is known as cerebral internet (a network of chips and nanobots within the brain). It sounds like science fiction; it is all recorded, documented and now declassified.

Take a long breath, take a pause... I understand that finding out about these appalling experiments can be disturbing... But there is worse...

The Weaponization of Mind Control Techniques and Technology

These experiments allegedly stopped in 1964, but the usually well informed say that of course they closed a program to open a new one, also because MKUltra was starting to "leak" to the press and — above all – to the People anyway...

But what we know for sure is that these experiments did not remain such: the results were then transferred to DAPRA, or Defense Advanced Research Project Agency, which developed actual weapons. Nowadays, the UN itself is investigating actual **weapons of mind control** in use in the USA.

These are called "non-lethal weapons" and they are not all aimed at mind manipulation, but some are, in particular **V2K (Voice to Skull).** This is no "conspiracy theory" as there have been court cases (more than 300) about its use on citizens, and all ended with compensation being imposed by the court for its use. And of course, the UN is investigating it. But what is more, the US Defense Dept openly admits its existence and use.

There is a letter from the Department of the Army, United States Intelligence and Security Command, Dec 13 2006, in response to a subject freedom of information request which clearly states that this is in use in the USA, details its effects on victims, causing "aural bioeffects" ... This means that people "hear voices" that don't actually exist.

They use very "radiofrequency directed energy" (radio waves) to make people hear and see things that do not exist. They basically induce hallucinations in people's minds. And of course the victims, called "targeted individuals" (or TI's) have no idea what is going on, and in many cases they see it as a form of torture...

The letter now regards the information on this weapon of mind manipulation "declassified" but only with information up to 17 February 1998.

Who knows what happened next?

Take another deep breath, take another pause. This is the worst use of mind manipulation we officially know of... But the levels we have gotten to are chilling.

The Rise of Social Media and Mind Manipulation

Now back to the more "overt" side of our story. Mind control and mass manipulation – not the experiments on a few but the daily practice of the media...

Let's recap again, from paintings and songs to the radio, television and movies, and with the new "variant" in it, *advertising*, which is what *has made mind manipulation immediately profitable.* What has changed since the 1950s?

The most glaring difference is that now we have the internet and social media. And it is very topical now to talk about how social media are manipulating our minds. In fact, we will dedicate a whole chapter to them. Because *social media* have some very weird characteristics:

- *They isolate you from others:* this makes you more vulnerable to mind manipulation.

- *They are very quick and full of stimuli (with quick rewards like thumbs up or little hearts etc.)* Any psychologist can see that they are designed along behaviorist lines and that they are clearly designed to manipulate your mind.

- *They are available all day long now.* This is really dangerous. We moved from being exposed to mind conditioning a few times during the week, to every night, to a few hours a day, to all day and all week, from when we wake up to when we fall asleep.

And this leads us to what scientists call "the state of the art", which means "how things are at the moment". On the one hand, hidden (but then declassified) *studies on mind manipulation have used the most atrocious and inhumane techniques possible.* They have been kept hidden from view, and applied against people's will. Ok, it's hard to get someone's consent to be mentally manipulated, but it does not matter. It is unethical to experiment without consent, even more to cause damage to people without consent, even more to torture people, anyway.

On the other hand, *"low level", diffuse and not hidden mind manipulation has become more and more pervasive, powerful, and even invasive in our lives.* These are the two threads of the story so far.

Key Elements of Mind Manipulation

But we can already draw some conclusions, just from the history of mind manipulation (in modern times). Mind manipulation has some *key elements:*

- *The use of communication media;* the more powerful the medium, the more effective the mind manipulation.

- *A hidden motivation;* this is *profit* in the vast majority of cases, but extortion, espionage and making "enemies" non-functional are common motives for the more serious cases, even political adversaries can be targets, and often are.

- *It uses Behaviorism;* "targets" (as they call us) are given *repeated stimuli* followed by *positive feedback* for the response they want from us and *negative feedback* for responses they want to discourage. *This is how they "rewire" our brain, i.e., and condition it to do what they want.*

Well, not bad. You already know the history of this field (I did concentrate on modern times; it's more relevant and we know more about it). But you now also know the basic workings of mind manipulation, the basic science behind it and its basic techniques. We will see them in detail in future chapters, of course, and we will, naturally *learn many ways to prevent, slow down, block manipulation, and even to decondition and "rewire" your mind.* But next I'm going to take you into a very surreal world, a world, a bit like a painting by Salvador Dalì... The world of the subconscious...

Chapter 2 – The Subconscious

The Strange Case of Seb and the E-Cigarette

Seb is a great friend of mine. Yesterday he told me a story he thought was strange… Guess what, it wasn't to me, but let me tell you, maybe you will disagree…

First let me give you some background information. Seb (Sebastian, of course) is 35, he has a good degree in biology. He is a very rational person, with a high IQ and a successful job and life. He does not drink in excess and he does not take drugs. He used to smoke, though. But he is giving up…

Like most people who give up smoking nowadays, he is using what is in fact replacement therapy, only a very fashionable one: vaping. It is in fact by far the most successful replacement therapy for smoking ever. You know that e-cigs can be fairly expensive and trendy, and that "vapers" now are so specialized and even "geeky" about them… anyway, he just got a new one through the mail yesterday, because, apparently, it's best to buy them online…

He got it, and he was very proud of it. He showed it to me; I must admit it looks great, with a colorful display and even a cool look… The fact is that he had been waiting for it for a few days. The old one was broken, and he gets a bit nervous, he even gets cravings for cigarettes still, if he does not vape… But he got it… He went out with it to try it out…

He got home, and you know what? The e-cig was gone! Gone! Vanished! Not on him anymore! So, he thought he'd dropped it… He went back and did the stressful thing of retracing his steps. Exactly and all… He has a good memory anyway… He looked everywhere but he couldn't find it anywhere…

Then he passed by a baker where he had stopped to buy a bun… And a man came out and said, "Are you looking for something?" He was taken aback, because he couldn't possibly have dropped it on that tiled floor… I mean, the noise alone… Anyway, he said, "Yes, my e-cig, it looks –"and the man stopped him… "Yes, we know," he said, "you put it on the counter and walked off; we even called after you, but you didn't respond…" and he handed Seb the e-cig back…

"Now, how is it possible that I put my e-cig on the counter? What for," was asking Seb when he saw me that night. You see, for him, he couldn't possibly have done it and, above all *he did not remember doing it*. Not at all! Even trying to remember – nothing! So, what happened?

The Subconscious Exists, and We "Do Things" when We are Subconscious

To me, the answer is simple: *he did not do it consciously, but subconsciously. Something in his mind made him do that action without him even being aware of it.* It happens, and it happens much more often than you may think.

We may speculate on what caused this "deviation" from normal behavior. *In many cases, stress can be the cause of these events.* Mark these words, because we are going to come back to them! So, maybe the stress of waiting for the e-cig, or work-related stress etc. But I didn't pry too much, so, for the time being, we cannot make a full diagnosis.

But I needed this example to show you that *we have subconscious behavior, and that it is not at all uncommon.* If *stress can cause it when unexpected and unwanted, unconscious behavior is actually very common in routine actions.*

Do you drive? Can you remember all the driving operations (pressing down on clutch, accelerator, brake, changing gear, turning left, right, using indicators, reading road signs etc....) from the last time you got home from work or school or college? Or even the stores? No, of course you can't! And the reason is simple, *all these actions, especially common and repeated ones, happen "under the radar of our Consciousness".*

When was the last time you forgot your keys? Why do you forget them? Or better, do you usually remember when you pick them up? No, of course you don't. You do lots of things mechanically. You do things and you are not actually conscious that you are doing them!

It happens to everybody, all the time, and at a very "low level", especially with common and repeated actions. We will see how *social media takes advantage of repeated actions to send things, including instructions on how to behave, into our subconscious.* But for now, think twice next time you put a "like" to a post, that they are actually giving you *stimuli* to respond to, like Pavlov's dogs, or a mouse in a maze...

What Is the Subconscious?

Yet, for the time being, we need to focus on the **concept of subconscious.** So far, we can say that *not all our mind is conscious, and that there is an area which is subconscious.* Now, let's look at what this area is like...

It is not fully unconscious, because sometimes there is *peripheral awareness of it*. You can't drive when you are asleep or totally unconscious, but you only need to give this activity your... well you guessed it... peripheral attention, and awareness.

The Conscious and the Subconscious Mind

However, *the subconscious is in contact with both the conscious and the unconscious.* Let's look at the last one first. In the *unconscious mind, we have all those mental processes that we are not aware of*. Automatic thoughts, dreams, forgotten memories etc. all "rest" in this part of our mind. When I say "part", I don't mean a "physical" place, because the mind is not the brain; the brain is physical, the mind is not.

The **conscious mind is where mental processes we are focusing on take place.** It is the center of our attention. If I am driving and talking to my friend, my conscious mind focuses on the conversation, not on driving. One of the reasons that we can do more than one thing at a time is that we can put our main focus on our main activity, and "peripheral awareness" on another one, usually a more automatic one.

The subconscious mind is out of our focal attention, but not fully unconscious. So, when Seb put the e-cigarette on the counter, he was focusing on buying a bun. On a "normal day" he would notice that he took out his e-cig (maybe by mistake), but this time he did not. So, he didn't shift his focus to the "unusual event", and he didn't notice it nor remember it at all.

We owe a lot to Sigmund Freud when it comes to the subconscious. Freud, as you may well know, is arguably by far the most famous person in the history of psychology, psychoanalysis, and psychotherapy. For Freud, things that are not needed immediately, but may or may not be needed at some stage soon, go into this area, where they are ready to be used, but "resting", like goods on shelves ready to be picked.

That indeed is what happens when you are driving, isn't it? If something happens, you immediately shift the focus from the chat you are having with your friend to your driving. And all the recent driving operations suddenly become very clear to you.

Conscious, Subconscious and Unconscious Mind

Although there is no exact calculation, experts tend to agree that **roughly 10% of the mind is conscious, 50 – 60% is subconscious and 30 – 40% is unconscious.** Not everybody agrees on this, but one thing seems to be met with consensus: **the conscious mind is only a small fraction of all our mind.**

A typical image we use to describe this structure of the mind is that of the iceberg. The conscious mind is the tip of the iceberg. The subconscious is the level floating up and down on the water surface, and the unconscious is that part that never reaches the surface of the sea.

How to Manipulate the Subconscious

Hold on, though, **how easy is it to make people do things subconsciously?** I am really sad and sorry to have to say that **it is fairly easy, easier than people may think, but it depends on many factors.**

A key technique to make people do things subconsciously is repetition. The first time you drive, you do it very consciously indeed. The more you do it, the less attention you pay to it, and the more subconscious it becomes. Oddly enough, doing things subconsciously may mean being very experienced and good at these things.

But, this, when it comes to fighting mind conditioning, also gives us a **key solution and principle to avoid, break and fend off mind manipulation: break the repetitiveness of the action.**

Let me give you a simple but fun (and useful) example. Do you always make the same typos? Like, many people spell "ten" instead of "the" or "ut" instead of "it" or they invert letters, like "teh" and "and" ... If they are repeated, it means that they are habitual, doesn't it? So, do you know how to correct these mistakes? **Turn the typos from subconscious to conscious!** If you type "teh" instead of "the", sit down and write "teh" wanting to write it, paying attention to it, and do it a lot of times... This way you will rewire your brain, and you will (promised) stop making that silly typo.

And if you do this, it will be your first, easy and practical rewiring and de-conditioning exercise! Well done!

How to Access the Subconscious

So, **how do things (thoughts, processes, desires etc.) get into the subconscious mind?** You have the answer now: **repetition of stimuli...** This is also true of small things, like the many small items we think we need every day. You see a new brand of candy one day, fine. You don't really care about it. But if you see it over and over again, then it becomes "familiar" and that convinces you subconsciously that it is "part of you" and that you "need it to be happy".

It gets a bit more sophisticated than that, and we will see it very soon. But **the core principle of advertising is repetition.** I don't know if you watch YouTube but it's a very good example of how they "invent our needs". If you do, you will notice that the ads on YouTube go in phases... At the time of writing, the "invest in the stock market phase" is over and the "take a marketing and managing course" is in full swing.

What's happening? Why so many ads of stock traders at the same time and then, as that is over, ads of webinars and online business courses? They really are the majority of all ads on that platform. More than 50% and at peak times far beyond that. Why?

Because **the more you see an ad about a product the more your subconscious is trained to recognize it as "normal" and if something is "normal and familiar" it is something you think you need.** Consciously you may well know you don't need that awful gadget. But as long as your subconscious is convinced, it just takes one "Seb moment" and you buy it!

Do you see how it works? Look back on your life and try to make a list of useless things you have bought... I'll see you back here in three minutes, just make a list, jot them down...

...

Here I am! I went out to water my roses; you should see how beautiful they are when they blossom... Anyway, it took me a second and I finished it. I bet you never managed to finish your list though, did you? Of course not!

This is proof that most of our minds are manipulated. But what matters most, this "shopping example" shows that **many if not most of our choices are manipulated.** You can consciously say that **all those**

24

useless gadgets were not the result of your conscious choice, and of your rational decision to buy them. Some, maybe – and even those, well, if you found out that they were useless, then you had been conned anyway. And that is mind manipulation too.

Can I ask you another question? When did you buy most of those useless things? Think about it and I'll just check on my wisteria...

....

I'll tell you something about gardening and de-conditioning or rewiring the mind later in this book... For now, I'll just tease you... But it is to show you that the way out of mind manipulation can be very pleasant indeed. Where were we? When did you end up buying most of those useless trinkets? Maybe you said, "After I split up," or "When I was stressing about work," or maybe you focused on a long term, low level condition, like "When I am tired," or, frequently, "When I am down", or even "When I get back from work."

Fine, all these have one thing in common: *your conscious guard was down, and you were more vulnerable.* That's what possibly happened to Seb, though his case is a bit drastic, unusual. But the fact that when it comes to low level but pervasive mind conditioning, like advertising, when you are tired, stressed, ill (yes!), demoralized, worried etc. is when *your conscious mind has too much on its plate, and things that you would normally manage in the conscious mind end up being dealt with by the subconscious mind.*

And advertisers know this perfectly well. They know that when we are weak, they decide which behavior they can get from us. Which is, in this case, to buy their product.

Cultural Factors and the Manipulation of the Subconscious

Can this technique be used also for other ends apart from selling products? The concept of convincing someone that something is good or right subconsciously is the same as that of convincing the person that it is necessary.

In many cases, this can be traced to *cultural factors* too. If you are brought up in a family where every weekend, or worse every day, you do a certain thing, you will end up pushing this activity into the subconscious as "normal" and "part of yourself". And you will find it very hard to break away from it.

Let's take food for example. Fried fat is bad for you. Who does not know that? So why do so many people eat it all the time and in disproportionate amounts? There are two factors at play here:

- Continuous and ubiquitous advertising of "junk food".

- Having been brought up eating junk food.

If both happen together, then the mind manipulation and conditioning is very strong indeed! Let me explain...

You may say, "But junk food is very tasty." Yes... - and no! It is tasty because it has a very *recognizable* and *habitual* taste for those who like it. For example, I don't find it exceptional at all, I find it much less tasty than healthy food, honestly. But I grew up eating organic food from my father's garden and I *acquired a taste for it.* Even objectively, there are far more and more varied flavors in healthy food than junk food.

So, what is the difference? You see, most people are exposed to junk food commercials, especially in the USA. But not everybody falls for them, do they? People who were brought up eating healthy food are far less likely to feel they need junk food. What's happened then?

We can say that *junk food commercials target mainly people who have "internalized" the idea that junk food is very good, normal, part of their identity and "tasty".* And *"internalized" means received into the subconscious,* or, in very serious pathological cases, *even into the unconscious mind.*

And if your social and family background has done all the hard work of pushing ideas into your subconscious, then advertising will find it very easy to trigger the response they want from you.

And this is true also of other aspects of life, including views on life and political views. The process of *radicalization of terrorists and criminals is one of mind manipulation.* You will find it hard to turn an open-minded person who has had a very liberal childhood into a radical terrorist. But if you get someone who has already internalized wrong ideas, like discrimination, the idea that "some people are inferior" and even "subhuman", then it's easy to trigger a violent reaction, even on cue. Yes, it is!

Hitler knew this quite well, and that is why he insisted on the process of "internalizing" the concept of "superior and inferior races" and similar scientific and humanistic blasphemies... It does not matter even if you know it's not true; as long as you are brought up with that concept as "normal", there is an open door in your subconscious, a "button ready to be pressed", and when this is done, *you will do as ordered unless you have built a resistance to it.*

So, *understanding consciously that something is wrong or right is the first step towards building that resistance.* If you watch the Nuremberg trial, you realize that the Nazi leaders had totally internalized the idea that murdering millions of people was perfectly fine. For them, they were subhuman, because they had it in their subconscious, most likely in their unconscious and because their conscious did not confront them with the reality. Watching their straight faces when they say things like "I was very efficient with gas chambers," not even realizing what was wrong with it shows how far mind conditioning can go.

The First Step against Mind Manipulation

Let's take another example and look at this topic in even more detail, or better from another perspective. Do you know the first step towards beating an addiction? You need to admit (consciously) that you have one. Fine, it is only the first step and a small one. It's by no means enough... No way!

But it's the first step... However, some people have internalized the idea that they can't beat the habit. Let's take cigarettes as an example... Have you ever heard people say, "Yes, smoking is bad, but I can get run over by a car tomorrow, so why should I bother?" This and similar answers actually are not honest. I don't mean that they are not honest to you. In fact, they are! They are not honest to themselves. It is **their subconscious** that it **is telling them to invent excuses to deny or stop what their conscious mind is saying. They are, in other words, "self-deluded".**

Now, can you see how the conscious mind and the subconscious mind are continuously conversing? The same applies to the subconscious mind and the unconscious. The divide between conscious and subconscious is blurred and "shaded" if you wish... Let me explain...

Do you know when you go to sleep? If you are very tired, you just fall asleep immediately. Basically, you drop from conscious to unconscious in a matter of seconds. But if you are not so exhausted, there is a time in between... In that time, you are still thinking and maybe even imagining things, but it all appears random, doesn't it? It's like your mind is roaming free and you abandon logical and rational thinking...

That is technically called **hypnagogic phase**, and it is a time from when you stop being fully conscious and in control of your thoughts and when you actually "switch off" and fall asleep. This is a **window into the subconscious.** It does have thoughts, but they are not "guided", not "controlled", not "directed" ... The great Irish novelist James Joyce wrote a masterpiece chapter, the last one in *Ulysses* expressing Molly Bloom's hypnagogic phase. The longest chapter (40,000 words) with no commas, no full stops, just thoughts following each other freely.

We can imagine the subconscious as being a bit like that phase. But there is no "exact moment" when you switch in and out of it... It's more like "gliding into it" or "thoughts melting slowly" ... There isn't a clear-cut boundary. That "area of connection" between conscious and subconscious is where the **two parts of our mind talk between themselves.**

In fact, if you train yourself, when you are in the hypnagogic phase you can get out of it for a second, change your train of thoughts, then fall back into it. This is good to avoid negative thoughts; it will have a positive effect on your dreams...

But this also tells us one important thing that mind manipulators know quite well: **if the conscious mind keeps repeating an idea to the subconscious mind, the subconscious mind will accept it.**

When we are "fully awake" (fully conscious), **the conscious mind works like a "guardian" for information it filters through to the subconscious.** Basically, if I told you a whopping nonsensical lie now, like, "the Moon is made of cheese", your conscious mind would bounce it back as "false". But does this happen all the time? And is it possible to **"bypass the conscious mind"**?

Levels of Alertness in the Conscious Mind

One question at a time, as the first answer also explains part of the second. No, it does not happen all the time. **The more we are alert, the more we are capable of rejecting thoughts and information.** But let's go back to the hypnagogic phase to see this in action. In that time before you go to sleep, your thoughts are not divided into "good and bad", "real and false", "positive and negative" ... You see, in the subconscious, thoughts and "things" simply "are". **We do not rationally discern between good and bad in our subconscious mind.**

You can already see how this is a goldmine for mind manipulators. If you pass a thought into the subconscious mind and then also pass the idea that that thought is good, you have literally bypassed the person's rational, moral, and ethical mind... **We decide between right and wrong in our conscious mind, not in our subconscious mind.**

Here is the big trick, isn't it? To start with, **we are not in "conscious mode all the time"**. If you catch someone when s/he is not in "conscious mode", you can easily pass on even wrong ideas, instructions, desires, etc.... This is because you don't have that "barrier", that "guardian" that "protection" you get when the conscious mind is switched on.

What's more, **even when we are conscious, there are different levels of alertness and of consciousness.** Let's stick to the word "alertness", which is far more correct, because Consciousness is a very complex topic, the "hard question" as scientists call it... Let's see this...

Think about yourself during the day, from 1 to 10, how alert would you say you are:

- Just after you wake up.
- After drinking heavy coffee.
- When you are working.
- When you are watching TV.
- After a heavy meal.

...

I was thinking about growing some herbs in my garden... What do you reckon? They keep pests away... Sorry, you know I take these breaks to do some gardening... Yes, you may have given different numbers, but for sure, you will have noticed that your alertness levels change throughout the day. For sure after heavy coffee, you are more alert. After waking up really depends on the person, as you know...

But the one I am most interested in is when you watch TV... The fact is. **When you watch TV your alertness levels drop significantly.** In fact in the long run, it makes you sleepy. What does this mean? That **the commercials you see on TV have a better chance of bypassing your conscious mind than others...**

But this is not only true of commercials: it is true of the news, information, ideas, opinions... The power of the television is far bigger than what people think...

Now, do you understand why so many experiments on mind control focused on subjects under the effects of psychotropic drugs? I would like you to think about it for a moment...

...

Whichever way you put it, let's see if you agree with what I am about to say: *experiments on mind control focus on people under the effect of psychotropic drugs because these induce altered states of consciousness. The researchers wanted to find out how changing your conscious state aided or prevented mind manipulation...*

It is not simply a matter of awareness, don't get me wrong. Consciousness is a vast topic. Actually, now Consciousness studies is becoming a whole new discipline, a branch of psychology but also of philosophy and anthropology (even physics actually!) But let's stick to the main concepts.

Your mind's alertness level can be changed artificially. In fact, the list of things that lower or your alertness is huge:

- Fatty foods
- Sugary drinks
- Dairy products
- Video games
- The television
- Social media
- Stuffy and polluted air
- Fluoride (this has a long-term effect on the mind).

These are actually "drugs" in the technical sense; they have a psychotropic effect on the mind. And note that most of what the modern world pushes for (in ads and not only) is within this list!

Activities and Substances that Raise Alertness

"Are there things that raise our level of alertness," you're rightfully asking? Yes, and we will see them all in detail, because these are the solution. Because not each single one is good... You see, as I said, it is slightly more complex than "simply being alert"; it's *"being alert in the right way" that matters*. But I am not going to keep you guessing for ages...

Here are some *practices and substances that make you alert in the right way:*

- Water
- Green tea
- Sleeping well
- Fresh air
- Contact with Nature
- Meditation
- Yoga
- Relaxation
- Martial arts
- Reading
- Vegetables
- Raw and unprocessed food

No, coffee and cocaine, even cigarettes, for example, make you very alert, but they only switch on part of your mind, and they leave the other part open to influence... Got the tick?

Bypassing the Conscious Mind

Now, on to the second question. As we said, you can now see how manipulation lowers your alertness levels and how we are not always 100% alert anyway... But now I am going to ask you a question.

I will ask you to stop reading for a minute and note down everything you can actually perceive, from the smallest noise to the quality of the air, smells, aromas, perceptions of light, voices, even far away in the background...

...

You won't believe how peaceful it is out in my garden... And you're seeing why I am linking gardening and preventing mind manipulation already... My little friendly hide and seek game is almost up... I'll come clean very soon.

I can tell you what I perceived though... I heard birds chirping, I smelt flowers (it's spring here where I am writing), especially daffodils, I felt a light breeze and, unfortunately, very much back in the distance, the noise of cars... There's a road about a mile from here, not a busy one, but I heard a car swish by...

You will have noticed different things, but for sure one thing we have in common. We could not perceive these things when we were intent on reading and writing... the same happens when you are talking, driving etc.... How many advertisements are there on the road? You actually see them, even if you are not aware of them... So, they bypass your conscious mind, and your judgement!

It is very easy to bypass the conscious mind with low level stimuli. These go under the radar of our alertness, because of course, we have a limited level of perception. We cannot focus on everything all the time, can we? And if you "receive them but you are not aware of them" they do not meet your conscious judgement, instead, they speak straight to your subconscious!

So, we have seen that *a key trick of mind manipulation is to bypass your conscious mind and speak straight to your subconscious mind*. This is done by:

- *Altering your level of awareness.*

- *Using low level but repeated stimuli that "go under the radar" of your conscious mind.*

Fortunately, there are solutions. For example, did you know that you can actually *train your conscious mind to be far more alert?* And because I am not so evil and I can't keep you waiting for solutions any longer, we are going to talk about it, right now!

Actually, I am going to do a spot of gardening first, but I'll be back as soon as you turn the page. Promise!

Chapter 3 – Training Your Conscious Mind

Welcome back! I bet you want to know about my "spot of gardening" now… Well, I just looked around my garden for things to do… It's quite nice, you see… that part of gardening where you just go round and let the garden tell you what it needs. It's nice in the morning. It's also a way of **training your mind to become aware of quiet stimuli…**

You see, it's so easy to focus on a noisy car passing by, or a person shouting in the streets, or a glaring commercial sign, or a massive flat screen… It's much harder, at least to us modern people, to let the odd sick leaf, maybe just discolored, catch your attention…

This is made worse by the fact that we live in a world where we are continuously bombarded with strong stimuli vying to catch our attention. And as you know, it's with the low level, hardly noticeable stimuli that they manipulate us. Even if we look at **grifters**, they **do the conjuror trick of distracting you with very showy and visible gestures with one hand and carrying out the trick with the other.** The concept is the same: **making sure they can bypass our attention.**

Increase Your Basic Attention and Awareness Levels

So, the very first solution would be to **increase our basic attention and awareness levels!** Everybody has his and her basic attention and awareness levels. They do change according to many factors, including:

- **Stress**

- **Mental fatigue**

- **Physical fatigue**

- **Illness**

- **Personal situations**

- **Worrying**

… and other factors.

These of course will lower your awareness levels. So, one thing to do is to **reduce these factors.** The simplest solution is to **have a healthy life.** But of course, this is not always possible, and I fully understand you. There are work problems; there are family problems; you may live in a chaotic city; there can be unforeseen events etc.…

On top of that, **most of modern life is designed to keep us nervous, stressed, and constantly tired.** So, leaving the modern way of life would be an excellent – if drastic – solution. Among the least "mind controllable" people on the planet you will find monks... of any spiritual or religious persuasion. Why? To start with they are not under the constant stress of most people's lives. Secondly, they have actively trained their minds to be more aware. But...

What Does It Mean "to Be Aware"?

Being aware does not mean being edgy and nervous. There is this weird idea (that comes from the business world actually) that if you are "hyper" you are "aware and productive". Nothing could be further from the truth. Even socio-economic studies show that this myth of "hyper means productive" is just that. The most productive people don't run around like headless chickens... they are usually calm, older (yes!) and they have built stamina and techniques...

"Hyper" people in fact are easily manipulated. They have a **very narrow focus; all** their thoughts are centered on that focus. So, their awareness is actually very low when it comes to everything else... You see the point?

So, what does it mean? It means a few things and it has some characteristics.

Good awareness:

- **Has wide focus,** not just in one object, but on everything that surrounds you. In fact, the more aware you are, the farther your attention can go.

- **Is calm and peaceful;** people who are highly aware of their surroundings do not fret or stress about things easily. **Peace means having your mind free from thoughts; these thoughts actually distract your conscious mind from external stimuli.**

- **It's constant through time;** of course, it changes too, but slowly and to lesser extents than people who have peaks and sudden drops do (sugary drinks cause this, and when you have a "drop" your awareness collapses, as teachers know quite well!)

- **It uses all senses;** the ability to rely in many perceptive forms and many senses is very important to avoid mind manipulation.

- **A person who has high awareness also has an open attitude to others;** by "others" we also mean animals and trees and even ideas. Yes, it's the opposite you see? You may think that you can **close up to shield yourself from stimuli – but this is a mistake!** It means using a lot of energy and the trick is to **be aware of the stimuli and quickly "deselect" negative ones.**

But how can you do it in practice?

Activities That Increase Your Conscious Awareness Levels

I bet you already guessed that there are activities that actually help you improve your awareness skills and raise your awareness levels. Maybe you already know I will be presenting gardening among these – and you are right; I will!

Let me give you an example though… Do you know that when you train for many sports, especially professionally, they teach you how to keep your eyes focused on the ball (for example) and at the same time look sideways to check what the other team members and your team members are doing? Well, *that* is actually awareness, not being totally focused on a page (paper or virtual) or on a specific client!

So, here we go, some activities that will increase your awareness… I am presenting them to you now, before everything else, for two reasons:

- *They are "groundwork"; they help your overall ability to counter mind manipulation.*

- *They take time – to learn, to be effective on your awareness and even to choose…*

So, start now!

Sports – Especially Team Sports

Sports teaches you a lot in terms of awareness, as we have seen. They teach you to be aware of the game, to focus on one point while keeping others within your peripheral vision. They teach you to keep an eye on your team and the competing team. They teach you to pick on small signals, from your team members and from your adversaries too.

You also have to heighten your attention during games (and training), and like with all things, practice makes perfect and training a skill or a sense actually improves it!

They also teach you stamina, a wonderful skill (or is it a quality?) that can really make a huge difference in life, not just when it comes to mind manipulation.

They also have other great beneficial effects too. For example, when you are playing sports you are usually in a "free zone" from mind manipulation.

Finally, they reduce your stress levels overall and they make you healthier.

Strolling

Strolling is physical activity, but not actually a sport… Still, it has excellent qualities when it comes to improving your awareness skills. When was the last time you actually took a stroll? Just for the sake of it, I mean? Dashing to the corner store to buy salt is not strolling! Oddly enough this activity is far less common than we may imagine. Some people hardly ever take a stroll, and most do it once a week or so…

But strolling, **especially in a natural place**, teaches you to allow your senses to be guided by the environment. You see we spend most of our lives **directing senses towards stimuli**, and we lose focus on **what our senses pick up without us looking for it…** This second type of perception, **passive perception** (as opposed to **active perception**) becomes "demoted" even fossilized in our minds… And **it's through passive perception that manipulation takes place.**

Strolling is also good for your health and stress levels. And it can also help you clear your mind.

So, if you really have no time to take up any other activity, promise that you will go for strolls every day. Yes, every day…

Martial Arts

Martial arts is literally designed to improve your awareness levels. They are just impressive. If a football player is aware of the teammate running next to him or her and of the adversary coming to intercept the ball, well… Compare it to a martial art master who knows if someone is simply looking at them – of course from behind!

Secret agents and special forces learn martial arts just for this reason; you become aware of all "presences", even those you cannot physically see. And you become aware even of the smallest stimulus, of a twig breaking in the forest, for example…

Naturally, martial arts teach stamina like few other sports, and in fact you can keep practicing them till you are very old, even till your death if you are healthy. But they are also good against stress and great for your health.

If you can, martial arts would be an ideal choice.

Meditation

Meditation is the best way to **clear your mind and relax**. You see, our minds are quite talkative in most cases. They keep talking to themselves all the time. Think about it, you hardly spend a minute (in most cases) without thinking rationally every day. What is more, the modern world encourages lots of verbal, rational thinking.

And **when we talk to ourselves with rational thoughts our awareness of external stimuli drops.** So, doing meditation is excellent against mind manipulation. It teaches you to "stop that voice at the back of your head" which, in most cases is distracting you from other things and stimuli.

It also teaches you to use all your senses; when you meditate, you perceive smells, sounds, colors, light, even gravity, heat, moisture, feelings, emotions, states of being... the list is longer than we think...

Finally, meditation actually increases mental ability and IQ (and EQ) levels, and many studies show it, and it does it very fast! According to neurologist Fadel Zeidan and psychologist Paula Goolkasian, it **only takes four days (!!!) of meditation to see clear improvements in cognition** (mental abilities)! Their research appeared in the peer reviewed journal *Consciousness and Cognition* in June 2010 and it is titled 'Mindfulness and Meditation Improve Cognition: Evidence of brief mental training', if you want to know more.

Finally finally (sorry), it's excellent against stress and it builds inner peace.

Visiting Parks and Other Natural Places

Being in contact with Nature is an excellent cure for stress. It is no hippy hypothesis: the science is out and being in touch with Nature has healing properties. But apart from the direct effects it has on your physical wellbeing, as with all things healthy, it also positively affects your mental wellbeing.

Just the idea of cutting off the "hum of the city" for some time is excellent for your mind and awareness levels. But apart from the background hum, there are all those violent noises and visual stimuli which literally tire our brains. Especially in modern cities. An old town with pedestrian roads and old signs is not the same as a modern city with neon signs and a cacophony of clashing noises.

What is more, the modern world overwhelms our senses; sight, hearing and smell in particular. Taking a break from this and instead allowing our senses to re-align to gentle, natural stimuli is perfect to improve your awareness skills and level.

Of course, this activity too is good against stress. So... remember that outing to the nearby national park? Maybe it's time to get a picnic hamper?

Mindfulness

Mindfulness is a lesser-known practice unless you are into healing practices. But it's growing very fast and as you can see there is very strong academic evidence that it increases your mental and sensory abilities quickly and significantly.

Mindfulness is a very special "activity" because it is based on "letting your senses talk to you". You can see how this is **just perfect to train your senses and passive perception.** And mindfulness can be practiced anywhere and for any span of time. You can do it when you are queuing at the post office, while at work, while walking, while eating... As long as you suspend judgement and rational analysis and just "enjoy your senses" it works and it does not matter what you are doing and for how long.

Eating Slowly

While we are at it, slow down your eating... Even this can help you improve your senses and awareness levels – as well as your digestion... and it makes you slim down... but it gives you more energy and better nutrients!

We have lost our correct relationship with food... We tend to eat fast and "assault food"; this teaches us to focus on "strong stimuli and active perception". Eating slowly, on the other hand, teaches you to "listen to food" and taste is such an ancestral and visceral form of awareness... Then of course, eating involves sight, smell etc....

Painting and Other Arts

Take up painting, take your easel and go to a park...Sit there for hours and try to express what that wonderful landscape is telling you. It's not just a beautiful hobby (at least, and Art, anyway...) It is meditation on one level, it is expression on another level.

It teaches you to let "the world with all its stimuli and nuances" speak to you... And of course, it heightens your awareness and ability to recognize passive stimuli. It's also a good way to clear your mind and relax!

Gardening

We got here! You see, gardening is a bit like meditating, it is mindful, it is a nice hobby, it can even be productive, but there is more... It teaches you to be in touch with Nature, and it's a bit like martial arts: very harmonic. It too teaches you to recognize passive stimuli. It increases your awareness levels, and it widens your focus...

No need to say that it's also good physical activity, and is excellent against stress....

So, well, can I close this chapter with a "hippy" statement? ***Mind manipulation uses the most appalling techniques and has carried out horribly cruel experiments, but the cure can be fun – in fact you can even avoid it and heal it with flowers!***

Chapter 4 – Signs and Symptoms of Mind Manipulation

How would you know if someone is trying to manipulate your mind? Are there clear signs and symptoms that someone is working on your subconscious mind to make you do what they want? You're in luck! The answer is actually a resounding yes!

But first of all, **remember to read signs together, not individually.** Imagine you go to your doctors with a complaint... For example, you feel tired and fatigued. That is the clear symptom that something is not 100% right with you. But is that enough for a good diagnosis? And, above all, would a good doctor not ask you more questions, look for other symptoms? Of course she would (or he would)! Your doctor may ask you a whole range of questions like how your appetite is, your sleep, if you have had lifestyle or dietary changes, if you are taking any medication etc.

So, let's take a leaf out of a professional doctor's book and do the same: **when you notice a sign or symptom of mind control, look for others before you draw a conclusion.** But why do I keep saying, "Signs and symptoms"? Aren't they the same? In some cases, yes – in ours they are not.

The Difference between Signs and Symptoms of Mind Manipulation

For the sake of our topic, there is a clear and important difference between signs and symptoms of mind manipulation. It's because in mind manipulation we always have at least two participants: a manipulator and a victim.

So, we need to distinguish between what we find out by observing the manipulator and what we find out by observing the victim... I think you already know what I am going to say now...

- **By symptom, we mean a detectable effect of mind manipulation on the victim.** In extreme cases, these can be quite disturbing, like blank stares etc. But in most, less serious cases, they are much lighter symptoms. That is good, but it has a flip side: they are harder to detect.

- **By signs, we mean behaviors, words or actions we detect in the manipulator which indicate that s/he is trying to manipulate our mind.** You will notice typical use of words, patterns etc. which should raise suspicion... We'll get to them straight away.

Spotting Signs of Mind Manipulation

You will need to keep a close eye on the **person and / or medium** you think is manipulating you if you have some suspicions. Nowadays, very often the manipulator is "remote", hidden "behind a screen" or "behind a telephone". Do you get annoying cold calls trying to sell you something? I do... And I also know why they prefer a cold call to a face to face transaction... It's quicker, maybe, but there is also another reason: you cannot see the interlocutor so s/he can hide body language signs that s/he is lying to you.

Do you get lots of ads on social media? Well, be aware that behind every post or every pop-up window, there is *a person (company) with a clear intention, and that intention is to get you to do something...* Then it may be more or less honest, and even this is very much up to your standards... If you want my personal advice though, keep those standards very high! I do...

But which signs can you look for? There are some *areas, patterns, and techniques that often give away the manipulator's intentions.* And we are going to see them right now.

Repetition

You knew this was coming. We talked about it with the example of advertisements. But even if you are face to face with someone who is trying to sell you something, beware of repetitions! Listen to *salespeople* and you will find that they *repeat key selling points, key words, phrases etc.* That shows that they are very keen to get you to fall for these concepts.

I'll give you a funny example... Once I went to visit a flat, and it was so small I could not believe it! It must have been 200 sq feet maximum. There wasn't even room for a small cupboard... The estate agent, a very nice lady, of course was a bit at a loss, but I went a bit along with her, and she kept repeating, "It's convenient" ... The fridge was not "tiny" (and you couldn't even open it while you were in the kitchen you had to get out and open it!) It was "convenient". The fact that the inky storage space was in a hole with the electrical panel and the boiler was "convenient".

You get my point. She was in a bad selling position, but still she repeated the only selling point she had. Or thought she had at least! But this leads us straight into the next point, because the example is quite fitting too.

Doublespeak

If you have read *1984* by George Orwell, you will know quite well what that is. If you haven't read it, may I give you a little reading suggestion? It's a novel everybody should read. Ok, in *1984* there's a dictatorship that tries to control everybody's mind. And it does it in many ways, but one is *controlling the language and changing the meanings of words.* Using a word with the wrong meaning is called *doublespeak.*

It is very common indeed; newspapers use it all the time and promote it. Especially when it comes to politics and political views. Of course, the USA has seen massive use of doublespeak in recent years, but I will give you an example from outside...

Not long ago, in Italy, there were demonstrations, like normal demonstrations, nothing violent or anything. People marching peacefully in the streets. The newspapers started calling them "antagonists".

Now everybody expressing an opinion is an antagonist to the opposing opinion, right? But "antagonist" sounds bad, as if you are "against the reader" not against injustice or even the loss of democracy (which is what they were demonstrating against) …

That is a clear example of doublespeak. And newspapers and the media use it all the time and consistently. Doublespeak words just spread very fast and become established, by doing this, the **perception of reality people have is changed.** In Italy, they were clearly trying to present people who were actually demonstrating to uphold the Constitution as "the enemy" (and "antagonist" and "enemy" are very similar in meaning).

I must say this was one of the few cases where there was an outcry about the use of doublespeak and if the papers have not fully stopped using the word, they are using it far less now. This is something sociologists should study, because to my knowledge it's quite rare that doublespeak gets challenged, but it shows that if you do, it "pushes it back".

And that gives us a good clue on how to protect ourselves from mind manipulation. But we will talk about it in detail later.

Over-Emphatic Language

Now, US citizens are naturally (culturally?) emphatic when they talk. But within the cultural parameters of the people involved, using over-emphatic language is usually a sign of wishing to manipulate. Think about those old adverts you would see on TV. The key strategy was to emphasize how cheap the cars were, how "great quality" they were etc. Words were often over the top; things like "The best second hand cars in the country!"

Salespeople will often say things like, "This is a once in a lifetime chance," or, "The best on the market," etc. This excessive emphasis is an attempt to convince you, to change your mind, even using "exaggerations" or faking enthusiasm.

Now, there are really enthusiastic people, and maybe for good reason. People may really love an idea, an object, a person, a work of art etc.… But in most times, especially with salespeople, politicians, and the like, the speaker is not actually all that enthusiastic about it… Trust me; it's a show. And in many cases, we can spot it very easily.

The problem is that we have become accustomed to fake enthusiasm, so, this too often goes under the radar of our conscious observation… I have always found fake enthusiasm "grating and annoying". So, when a salesperson uses it, it actually works against his or her purpose and aim. If you can find it in yourself to feel the same distrust and rejection for fake enthusiasm, you will have a powerful tool to defend yourself from manipulation.

Empty Claims and Incorrect Use of Data

Fake emphasis and empty claims are related and often occur together. These two can be very good signs to tell you that someone is trying to manipulate your mind. What are empty claims? These are claims that have no evidence, but also claims where the evidence is picked on purpose. A typical manipulation technique is to **choose only those facts that are useful to the manipulator and ignore the others.**

Unless you know the topic you are talking about in detail, this is often difficult to understand. However, note a typical pattern here: the manipulator starts with some statistical data, which can also be true, but it is taken in isolation and only used to prove that his "pitch" is right. The manipulator will not stop on the details, context etc. of the data. He or she just uses it and jumps into the selling pitch straight away.

Have I talked to you about YouTube ads of online courses and webinars? They very often use this pattern. I'll simplify but the gist is this: "50% of businesses that fail don't use the right marketing technique. Our course will teach you just that."

To start with, do we actually know that the course teaches the right marketing technique? I mean, it looks like it because it gives us some data. But that's a mystification. Why? The data may well tell us the problem, but it says absolutely *nothing* about the validity of the course.

But the fact that they say it very fast and one following the other *makes it seem as if the data backs up the validity of the course or webinar.* It is not illegal, but it falls well under my bar of "correctness". To me it shows that they are ready to "bend the truth" to obtain something from you... Draw your own conclusion.

In my example (which I have slightly changed for copyright reasons), then, there's another "twisted fact. Note: "50% of businesses that fail don't use the correct marketing technique" only puts two details together, but does not link them. Put simply, we don't know if the lack of the correct marketing technique is t*he reason why they failed...* Maybe even 50% of those that don't fail use the wrong marketing technique?

Yet to the vast majority of people not even reading the data, but hearing it, delivered fast, maybe when you are half distracted, the **impression is that the data backs up what the manipulator is saying and will say next; but it's just spin!**

Before parting with your hard-earned money, before making any important decision, **beware of spin doctors and spun stories...** Those ads, to be honest, struck me as being very much below my standards, very "insistent" even "aggressive".

Insistence and Aggressiveness

I would by any means avoid anyone who is insistent or even use "aggressive marketing techniques". These are clear signs that they want something from you, and they cannot get it by simply giving you the facts and asking you if you actually need it, want it, or even can afford it or not.

They are trying to:

- *Prevent you from thinking properly, and reflecting on what they are saying.*

- *Prevent you from weighing pros and cons.*

- *Prevent you from fully and clearly understanding what is being proposed.*

- *Give you a fake sense of necessity, urgency etc.*

I am here talking about the greengrocer at the market who shouts out, "Ripe tomatoes 50% off! Hurry up!" That is straightforward, you see, he or she is possibly telling the truth and not hiding the fact that s/he wants you to hurry up…

When they actually hide the fact that they are hurrying you up, however, then it's a problem…

Linking Unrelated Things, Images, Thoughts

Think vodka, gin etc.… I know, you already got a picture of "summer holiday" and "half naked women" (or men) and "party time on the beach" in your mind. Why? You know why… For years they linked the idea of spirits with these images in commercials.

They are totally unrelated… Would you really naturally go for vodka when it's 100 degrees in the shade? Maybe a cold soft drink, maybe a beer, an ice pop? Vodka, really? And before these ads, people thought of bearded men dressed in heavy furs in the snow when they heard the word "vodka". Gin too was linked to "poor and destitute people in northern Europe", not a catchy, "sellable" image…

But like you saw in *Clockwise Orange,* and now you know how Behaviorism works, you will understand that linking half naked women on a beach with vodka is like giving food to dogs when you ring a bell… The dog will salivate even when the food is no longer there – and I'll stop the sentence here… But that's exactly how they are treating you…

Body Language

Body language is a whole branch on its own, and if you want to know more, I will add a link in the resource page to study body language and how to use it against mind manipulation. For now, be aware that *incoherent, contradictory, and nervous body language may be a sign of dishonesty, thus an attempt to manipulate you.*

Of these, nerves can easily be due to other reasons, and you always need to read all signs in conjunction. Look out for signs like:

- *Hiding hands.*

- *Avoiding eye contact.*

- *Keeping physical distance.*

- *Closing up (crossing legs, arms etc.)*

- *Sneering.*

- *Trying to gain a "vantage point, a higher position".*

- *Contradictory signs in general.*

Body language is one of the best ways of telling if a person is "comfortable" or "uncomfortable" with what s/he is saying, and even great liars are never fully comfortable with lies...

Talking too Fast

We have already seen this, but it's worth stopping on it for a second. Yes, expert manipulators will use a speed which is adapted to the victim: just a bit faster than the victim can manage. And by manage, we don't mean hear, but "understand fully".

In other cases, like when you see posts in your timeline, then they are timed so that the average person will never be able to comprehend them fully unless they expand the post and read it...

Some ads are fast, on purpose. They want to sound intelligent; they also want to look like they have a lot to say; it creates a false sense of urgency and, of course... they bank on viewers not understanding what they are saying fully, correctly, or critically.

Elusiveness

And of course, you can get as much from what people don't say as from what they say, and how they say it – maybe even more! We will look at techniques for how to reflect on what people say later on. But for now, keep these three ideas in mind.

- *Hang on to what you think the person has not said, and you noticed during the speech.* Make a mental note when you feel there's something missing. You can do it in many ways. Of course, you can write it down, if you have a chance. You can make a mental note if you have a good memory. I count, using my fingers... I count a finger at every question I have, every doubt I have, and keep them in mind. And you know what? It seems to put manipulators on the back foot. They will notice you, and they will know their story is not working...

- *After the encounter, the speech, the advertisement, the meeting etc. take time to reflect on it and ask questions about it.* This is even more essential if it is an important matter. Never buy anything of value on the spot, take your time... The same applies to big choices in life. You have a *right to reflect and consider all the points, doubts etc.* And if there are points that are not clear, if you have doubts, again, make a note. Write them down... *The more important the choice is, the closer you need to be to 100% certainty.*

But let me tell you a trick... You can turn the "missing information" to your advantage. How? Here is the third idea to keep in mind:

- *If you have doubts, or feel something is missing, ask questions.* To start with, you should never trust anyone who does not even want to be questioned. But sometimes we can become a bit "shy" just when we should not be...

  By all means, ask questions about what does not convince you, and keep pressing. Even if there is nothing specific you have doubts about, always ask questions about details. Then, keep an eye (ear) on what the response is like: is it confident, straightforward and exhaustive? Is the other person trying to evade the point? Or the answer is not as straightforward as you would like?

Whether the person's words are elicited or not, the *elusiveness in a speaker is always a very good sign that s/he is hiding something from you.*

There is, of course, the chance that the person simply does not know the answer. This, again, is something many people can "sniff out". Ignorance in itself is not "incriminating", but if you notice a willingness not to answer, and a few other signs that go with it, then you are really on to something.

Symptoms of Mind Manipulation

Let's now turn to the victim. The symptoms of mind manipulation are many, varied and they depend a lot on the gravity of the manipulation.

A good example would be Othello, the protagonist of the eponymous tragedy by Shakespeare, and a play I would suggest you watch or read if you are interested in mind manipulation. At first, he is fine, he only becomes a bit suspicious when Iago "sows the seed of jealousy" in him. Then, he becomes nervous, more suspicious, he "wants more and more information about his wife Desdemona"; he then becomes antisocial, he becomes distracted from his work, he becomes paranoid and, in the end, even murderous.

This is a play, but it shows the *escalation of symptoms as the mind manipulation progresses.*

At the same time, when you are under continuous and low-level *mind manipulation, you most likely will have no symptoms at all.* The trained eye may notice them, but for most people, some symptoms are seen as "normal behavior".

Now, let me give you a simple example. I have a friend; his name is Jeremy and he's overweight. He knows he is, but despite all this, Jeremy cannot go by a fast-food restaurant without stopping at least, casting the desirous eye to the window, and in many cases, he walks in...

Even if he did not walk in, you would still, from an external, objective, and independent perspective, notice that there are symptoms of mind control, in this case...

Cravings and Unhealthy Interest in Something

Cravings for food, alcohol, shopping items, cigarettes etc. are all clear symptoms of mind manipulation. "Hold on," you may say, "cigarettes are addictive." True, but they are part of the mind manipulation strategy themselves, while also being the aim of the manipulation. It happens a lot with addictive products (and remember that sugar, fat, coffee etc. are all addictive substances).

Also, morbid interest in a topic or "fetish" (by no means sexual fetishes, others, like the new phone, a brand, an item of clothing, a particular car etc.) can be clear symptoms of mind manipulation. I think the explanation here is straightforward. It's fine if you like something in a healthy way; but think about cell phones, in some cases, the interest in the new model is literally morbid. Long queues to get model 1235782901457/bis-ABRTF75 of the famous "uPhone" (I didn't want to give them a free commercial!), especially with people who already have model 1235782901457/bis-ABRTF74 is not healthy behavior.

These people actually think they are "cool", because they appear as the "top of society" especially in particular parts of society, modern, technological, urban, "connected" etc.... The reality is different; in some respect, they are more serious than Jeremy. His addiction is really bad, don't get me wrong; but at least he knows he has it and he does not feel "cool" anymore for eating fast food.

Note how all this can be explained away with the old bell and salivating dog... They want the new phone not because they actually need it, but because they associate it with *social clout (a very common "reward" in mind manipulation).*

These are the most common *low-level manipulation symptoms.* At higher levels, the list is quite frightening, but we will go through it fairly fast, because they are comparatively (sigh!) rare, and in these cases, the victims would need professional help.

Symptoms of Serious and Advanced Mind Manipulation

You know by now that mind manipulation can reach unthinkable levels. Usually, low-level mind manipulation has few visible symptoms. But when it becomes serious, then there can be a long series of symptoms, including:

- *Eating disorders*; here we are not talking about Jeremy's case (which could still be an eating disorder), but people who are being manipulated for things other than food, and yet the manipulation affects their eating habits.

- **Sleeping disorders**; these are quite common, sometimes even at low levels, with dreams about a product, waking up wanting to smoke etc.... But in serious cases we talk about either insomnia, uneven and discontinuous sleeping patterns, or also unusual dreams or even continuous nightmares. The latter is tantamount to torture, and many targeted individuals report appalling things, like, "Every dream for months was a nightmare" ... These are extreme cases (and many got compensation for this).

- **Problems socializing;** it is not unusual that people under severe mind control find it hard to relate to others; in many cases, their plea for help is in itself a problem. People do not understand what they are going through and they themselves are often unaware of the root problem and they cannot explain it, nor prove it, very often. So, acquaintances, friends, and even family may think they are "weird" or even "crazy"...

  In other cases, anyway, the strain mind manipulation puts on victims can result in lowered social skills, the need to sleep, to stay alone, to avoid crowded places etc. This and other behavioral patterns can negatively impact on their social life.

- **Addiction;** severe mind manipulation can be a real strain on the individual, as we said. Quite a few turn to alcohol or other drugs, including prescription drugs... If you met them and listened to their stories as I did, you couldn't possibly blame them for it.

- **Inefficiency at work;** yet another consequence can be that people lose focus at work, which can also happen in small doses at low level mind manipulation. The time you spend browsing for the new iPhone model is not really spent efficiently for work. But in serious cases it can turn into a regular and unmanageable lack of focus. No need to say many targeted individuals lose their jobs, or find it hard to find another.

- **Mental blocks and "blanks";** strained minds sometimes stop when they are pushed. Also, serious mind manipulation interferes with the normal cortex workings of the brain. Some mental paths may be "cut" (weakened), or the brain and mind may become very tired, and the "lapse" or *lapsus* becomes common, at times frequent.

- **Memory loss;** this is common with everybody under strain, thus, it does happen that people under mind control end up suffering from memory loss.

- **Erratic behavior;** of course, mind manipulation has the aim of changing your behavior; this can have all sorts of side effects, including behavior that onlookers cannot explain logically. In serious cases, people may shout at "invisible things or listeners" in the streets, for example.

- **Repeating the same story;** some people who have suffered seriously from mind manipulation may keep repeating the same story, often about themselves, often about an injustice received, to people they meet, even very early on in the encounter.

- **Blank stares;** once you are "under" in serious ways, your eyes will look very intense at one stage, but looking blankly and past people. This is a sign of actual mind control. These are looks you find in people who belong to death cults, sects (and other cases, like secret service "unwilling agents" etc.)

- ***Violent behavior;*** this is a rare, extreme, and very serious symptom. It may happen because the person needs to release tension, in which case it is still bad, but not as bad as when the violent behavior is actually the aim of the mind conditioning operation. Yes, it is possible to get people to commit violent crimes through mind manipulation, the word "assassin" itself is a case in point.

And we shall close this chapter with an intriguing story, one you can add to the history of mind manipulation, one that shows how old it is and how efficient it already was almost a thousand years ago already, and one that tells you the origin of a word...

What is the origin of the word "assassin"? Assassins were actually a group of heretical Muslims of the Eleventh Century BCE. They lived in the Middle East, especially in Persia and Syria, and their actual name was *Nizari Ismailis.* Why then this "nickname?"

Well, they used to take a lot of hashish before going on murdering expeditions. I know, weed smokers nowadays are peace loving dreamers, mainly, but the fact is that when they smoked, they were told all sorts of stories about how fighting for their cause would send them to Heaven...

So, it was a way of manipulating their mind, like Pavlov did with dogs, or better almost like the CIA did with LSD and the Nazis with mescaline... The difference is that they were only manipulated with ***positive reinforcements to stimuli***, not negative ones, so... Not so cruel (and effective) as modern mind manipulation...

Still, in Arabic, *"hasisi"*, *"al-Hasishiyyun"* or *"hashashin"* all mean "hashish eaters" and that was their nickname. It was then transformed into the Latin *"assassinunus"* and you can see that it is basically the modern English word we use nowadays: "assassin".

Imagine what they can do nowadays!...

But did I drop a little clue to what we are going to see next? Yes, I did! Because in the next chapter we are going to look at the very, very core of behaviorism in detail. You know a lot already, but this is going to give you a very technical insight and – of course, ideas on how to counter mind manipulation...

But can I ask you one thing before we move on? Would you do something you really like before you turn the page? Guess what? I'm going to look at my garden – you do what you like best, even for a minute...

Chapter 5 – Behaviorism, Positive and Negative Reinforcement

Did you fully enjoy what you did? No, don't tell me... I am not a curious person... Anyway, you are right – I couldn't possibly hear you... I haven't got mind reading skills, though apparently some people do, so we find out in the CIA files from **Project Stargate** reveal... The declassified files (2017) showed that they used mind readers to spy on the Russians from 1972 to 1995, a "hell of a cheap system," according to US Congressman Charlie Rose of North Carolina, of the House Select Committee on Intelligence...

This just shows you how far this side of "underground psychology" has developed... But you are safe with me and now I am going to tell you why I asked you to do something nice before reading this chapter... Because *I wanted you to associate reading this book with something positive...*

The difference with mind manipulators is that *I didn't force the reinforcement on you (a)* and above all *I came clean and was honest and open about using it (b).* That makes a huge difference from when you watch the proverbial vodka commercials with half naked women (and/or men) dancing on the beach... That's not something you choose and they (badly, ok...) conceal *making a link, a connection in your mind between a stimulus and a reinforcement.*

What is more, this *reinforcement can be positive or negative.* What we saw "between the chapters" was *positive reinforcement,* which, in Pavlov's case, was food for the dogs, for potential (male) vodka drinkers, it is the image (hope, desire etc.) of a beach party with half naked women (the odd half naked man thrown in makes sure that it is not only "targeted" at heterosexual males...)

Now, sorry, the word "targeting" that market experts use all the time always brings up a very bad feeling... Where were we then? There is a *reward, or positive reinforcement* but there can also be a *punishment, or negative reinforcement.* We will come to this last one in a minute...

Positive Reinforcement

Positive reinforcement is not in itself unethical, dangerous, "bad". In fact, while mind manipulators have developed ways of using it to "bend your will", it can be applied to very positive ends...

Think about the teachers you liked most at school; most likely they were those who noticed when you did or said something right, those who encouraged you, those who said little words like, "well done," or "great idea," or "good point!" They were, in short, those who used positive reinforcement.

Virtually all *modern pedagogues believe that good education is based on positive reinforcements.* Teachers now know that if they give rewards to students, they will encourage them, boost their motivation, their stamina, and even their willpower. Not only, but they also know that their students will love their subject, and pursue it (unless something negative happens), even after they are no longer students...

And I am asking you to go down memory lane now, and think about the subjects you liked, the ones you pursued after school, formally or informally... Now, think back to when you were a student: how did you feel about them? How did the teachers make you feel about these subjects? Take a few secs (as long as you wish, actually) to think about this and bring back some memories...

...

I didn't go to the garden; I actually did the same exercise as you did this time... All sorts of things come up when we go back to our school days... We remember the oddities of teachers, their weird behavior (we do, and better than their lessons!) But we also remember "good teachers and bad teachers" ...

Sometimes we cannot put our finger on it, but with the good teachers we usually felt "safe", "understood", "encouraged" ... in a word, "rewarded". Maybe you don't remember exactly, or maybe now you know about it, your memories will bring up those nice words, the smiles, the nods that the "good teachers" regularly used.

There are loads of studies that show that positive reinforcement can improve a student's academic success. This also works with parents and their children actually. And there are many studies that show that **positive reinforcement can improve behavior in children and pupils,** one such research papers is 'From Positive Reinforcement to Positive Behaviors: An Everyday Guide for the Practitioner' by Ellen A. Sigler and Shirley Aamidor, which appeared in *Early Childhood Education Journal,* Vol. 32, No. 4, February 2005.

This study confirms that positive reinforcement works, but unlike other studies it can also see the drawbacks: there's a funny passage in it, a hyperbole, an exaggeration, but maybe not even such a big exaggeration:

> *"It is true that when a child is engaged in a creative activity, like drawing or painting, if you indicate, "I like the color you are using," you will indeed get an entire page of purple."*

I am sure you understand what the researchers are saying... But apart from the funny side, it has two important points in it:

- *Positive reinforcement is very powerful, and it can change behavior.*

- *Positive reinforcement must be used correctly and ethically.*

And this second point is exactly what we are going to see next.

Using Positive Reinforcement Correctly and Ethically

Would you think that the now famous vodka commercials use positive reinforcement correctly? Ethically? Do you think it is acceptable to encourage people to drink spirits, which cause all sorts of health and social problems by falsely associating them with partying on a beach with half naked people? Think about it...

...

These ads are fully legal, but I can hardly find what **good they want.** Unless we accept that "making money is always good", I have an ethical problem with these commercials. And I bet you had already suspected I did! Using what is proven to have an effect on people's psychology and behavior to cause self-harming behavior cannot be defined as good, nor as neutral, but only bad. They are therefore totally unethical.

Now, in the study by Sigler and Aamidor we cited before there is a clue: **you must make sure that the behavior you want to obtain by using positive reinforcement is positive, good...** And this means for the person you are encouraging too.

Developing stamina, confidence, willingness, and even interest in pupils and children is certainly good. Helping people break a smoking (drinking or drug) addiction is good too. You know they will benefit from using positive reinforcement.

But many advertisements show that **it is possible (but unethical) to use positive reinforcement to encourage negative behavior.** You can give a sweet (or tell him/her something positive) to a child every time s/he does something bad, like throw a tantrum, or worse... This way you will encourage the child to do it again.

This is why it is true that when a child throws a tantrum, you should not give him/her what they want. That teaches him/her that bad behavior has positive consequences.

Similarly, **breaking mind manipulation only uses positive reinforcement.** To stop, get out of, recover from mind manipulation, we can only use positive reinforcement. This may look like a disadvantage. I don't think so. I actually think it's a bonus... It means that getting out of mind manipulation is a positive experience.

Now, I'll ask you to do an experiment. Choose something you know you don't need but you want "too much". Something bad for you. Choose something fairly small at this stage. You know exactly where I am going: choose something you suspect you only crave through low-level mind manipulation.

It may be a product, unhealthy food often advertised on TV etc. It may be using social media... Don't worry; I am not asking you to give it all up completely. But take about a week. Once a day, when you want it, just renounce. But that's not the end of it... Replace it with something healthy (physically, mentally etc.) and pleasurable.

Instead of going on HeadBook (I like changing names of brands, just out of spite) or Trotter, listen to some of your favorite (uplifting, please!) songs.

Instead of the burger, cook (or get) something healthy but tasty, high quality... There's a lot to choose from nowadays. Instead of the sugary fizzy drink, get some freshly squeezed fruit juice...

Do it once a week... We will come back to this exercise later in the book, for now, just choose what you will do.

...

Done? Best of luck with this experiment. You already see that we will be using positive reinforcement to break a habit. For the time being, I simply want you to **build the idea and experience that life can be more pleasurable without that habit, that addiction.**

If you want to reinforce this even further, add two things to the experiment:

- *Write down how good you feel when you do "the other thing".*

- *Remember the pleasure you got from "the other thing" just before going to sleep.*

One will make a more memorable mark in your rational mind, the other will help your subconscious mind accept the new activity as "part of you and good". Both will fix the new "other activity" more firmly in your memory as positive.

But now on to the other side...

Negative Reinforcement

Welcome to the "dark side". And dark it is indeed. We have seen that while the original "assassins" were motivated to kill with lots of hashish and lies about a reward, the Nazis and the CIA even used torture to change people's behavior.

We need to step back a little in time though now. Just after the Second World War, a study that came out in 1948, by a US psychologist by the name of **B.F. Skinner**. He is famous for what is known as "the Skinner box". I could call it a "torture chamber for mice" but let me know if you disagree...

It is a cage, with an electrified grid as the floor, a green light and a red light, a loudspeaker, a lever that opens or not a food dispenser. You can see how it works; the loudspeaker gives a signal that tells the mouse that there may or may not be food. The mouse has to look at the lights: green means there is food (reward) and red means the poor little creature will get a "complimentary electric shock on the house". The mouse can either get the reward or the electric shock when it pulls the lever, according to the light.

Then guess what? The mouse quickly learns that when the light is red, that lever is better left untouched.

Skinner found out *three types of reinforcements:*

- *Positive*

- *Neutral*

- *Negative*

We have seen the first: the neutral has no effects, the third has strong effects. What's more - is that *negative reinforcement has very fast effects; fear acts very quickly on the victim's mind.* It does, in fact, work faster than positive reinforcement. The reason is actually simple: *when we are worried for our safety, it becomes a priority, and we want a fast solution.*

It also means that often we suspend critical thinking when we are scared and/or facing a threat to our wellbeing, happiness, even social status, or in extreme cases, safety and life.

Negative reinforcement is a very powerful tool. Some people will say that it's more powerful than positive reinforcement. It may depend on how heavy the punishment is, but what matters to us is not so much which is generically "stronger". What we need to state is that *negative reinforcement is:*

- *Faster acting*

- *Always unethical*

I mean, you can get permission to use very limited negative reinforcement from a volunteer to an experiment. That consent needs to be, however, signed in full consciousness, compensated (financially) and the extent of the negative reinforcement must be very limited and never leave any permanent or long-term consequence.

I can give you a bitter coffee, or if I want to overdo it, a salty coffee for an experiment after you have signed a full agreement and I have paid you for it... This is in the name of science. That's about it... No, an electric shock is not ethical. With or without agreement and with or without even massive compensation. It's not just illegal; it is a crime against Humanity.

And now I will show you some of the horrible things that have happened "on the dark side".

Uses of Negative Reinforcement

Unfortunately, people (even well-educated people) often forget the ethical issue and they like to cut corners and get quick results. So, guess what? Negative reinforcement has been used to change people's behavior even in institutional and "scientific" situations.

You will know that till not long-ago caning students (or other forms of corporal punishment) was acceptable. No, sorry, I got it wrong. It wasn't just acceptable. Educationalists swore by it. And of course, you would avoid making mistakes if you didn't want your knuckles birched, but you also became very wary about exploring (and presenting) new ideas. In the end, is education just "avoiding mistakes"?

Electro-shocks (or ECT, Electroconvulsive Therapy) have been used by so-called psychotherapists for decades, and in many countries the "therapy" is still not illegal, even if it's almost never used, and used with low electrical discharges. Well, it is torture, and torture is a crime against Humanity (we have seen a few already on the dark side...)

We have seen appalling experiments (even on children) with negative reinforcement and mind conditioning. The use of psychotropic and hallucinatory drugs like LSD was meant to worsen the effect of the punishment, to extreme levels (nightmarish, literally, just imagine being in pain and in a horrible nightmare sometimes for weeks on end...) Just thinking about it is sickening.

Lesser and more acceptable uses of negative reinforcement may be the "garlic nail polish" to make children stop biting their nails. But even that one raises all sorts of questions from a psychological point of view, for example:

- If a child bites his or her nails, this is usually a symptom of something deeper (insecurity, worry etc.) stopping the symptom does not solve the problem.

- Even worse, the child now can associate the attempt to relieve himself/herself from the problem with a bad experience.

- Then garlic is actually a super healthy food; are we sure we want our children to hate it?

On the whole we can safely say that very little good will ever come from negative reinforcement. And having said this, we will get out of the "dark side".

Hey, but don't jump with joy yet... We are going "somewhere in between" now.

The Trap: Positive and Negative Reinforcements Together

The effect of mind manipulation is heightened if you use both lights in Skinner's box, metaphorically speaking: *if you use both negative reinforcements and positive reinforcements you will have a huge effect on the victim.*

Guess what? Mind manipulators are very much aware of this. In serious cases, like with MKUltra and similar horrendous projects, these two forces were sometimes applied intentionally.

If you show someone that when s/he does something the punishment stops and not only, a reward starts, it's quite easy to condition this person to doing it as a habit. I will give you an example. Heroin, the drug... You see, people who use it feel bad when they are not using it, and very good when they use it. It becomes "second nature" to take it then. This is why the habit is hard to break.

If you give an electric shock to someone when this person for example waves with the left hand, and a reward when s/he waves with the right hand, you will soon find that the person not only will stop waving with the left hand, but will be very willing to wave with the right hand.

This concept works at all levels (of stimulus, reward, and punishment) and on all sorts of behavior. It can be drastic like the electric shock I mentioned, even more drastic if under the effect of psychotropic substances, or very light, like a simple smile and sneer… But maybe repeated over time and often.

Now, I will ask you a question… Do you use any social media? Have you ever posted something that got many "likes, stars, hearts, thumbs up, or positive comments"? Ok, we all did. But have you ever posted anything that got negative comments, people arguing with you etc.? If you have you know what it feels like.

Now, can you see that **social media has a system of rewards which is inbuilt, but a "hidden" system of punishments as well.** People who design these massive platforms know exactly what they are doing. They try them out in Beta format for a long time. They study users' reactions. And they know the social context they are working within very well…

So, what is the effect of likes for some posts and (sometimes long and exhausting) arguments for other posts? Which posts get the most likes? Which gets the most arguments? Think about it for a minute…

…

I hope you remembered to do something positive in the meantime. Maybe replaced a bad habit with a good and pleasurable one like we said at the end of the last chapter? Anyway, I am sure this exercise opened up a lot of pathways of investigation to you…

We will get round to discussing social media in great detail very soon. But for sure you will have noticed that **the posts that get most likes follow a trend, a pattern**. This trend depends on the "bubble" you are in and on very typical "online conversation modes". Memes get lots of likes. But memes also teach you to disrespect others.

How about the posts that get contradicted etc.? These are often critical posts, posts that don't form with what most people think, especially in your bubble. So, we can say that **the overall effect of rewards and punishments in social media is to make you conform to some social patterns and avoid critical thinking.**

And this is not little in terms of mind manipulation… But there is more, and a final point I would like to make: the **effect of society as negative reinforcement**

Social Negative Reinforcement

Did you notice that while the social media themselves don't have an inbuilt punishment system in most cases, they use the behavior of users for it? YoTube (it's the young version of the other "tube") does have thumbs down, but most other social media avoid them.

Still, if you say something that goes against what people who watch, think, or like, and especially if it goes against what a particular group of people dislike, people who like to "argue their case on social media"... well, if you have had a long argument on one of these, especially "Trotter", you will remember that you had a horrible time, even a whole horrific day.

Let's go back to our vodka commercials... Can you see any "implicit" and "covert" negative reinforcement given by social values and society in them?

...

I bet you did! The idea behind it is that you have to be "cool". Those ads are mainly positive reinforcement, but even there, you will find the little thought at the back of your mind that says, "These are the cool guys," and thus the sentence, for the vast majority of people, those who have felt "uncool" at school has a very loaded meaning. It means, "Hey, if you don't drink our vodka, you are not cool". And that is how many **commercials and other forms of mind manipulation use society, social "values" (beliefs), patterns, and traditions as negative implicit reinforcement.**

Now you can see how deep this system of negative and positive reinforcement is; it uses society, it goes deep into our subconscious and it can be very insistent, repetitive and all pervasive.

But we have a few ideas about how to get out of it now... It has to do with positive reinforcement, but also with replacing a bad, induced habit with a good, chosen one... And this is what we are going to see next. But take a break now and guess what? Do something nice, healthy, and pleasurable first!

Chapter 6 – Replacement Therapy for Mind Manipulation

Mind manipulation causes a form of addiction, as you now know. And what is the best way out of addiction? There are a few working strategies, to be honest, including changing life or lifestyle. But, honestly, not everybody can afford to get the first coach and leave everything behind for a new life... So, the most practical, the most adaptable, and often the cheapest way out is *replacement therapy.*

Do you know that I gave up smoking a few years ago? I had tried in many ways... I tried chewing gums, patches, pills... It never really worked till vaping came along... Vaping is simply strong, effective, and even a fashionable replacement therapy. And it works so well looking at the numbers that the tobacco industry is really worried.

But do you know what my father told me when he saw me vaping? He said, "Son, I gave up from one day to the next – just with my willpower." Ok, some people may have done that in their life, but to start with, he "lied"; even my father, who does have amazing willpower, used candy sweets to get out of smoking... It's just a less effective replacement therapy, in the end.

Of course your life situation, commitments, quality, social relationships etc. are all factors that can help you succeed or not... And life has become more hectic and stressful. This means that it's harder on the whole to give up on bad habits and break addiction and mind manipulation...

In fact, communities and clinics for alcoholics and drug addicts are not in Manhattan and even fewer in Queens... They are in peaceful places, often in the countryside. They also offer that life change element that really works. For serious victims of mind manipulation, like targeted individuals, the suggestion of moving to a quiet place in the countryside is a very good one indeed. And these people have suffered so much that I do know some who have actually left their job and everything and moved to a peaceful place in the middle of nowhere...

For lesser problems, maybe selling your home is a bit too much to ask! So, let's stick to replacement therapy for the time being...

What Is Replacement Therapy

Most of us know roughly what "replacement therapy" means. It means *replacing a habit, substance, or behavior with another one you have chosen and which is healthier and better for you.*

But in the examples we have seen, we already have two types of replacement therapy. I said that my father changed smoking for eating sweets; I changed from smoking to vaping. For heroin addicts, the swap is from heroin to methadone in many cases... These are not the same "types" of replacements, are they? In fact, they are:

- *Replacing the way a substance is used with another way (smoking – vaping).*

- *Replacing a noxious substance (habit) with a less noxious one (smoking – candy sweets).*

These are typical replacement therapies. Note one thing, with vaping you can then easily reduce the amount of nicotine by degrees and reach no nicotine at all. The "smoking nicotine to vaping nicotine" is only the first step. The second step is the elimination of nicotine altogether. Store owners and assistants of vaping outlets actively encourage customers to reduce the nicotine till you get to naught in my experience, doing an excellent service to society.

The same idea applies to methadone and my father's candy sweets (and other food, mind you... most people who stop smoking eat more...) However, methadone has not proved that effective in the reduction phase...Anyway, the idea is that this replacement needs to go one way:

- *... all these replacements are then meant to reduce the quantity of the substitute substance/habit till you get completely out of the addiction.*

But when we talk about mind manipulation, we also need to look at a third type of replacement therapy... ready?

Mind Manipulation & Replacement Therapy

You have already started replacement therapy, have you not noticed? I asked you to change a habit by *replacing only part of the habit but with something totally different.* You see how this uses the same principle as "total replacement" therapy but instead of changing the whole substance/habit etc. with a "less bad one" all at once, and then reduce the less bad one... Here we ask you to introduce a positively good one, but start replacing the bad one by stages, till the positively good one has totally replaced that bad one.

We can use both strategies in mind manipulation cases; the latter though is particularly useful with mental patterns and rewiring... *Mind conditioning often leads you to thoughts you do not actually want.* It is at this stage that we can rewire the brain and strengthen positive thought patterns instead.

We will see this better when we talk about rewiring the brain, but *the more you follow a thought path the stronger it becomes.* The more you think, "I like sweets," the more it will be easy to think about it, the more often this thought will come and the more you will actually believe that you like them.

How about if, just at the "juncture" in your brain where the street "I like sweets" starts with you getting a fork, and then you get "I love fruit a lot" instead? At first, this second thought path will be small, like a little animal trail in the forest. But the more you repeat it, and you give it a strong, pleasurable positive reinforcement, the more this path will widen and become clear... Till it's bigger and more pleasant than the "I love sweet" street, and it becomes your preferred one when you get to that juncture.

See how this works? *We will slowly rewire your brain so that the mind manipulation path is replaced by one of your choosing. This way, you can replace a bad induced habit with a good one of your choosing.*

Do you want an example? Why not replace watching TV or being on social media with reading? It does not need to be "heavy reading" … If you're not a convinced literature geek, reading *Love and Peace* by Tolstoy maybe is not the best replacement for "FootBook" or "InstaGraph" or a light TV program. But there are newspapers, comics, funny books, magazines etc.…

And it's easier to read a quick magazine article instead of watching a TV program or going on social media, especially if it's meant to be a quick activity, and you have little time… But the chosen habit needs to be positive, good for you, and, above all, your choice and enjoyable.

Of course, unlike with methadone, sweets or nicotine in vaping, *with this type of replacement therapy we want you to increase, not reduce, the replacement substance or better activity because it is healthy and good for you!*

Replacement Therapy Must Be Enjoyable

Let's take an example. Do you know how many people have tried to become vegetarians or vegans and failed? That was especially true in the past. Do you know why? Try stopping eating steaks and replace them with lettuce and carrots!

Once upon a time (it looks so long ago now), vegetarian and vegan food was "boring". Mind you, you will get used to tasting a leaf of lettuce, but it's very unrealistic to think that you can replace the strong sensation of eating steak with it… But vegans and vegetarians came up with new recipes, food that tastes like (even better than) meat, with the same consistency (even juicier) … And in recent years, the number of vegetarians and vegans is in fact growing very rapidly…. In 2018, 5% of US residents were vegetarians and 3% vegan. In most European countries the number of vegetarians is even higher, usually between 7 and 11%.

But all these people had to go through replacement therapy. By having good, enjoyable, and even fun and visually attractive food makes it more achievable.

One of the great successes of vaping is that you can have all the flavors you want… That gives pleasure, and a wide range of "rewards" … It makes it fun to try blueberry rather than chocolate… This is an advantage over tobacco, which, for though different brands may have slightly different flavors, it is always tobacco flavor…

So, if you have a problem, like, your children watch too much TV – ok, then, first of all congratulations for focusing on this. Second, what have you been thinking as a replacement? Can I give you a list to choose from?

- Board or card games
- Doing house chores
- Playing football
- Doing homework
- Playing video games
- Playing with friends in the garden

Which ones would you choose? Which wouldn't you choose? Why? See you after a pleasurable break.

...

I had to change the radio channel, the music was too "harsh" ... You see, I replaced watching TV with listening to the radio in the morning... Ok, I think we will agree that there are three we can really choose: board and card games, playing football, playing with friends in the garden. You can add as many similar ones as you wish, like playing with dolls, playing with the dog, painting, dancing etc....

The point is that **you have to replace children's TV time with something fun!** But how many parents say, "Why are you watching television? Go and do your homework!". What happens here? That they give an unpleasant alternative and negatively reinforce the TV watching habit!

This must happen millions of times every day... If only they stopped to think... If only they understood what you know now! These parents must be in perfect good faith but in many cases, they are just making the problem worse.

So, homework and house chores are not functional, but how about video games? There is a double problem with this: they are *even more addictive* than TV and they are by no means healthy.

So, now you see how the **choice of replacement needs to be healthy, enjoyable, and not highly addictive.** You now have the keys to the solution of many problems of mind manipulation.

This does not just apply to children. Adults too want to have fun; they want to enjoy themselves etc.... Apply these rules to you as well...

By the way, how has your "long term replacement experiment" been going?

...

I hope it's going well, but maybe now you know more things about how to use replacement therapy, and you want to bring some changes? Maybe you want to change the replacement? Maybe you want a more positive one? On this point, social activities are always a good choice... Is your child watching too much TV? Invite one of his/her friends over! Quick solution, healthy and gold for social skills...

Maybe you think the reward is not enough? Then...

Add Extra Rewards to the Replacement

Do you know what some people who stop smoking do? They put their cigarette money into a piggy bank, even part of it… Then, at the end of the month or so, they open the piggy bank, and they find out how much they have saved.

This is excellent! Do you realize how many things you can do with the money you spend on cigarettes? It depends on where you live, in the USA the average cost of a pack is $6.28 at the time of writing; but in some European countries it can easily get to the equivalent of $10.00! Two packs and you can go out to the restaurant. Five packs and you can buy new shoes! Imagine after an average of thirty packs in a month… what would you get? A weekend break, a small holiday?

You see, this is *extra positive reinforcement.* You can always add it "from outside". For example, if you propose playing in the garden instead of watching TV to your child, add something more… Say, "If you do this I will…" – and add something nice but positive. Don't buy them off with sweets! Something like "I will let you play with your friend tomorrow," or "I will help you with your homework," or "I will get you new crayons," etc.…

The odd treat is always fine, I am not advocating a Spartan regime! But don't make it a habit of replacing a bad thing with another bad thing. Especially if you are caught unprepared, you are busy with something else etc., "I will get you an ice cream," every now and then is perfectly fine. Then good quality Italian ice cream is actually ok(ish) in terms of health…

You see, the more pleasure you introduce into de-conditioning your mind and rewiring your brain, the more successful you will be!

Planning and Structuring Replacement Therapy

Imagine your replacement therapy like a graph… You will need to increase the replacement by steps while at the same time you reduce the bad habit. One line goes up, the other goes down. And yes, going past that 50:50 point is quite important, one of the main turning points.

But how can you do this? Are there any strategies you can use? Of course, there are!

There are quite a few tricks you can use…

Choose the time to start well

People are more likely to succeed if they start replacement therapy at a relaxed time, a good time or "during a break". Stopping smoking when you change jobs, when you go on holiday, when you start a new relationship or anyway when you are not very stressed is always far more effective.

Don't expect too much too soon

Don't give yourself unfeasible, "athletic" targets, like, "I will stop eating sweets in a week," if that is your problem… No, give yourself plenty of time! Of course, this will depend on what you want to give up. Smoking is very hard, and I can say it from experience. I found not watching TV very easy for example… Yes, I have changed many habits in life…

Be flexible

Even if you want to set targets, be ready to change them. Leaving an open-end date is also possible. It depends a bit on you. If you know yourself well enough and you are aware that "open end projects are not for you" then avoid it. But if you trust that you have enough willpower and you can leave the final goal unscheduled, please do.

In any case, however, **be ready to change the timing, and even scale down the project temporarily.**

Keep in mind that life can be tough and "things happen"

Unexpected things happen in life. You may be perfectly on track one day, then the next day you get a "blow" from life… I don't wish it to you or anybody. But if it happens, just slow down, readjust, put it off… But don't give up!

Don't beat yourself up if things go wrong

And on this topic, if things go wrong, don't lay the blame on yourself. This too is mind conditioning! You see, we are taught that if we start a project and it goes wrong, it "*must*" be our fault. In some cases, ok, it's true. But in most cases, people have to give up because of unforeseen events and events that do not depend on them.

It is not your fault if the market changes. It is not your fault if a friend lets you down. It is not your fault if you fall ill. It is not your fault if you lose your job or it does not go too well. It is not your fault if your car breaks down and you need to buy a new one… Get the point?

Stopping smoking is a good example here. People have setbacks and they start again… Ok, it happens. But if they blame themselves for the setback, then they negatively reinforce their smoking habit… And no, I'm not completely saying that you shouldn't take responsibility for things that ARE in your control to just blame something else. Be mindful of this.

Start with about 5 to 10%, not more!

These percentages give you a rough idea. It's hard to quantify certain things. But for example, TV… If you watch it for 3 hours a day, start with a bit less, not half… Take away 15 minutes on day one, and then move to 30 etc.

With cigarettes there can be a double way to be honest. You can start reducing how much you smoke, by one cigarette a day (or every two or three days) and then stop altogether.

You can do it while vaping as well, but actually with vaping stopping cigarettes altogether is quite easy. Then again, you will start with high nicotine levels, then reduce it little by little. I actually started with the highest possible level of nicotine. I know myself… I know I like strong sensations… and I wanted to make sure that vaping would be stronger than smoking cigarettes. It worked. But then I cut down slowly, actually very slowly by other people's standards.

Add extra rewards at each stage

Every time you change steps, every time you achieve a partial success, every time you make progress, give yourself a treat, some extra positive reinforcement. Even thinking about it beforehand has a great, positive motivational effect: "If I cut down another cigarette, I will treat myself to a movie on Sunday…" Savor it as the moment gets nearer and your aim is getting closer. Celebrating success is vital in finding more success.

Involve others

If you can, by all means tell your family and friends you will be starting a project, no need to say, "replacement therapy". You don't even need to get into the details of mind manipulation. You can simply say, "I want to change this habit/this thing in my life," and then you can simply ask them "to be aware of it" or "give you a hand if they can".

In particular, if you have a partner, you should definitely involve him or her – if it is possible.

Reflect regularly

Every now and then, say every week, take some time off all other duties and activities and reflect on your progress. Reflection is key to success, whatever you do! Reflection needs to be done with peace and calm, not in a hurry and noisy place. It needs to have an "ameliorative purpose"; it cannot be a form of "inquisition".

It's purpose is to see what has gone well (which is positive reinforcement) and then find ways of doing even better. It is not an exercise in self-flagellation, ok?

It is simple: find a quiet place. If you want to do it with a friend, your partner etc., fine... Get a cup of tea (a glass of wine is fine, actually, red is better anyway; it relaxes you, while white wine makes you nervous), and *brainstorm:*

- *Three things that went well.*

- *One thing to do, to improve, or add to your schedule and plan.*

If you have more than three good things, fine! But do not add too many improvements. One or two maximum. You can always add the others that come to your mind next week. The task needs to be feasible, or you will set yourself up to fail... One good improvement and you will focus on it very well, instead.

What's inside a word?

But I want to tease you a little bit more... Did you know that you can actually use words, rephrase them, change them so that you can change people's minds and even long held beliefs?

Chapter 7 – Neuro Linguistic Programming (NLP)

What are you using when you think? What are your thoughts made of? The answer can be complex, but on a basic level, you will agree that "words and sentences" is a viable answer. And it is. We have already said it: we use words and sentences to formulate rational thoughts.

Now, I'll ask you another question: if I could manipulate the language you use, if I could influence it, would I also influence your thoughts, or even your way of thinking? Let's meet again after a short reflection.

...

Can I try and guess what you answered? I bet you thought it is possible. Now, I'll ask you a more personal question, one which you only need to answer in your mind: when was the last time you used language to sway a friend? Or to obtain something from someone?

...

Ok, I got it... You are one of the very, very few ones who never do these things. Or are you? Are you sure you've never even used a "more convincing word" to get your way? Of course we all have and do, and it's not really problematic; there is a range of linguistic choices we can make which is all fair and honest.

But how about if this *link between language and neurological processes could be manipulated?* Or, put in a different way, *is it possible to use language to induce neurological processes and then actions in people?*

This does not need to be used in a negative way; it can be used to cure people. And in fact, this concept has been developed by some psychotherapists, including *Richard Bandler* and *John Grinder* who, in the 1970s theorized a way of treating mental issues with language, or what we call *NLP,* or *Neuro Linguistic Programming.*

Does NLP Work?

I need to start by being very straightforward with you. Many scientists believe that NLP is not actually a functional method. Let's say that for many years, there has been large opposition to the validity of this theory.

But science does and must change its mind when new discoveries and studies come along. Recent peer reviewed research has started to show that its academic fortune may be starting to change. In a long and detailed study published in the *Journal of Cognitive Neuroscience, 18:12, 2006,* we find evidence of how actual effects can be identified and traced when NLP is used, in particular, so-called "garden path effects". This is when a sentence has a meaning when in isolation, but in the context, it has a different meaning.

In any case, if you want to read more, the study is long and full of data, and it's titled 'A Neurolinguistic Model of Grammatical Construction Processing' and written by Peter Ford Dominey, Michel Hoen, and Toshio Inui.

But leaving academic debate behind, it's still quite useful that you know about this very specific field.

Now, I just discussed the academic standing of NLP for correctness. But I also need to tell you that what we mean now for NLP is not the same as what Bandler and Grinder meant. You see, they had meant it as a psychotherapeutic method. By this we mean a set of strategies and theories that a psychotherapist can use to treat and / or cure people. Despite some positive signals, as a psychotherapeutic method, it's still regarded as being based on wrong premises and not functional. But…

Developments in NLP

If NLP has not found much fortune in psychotherapy, it has found fertile ground among manipulators, especially in sales, marketing, persuasion, negotiation and similar fields. You see, the idea that you can use language to convince people is pretty self evident, unlike the idea that you can build a whole set of strategies to cure people using only language…

Soon after its announcement to the world, NLP caught the interest of marketing companies, sales agencies, business training providers and the like. They took the principles fairly, freely, and roughly, but they developed a ***striking set of techniques and stages to "grab people's attention" and then convince them to change their minds and then act upon it.***

Applications of NLP

Let's meet our vacuum cleaner door to door salesman again (let's make him a man this time). Shall we give him a very trustworthy name? How about Ben? Ok, then. Ben has it all: he's well groomed, he has the gift of the glib; he's naturally pleasant, well educated etc… He still does not get great results though…

He tries and tries, but the vacuum cleaners he sells are still few and far between… So, he thinks that there is something about his speech, about his delivery, about his technique that does not work. You see, he's self critical…

So he looks around. At the time there was no internet but he found some flyers with NLP written on it… And he finds that there is an actual method, ***a script in clear stages and phases that can get you from grabbing someone's attention to actually getting them to do what you want them to.***

Basically, it's a **step by step guide to "persuading" people**... "Great," he thinks to himself, "I am taking this course straight away!" He did. He paid $50.00 (back in the days it was a lot) and – you guessed – his sales increased an awful lot!

And you know what? You can now get the same course Ben took – and for free! Just read what is coming next!

...Sorry, I identified a bit too much with the course trainer... Anyway, I'll show you what these steps are... For free, of course.

Anchoring

This is the "foot in the door" stage. For Ben, it used to be a door in the face before he realized that what matters is to strike the customer with an **immediate sense of bonding.** And that's where Ben had been going wrong! How can you establish a connection talking about a vacuum cleaner?

Now, look at advertisements – let's say something like food for kids. You have a problem here: you need to sell food for kids to adults. Ok, you are right, some ads are directed at kids (so that they nag their parents), but many are directed directly at the parents, aren't they?

So, what can they use as anchoring?

...

You will have noticed that many ads show happy families, smiling and healthy children, a playful but very "orderly" scene... You see, this is what parents want their children to be. This is what makes parents happy.

If you compare ads targeted at children, the scene is often much more colorful, crazy, dynamic, playful, even surreal... This is because these ads anchor to their vivid imagination, not to their parents' wishes and dreams...

You see, **you need to catch the other person's attention with an image, sentence, phrase, idea that s/he likes**.

Do you want to guess what Ben did next? He switched his intro... Instead of talking about the vacuum cleaner, he started talking about "cleaning up after children". He then developed questions as if he was carrying out a survey, like, "Do you ever get your child to clean the floor?" and "Would you like to?"

You see, he worked out how to anchor his speech. **Anchoring requires an emotional engagement on behalf of the "target", the person we want to persuade.** Remember that at the time most of the people Ben met were middle class women, with children etc. So, he got the "right way in".

Belief Change

Only after Ben was sure that he had fully anchored the customer, he moved on to the second stage: belief change. In case the first anchor did not work, he tried a second, then, on rare occasions, even a third. In any case, he would **never move into the "belief change" phase if the anchor had not worked**.

And he realized a big mistake he had been making... Talking about the vacuum cleaner straight away meant trying to change the customer's belief without having made an emotional connection first.

After the course, he already knew that if the anchor had not worked, he was wasting his time. There was no way the customer would end up changing her or his mind.

And this is exactly what all his job was about, isn't it? Making people change their minds and believe they need a new vacuum cleaner. At least in 99% of cases...

How can you make people change belief? First of all, you need to believe that they can change their mind. And this is a basic tenet of NLP. If you use the right words, the right ideas, the right images, most people can be made to change their mind. The question is, however, "how?"

There are some guidelines that NLP experts use:

- **Take it slowly and in small steps.** You cannot change someone's mind in one big step... You will need to "move" the person's position very slowly. Experts actually visualize the person, and watch carefully how she or he moves, making sure that they don't revert back to their original position.

- **Ask questions.** NLP users will ask lots of questions about the issue they are focusing on. This way they get two results:

  1. They collect information about the person and his / her possible problems.
  2. They instill a sense of doubt and uncertainty within the person.

  Don't forget that if I ask you a question, I force you to doubt your position. This way, I am already taking you to a position where making you change your mind is easier.

- **Offer solutions.** Offer solutions to the problems that arise from the questions. This will make you look knowledgeable and trustworthy. But also make sure that **the solutions lead to your final goal.** In Ben's case, the final goal is selling a vacuum cleaner, so, his solutions will be "masked ways of saying: you need a vacuum cleaner".

  I want to give you an example here, to make it clearer. A potential customer complained that children play football every day and they come back with dirty shoes. And of course, he could have told her, "Get them to take their shoes off," instead he said, "You can change the carpet with wood flooring, but even then, cleats would scratch it," and then of course he said, "But it's so beautiful that they like sports, they are growing very healthy!" You see how he left her no real choice, but didn't even mention it by name?

66

- **Narrow the circle.** This is quite a haunting image. Have you ever seen hawks hunt? They start with large circles and make them smaller and smaller in the sky. Basically, they "close in on the prey". And trust me, many NLP users see it exactly in these terms.

  What Ben did about the footballers is also an example of "narrowing the circle." You basically have to show that all other options are "dead ends" and in the end, when you offer yours, after the person has been struggling to find a solution, you will look like a hero, or heroine!

You see, it's a step by step strategy where you know the final goal, and, with well chosen questions, words etc. you close some "paths" and only leave the gates that lead to your pre-decided solution open. When the person you are trying to persuade gets there, *it must look to the person as if s/he had got to that solution freely and independently.* In reality, you led him / her there and s/he has not even realized it.

Along the way, there are also other techniques you should use. And here they are...

Reframing Content: Rephrase and Reformulate Sentences

Have you ever noticed how professional salespeople (like for insurances, cars, technical items especially) like to rephrase what you say? They don't just add a technical tone to the conversation, they do two more things this way:

- *They show you that they are the experts, not you, so you need to trust them.*

- *They put things in a way that make your perspective look better.*

Let's go back to our footballing kids. How would you rephrase, "They come in with dirty shoes and the dirt doesn't come out"?

...

Fine, this was a tricky question, First of all because you are not an expert, second because it does depend on your aim... Well, you know what Ben said before giving his "loaded solution?"

  "True, grass and mud get caught in the fibers of your carpet, I see. If it's wet then you need a lot of power to get it off."

You see, he shows that he knows a lot about the problem, and he also hints that the solution is "lots of power"... Not that it's "taking those dirty cleats off..."

Also, people who want to manipulate users with NLP will rephrase verbs in a very skillful way. For example, "want", "desire", "would like" will become "need" or "can't do without". You see, this way they switch a simple "wish" to a need! Similarly, if you say, "I can't afford it," they will change it into "You could afford it if," or similar constructions.

But there is more to language in NLP techniques... There's also body language.

Mirroring

This is a common technique used by manipulators to give you a subconscious impression that there is "feeling" or that you are "both on the same wavelength". You see, psychologists and sociologists have noticed that people who really get on well together naturally coordinate their movements. Research shows that if you are fully in tune with a friend, the chances that you pick up the glass at the same time increase enormously.

And there is more; they also noticed that if people really get on well, they tend to sit in the same way, or stand in the same way. They also tend to face each other perfectly (and not lean or turn away) and sometimes they literally mirror each other's actions. Like when your friend strokes her hair and you do the same...

Now, I'll ask you a little favor. You can do it now, if you want, or later... Just take a walk where people have fun, like a park, especially where people play sports or have lots of leisure facilities. Even a movie theater is quite good. While you are there, look at couples and groups of people. Check out which ones you think get along really well together, and those who don't. What can you say about mirroring each other's actions?

...

This time I had the chance to go to a flower show! Loved it. I also noticed that there were couples there, and some would focus on the same flower. Some even touched the same plant at the same time! Others, however, were focusing on different things, one looking one way, the other the other way...

Naturally, I formed an idea in my mind: those who acted in unison seemed to be more "attuned", more in agreement with each other. I don't know if they actually were. But that's not our point. Our point is that, **when we see people mirroring each other, we assume that they are on the same wavelength.**

I bet your experience was not different from mine... Now, here is the trick... How about if, say our Ben, learned to copy his customer's actions, movements, position, posture etc.? Wouldn't he be giving his customer the impression that he is a "similar person", or "someone you can get along with easily?"

I am sure you can see how the trick works. In this respect, NLP has developed beyond pure linguistic techniques. Then again, we still call it body "language".

Synonyms Matter

We have looked at rephrasing, and this is part of it, in a way. Let's say that we have a wrong idea of what a synonym is. In fact, ask the person in the street and you will get, "Synonyms are words that mean the same," but do they?

Now, look at these synonyms and find differences between them.

- Like and love
- Work and toil
- Old and ancient
- Fresh and cold

...

I'm sure you got the point... It's very hard to find words that mean exactly the same. Most synonyms are "words within the same area of meaning but with different shades of meaning". They are "very similar", not the same...

Even words with super similar meanings have something slightly different: "choose" and "select" are very similar, but if you say "choose" you sound more friendly, more informal, if you say "select" you sound technical or, depending on the context, even "clinical and cold"... You won't tell your son or daughter, "Select the cake you want!"

This difference in meaning is the **connotation**, which is the "added meaning" we have to words. For example, "home" means a place where you can live, but the connotation is also usually of "pleasant, safe, warm, private" and similar meanings.

NLP manipulators are very good at using synonyms to shift your position very slowly. I am sure you can see how it works. If you want to move someone away from an idea, you rephrase and choose synonyms with more **negative connotations**, while if you want to "invite someone towards an idea", you will choose synonyms with **positive connotations**.

Also note that it's the **connotation of words that often carries an emotional charge.** This way, by using the emotional perception of words and ideas, it is far easier to change people's minds, rather than having to go "the rational way"...

It takes training and experience to play with words that way, but if you are worried that someone is using NLP techniques on you, sniff out the use of rephrasing and synonyms and you are on to something!

Visualization and Metaphor

A picture speaks a thousand words. Even a picture in your mind! And if a mind manipulator can manage to get the "target" to draw pictures in his or her mind, the manipulator can communicate much more effectively, vividly and convincingly.

Sometimes teachers use visualization to engage students. But you can also induce it in people. Sentences like, "Imagine a big field full of flowers in bloom," can be used to bring up visual images in people's mind.

So, our friend Ben started saying things like, "Imagine getting home and finding it spotless," or "Could you imagine if you could clean your whole living room in three minutes? Even before guests come?" You see, these images are far more effective at selling vacuum cleaners than technical descriptions, aren't they?

Metaphor, which I have added in this section is a more complex issue. We know since the times of Freud that our mind does use metaphorical language to think. In fact metaphor is so key to psychology that there are whole books written on it. Some metaphors have very deep meanings that sink into our subconscious.

Staying on the theme of home and home appliances, for example the "hearth" metaphor is very powerful. "A crackling fire in winter" brings up all sorts of connections, and of course Ben would add that with his top of the range vacuum cleaner you can clear the ashes in ten seconds afterwards. But what he is selling here is the idea of a romantic evening, or maybe a time of hugs and warmth etc...

Using metaphor means bringing up unspoken meanings in the metaphorical language used. It's like talking about something already sunk into our subconscious without mentioning it.

All you need to know to protect yourself is to *be very aware of the power of images and metaphor, and if someone uses them too much, that should ring an alarm bell.* poets excluded, of course!

The Bright Side of NLP

Don't lose faith in the Human family though! While there are people who will take advantage of anything to grift or manipulate your mind, but others have a positive outlook on life, and they can turn even very unethical and evil techniques into positive ones...

It so happens that many psychologists and other professionals have asked themselves a very deep question: "Is it possible to use NLP in a positive way?" They thought about it, tried out a few techniques and... Yes! Of course we can!

The key differences between using NLP to manipulate or even to heal are two:

- *That NLP techniques are used on a consensual person (even oneself).*

- *That NLP techniques are used for a positive goal.*

Georgina, for example, has very low self esteem. She is one of those lovely, sweet, intelligent and very gifted people who is not achieving what you would expect from life. Why? Put simply, she has a negative attitude towards achieving. She has that mindset many people have, that "things are hard to get" or even "impossible".

You know the sort of person we are talking about. People who say, "Yes, it will happen to someone else and not me," every time a positive idea comes their way.

Can I ask you a question? Now that you have learned a lot about NLP, could you see ways in which we could use it to help Georgina?

…

I suppose you have come up with a few ideas already. Maybe you thought that if we help her rephrase sentences with positive synonyms, positive verbs, strong expressions of willpower, little by little she will start building her confidence. And you would be right!

NLP is a technique to change people's attitudes and ideas, and that can also be used to change bad ideas into good ones!

How to Use NLP for Good Reasons

You can use NLP on yourself. Using positive affirmations (which we will see later in this book), is a way of changing your mindset. Visualizing positive results is another (again, look at the last chapter of this book for these techniques with practical exercises). In fact, lots of the exercises in Chapter 13 are based on NLP. But I know you are patient to wait …

Ok then, just because I am a "softie" as students say… First of all:

- ***You need to know your traits well and be honest about them.*** Asking a friend or significant other to be "tough but fair" with you could be a good idea. There are things that, despite all our efforts, we cannot see in ourselves. But take what s/he says as a "chance to change it", not as a critique to you.

- ***You need to focus on one single trait or wrong idea at a time.*** You would make a mess if you tried to change all your improvable sides together. Don't even go there, for your own sake of sanity!

- ***You need to decide exactly where you want to get to.*** Write it down if you need to. For example, "Now I believe I am not good at my job. I will believe that I am very good at it".

- ***Make a list of "negative sentences" you regularly use***. This needs to be very long and detailed. These are the sentences that "build your thoughts in a negative way."

- ***Cross them out and write positive versions of them.*** You don't need to memorize them. Use these as "inspiration" and then…

- ***Use every chance you have to rephrase and reframe.*** This needs to be ***regular and frequent.*** It's fine if you sit there in the evening for 30 minutes and you look back at your day and say, "I said this and I should say that," and go through all the negative thoughts of the day.

But you must also do this with small but regular changes. Change many, short, simple sentences several times a day. Imagine a spider weaving a cobweb that catches bad thoughts… The more regular it is, the more frequent the individual threads, the better it works…

You can start now. Just make sure you keep it all positive!

For fully detailed (easy and fun) activities, please wait till Chapter 13. But now you know how to identify and defend yourself from NLP manipulators and you can even start using it for your own good.

Getting Personal

So far, we have focused on mind manipulation through the media and similar ways, but what happens if you meet someone in person who wants to manipulate you? I am not talking about the professional salesman, here… We'll get to them as well, but in due course. I am talking about that manipulative colleague of yours, or the store manager who always gets what he wants…

You know, those who do it – let's say by vocation? So, if you want to know about them and how to stop them… Well, first treat yourself to something you really enjoy, then just meet me in the next chapter…

Chapter 8 – Manipulators in Everyday Life

Have you ever worked hard only to find out that someone else got all the credit? Have you ever been tripped just in front of the finish line at a metaphorical race, at work, at school, or maybe even with friends, acquaintances etc.? I bet you have. I have. Most people have, and the exceptions are often "on the other side" of the fence in this case: they are the manipulators.

There are quite a few people who manipulate others in everyday life, especially at school and at work. "Why at school and work, especially," is the question you may be asking now? Let me tell you...

What Turns People into Manipulators

Alex is an adolescent student. His parents are quite demanding, and they expect him to be a top student... But unfortunately, while he is academically gifted, he is not "as gifted as quite a few other students in his class".

However, he finds out that a very intelligent girl, Asia, has a soft spot for him... So, he makes friends with her. He butters her up, he talks to her... Well, you know... He feeds her infatuation instead of telling her the truth, which is that he does not like her at all. But he knows he has something to get from her if he keeps flirting with her: he can get her to help him with class and homework, and, if all goes to plan, he can even get her to write his homework, essays etc....

And he manages... That goes on till he changes school, then, he starts all over again, this time with a girl called Rebecca. Then he starts work, and, well, the situation is slightly different, but the game is the same... And he finds that his colleague, Sarah has noticed his good looks...

This is a sample story, but the pattern is quite common. People learn that manipulating others is "advantageous" to themselves and they hang on to it at first as a strategy to meet standards expected from them, then they refine their technique, and they use it for "benefits" like career advancement, making money etc....

Let's make the ***factors that turn people into manipulators*** explicit:

- ***It usually starts as a tendency at a young age.***

- ***The future manipulator is often under social (family) pressure to "do better".***

- ***The future manipulator may (often does) feel that s/he cannot achieve the goals put on him/her.***

- *In other cases, the future manipulator is actually encouraged to manipulate by family members instead.* These are serious cases; they often end up looking at others as "objects" and even "inferior". But these also often end up being the most skilled manipulators.

- *The future manipulator achieves positive results from his early manipulation experiences (positive reinforcement).*

- *The manipulator becomes accustomed to doing it.*

- *Manipulation becomes normal practice in his work and/or social life.*

As you can see, society is, once more to blame. *A very competitive society (at school and work) is both the "motive" of manipulators when they start and the giver of the "reward".*

This is key; really, we will never get out of this cycle if we do not change society and make it less competitive. It is because of its competitiveness that young people feel "obliged" to manipulate at first... But this is also a *society which rewards manipulators, selecting them for key, well paid, and powerful posts.*

The focus on achievement, rather than honesty, the focus on competition, rather than cooperation, that we have in our social (working, school, politics etc.) structure simply means that *manipulators have an unfair, but often huge advantage over honest people in this society.*

We "select" the least trustworthy politicians... We don't, because by the time they get their name on the ballot paper they have been selected by... party, previous political life, work success etc.... And all these are already "filters" that select ruthless people, rather than honest people.

There are due exceptions, but this is very common. In my view, it is becoming more and more common, and even more pathological and grave.

How to Spot the "Manipulator among Us"

Fine, now we know what path leads people to becoming manipulators, but is there a way of spotting them, of finding them out, of identifying them? Yes, of course there is! Put simply, *everyday life manipulators will show the same signs of manipulation as "remote distance" manipulation,* the ones we saw in Chapter 4, 'Signs and Symptoms of Mind Manipulation' like, in particular:

- *Repetition*
- *Insistence*
- *False and empty claims*
- *Elusiveness*
- *Overemphatic language*
- *Contradictory body language*

They may also display the other signs too, but at this stage the usual warning: look at the signs as a whole, one single sign is not usually enough...

But there are more, specific to face to face interaction, like:

- **Excessive friendliness;** there are people who are naturally friendly, but you also have those who don't do it naturally. And, when you start a new job, when you get into a new neighborhood etc., you may know the type of person I am referring to... The one who wants to be "first in getting your confidence" ... These people often add a bit of insistence in the way they propose themselves as friends. Which leads me to the next point.

- **Willingness to skip stages in pushing your relationship to the next step;** they skip too fast from "being good acquaintances" to "being good friends". They want to get your confidence, as we said, and they often use the word "friend", "trust" etc. but out of context, in a forced way... **They want you to see them as friends even before you have done all the "routine safety checks" to regard someone as a friend.**

- **They flatter you;** being complementary to encourage you, to build your confidence is fine, but when they want to butter you up... Then there may well be a hidden agenda... This is linked to overemphatic language. If you did a good job and a colleague comes and says, "Well done," or indeed, "Good job," that's fine... But if for a decent job done you get a "I have never seen such an amazing job," or, "You are phenomenal!" then beware...

- **They are confident with asking favors;** note that they will have to test your "gullibility" (their word, not mine!) and they need to do it in stages. They won't try their big grift on you without testing the ground... They will start asking you little favors first, and check if you are "one of those who can't say no", or at least if you say "yes" easily, and/or how to get you to say yes... Beware of people who come back with the same request after you say "no" ... There can be exceptions, you may have a colleague who really needs that shift swap because of his/her child... But be careful...

- **They talk behind people's back;** this is bad behavior in any case, but **very typical of manipulators**. They do it because they want to influence ("manipulate") your social patterns. They want to decide your "enemies and allies"; they want to pitch you against their own "enemies", or they want your negative opinion on someone to come in handy when they need it... Never trust people who talk behind others backs. In the end, they may well do it behind yours.

Now, look out for these signs, because if you have a good quantity of these (and of those in Chapter 4), your new colleague may be bad news... By "good quantity" we mean:

- **Number of different signs**

- **Frequency of occurrence of each sign**

- *Level of each sign*, as each can be a small, little thing, or a big one, like asking you to pass a pencil is one thing... asking to take the slack for a mistake is another...

Now, we need to distinguish between "common manipulators" and even more dangerous individuals... Allegedly these are the greatest, most effective, most constant, most skilled, in a word, the most dangerous manipulators of all...

Psychopaths and Sociopaths

Psychopaths and sociopaths are becoming a "mainstream issue"; more and more, even non-professionals, "normal people" are realizing that our world has a major issue: *society favors the advancement of psychopaths and sociopaths.* It does it in exactly the same way as it promotes manipulators, by rewarding them, with better jobs, money, important positions in society, political power etc. And that is exactly what sociopaths and psychopaths crave most of all.

For them, these rewards, especially power and influence, control over others and money, are by far the most pleasurable rewards ever. And note that society proposes them as such, rather than happiness, health, good relationships, fun, being useful to others...

And sociopaths and psychopaths are perfectly adapted to this system of non-values and rewards for being "ruthless" rather than "honest". Why? It's in the name. *Sociopaths and psychopaths are incapable of feeling emotion and empathy for others.* This means that *they see people as objects,* or "things to use to their advantage".

Theirs is a serious condition, a disorder, that needs to be treated. They are actually dangerous to society, to people around them, and to anyone they get in contact with. And because they have no qualms, no sense of guilt, they are excellent liars and manipulators.

There are many symptoms that show you someone is a sociopath or psychopath, on top of being excellent manipulators, so, showing some/most of the signs we have seen so far...

- *They are self-centered;* their world is all about themselves. Everything that happens matters only for what it does to them.

- *They are not self-critical;* they don't admit when they are wrong; in their mind, they can only be right. *They blame mistakes on others,* and even see "conspiracies" against them when they get it horribly wrong.

- *They show no real emotions towards others;* they can try to fake them, but they are quite bad at that... You will notice that they "cut emotional displays short", they look "uncouth" towards other people's suffering and often don't even register that the "expected response" is one of at least faked sympathy.... They often miss the "request for empathy" from others.

Note that in many boards of directors, these are "qualities" … If you have to fire 10,000 people, if you have to tear a village to the ground to build a polluting power plant, if you have to push your company's interests above all others (including people's suffering and livelihoods etc.) the fact that you feel nothing about others is a massive career advantage. Huge. And this has now transferred into politics too…

We will look at how to deal with non-sociopathic and non-psychopathic manipulators in a second, that is a different kettle of fish… But for now…

If you spot a sociopath or psychopath in your life, in your social or working network…

- **Never trust a single word they say.**

- **Try to break every possible link. If you can get them out of your life altogether, even better.**

- **Don't try to be a good Samaritan and try to help them with it. Only, and I absolutely mean only professionals can deal with them.** In fact, if you try to help them, they will sniff it immediately and take advantage of it. I am not joking; I know people who have had their lives *totally ruined by sociopaths and psychopaths.*

So, **the only way to subtract you from mind manipulation from a sociopath or psychopath is to get them out of your life or at least keep them as far as possible from you.** There is no middle ground, no "solving the problem while keeping the person".

But now on to sunnier – or better "less cloudy" beaches…

Dealing with Everyday Life Manipulators

Let's see how you can counter the "intrusion into your life and freedom, or will power" from that disturbing colleague of yours that you have found out wants to manipulate you… There are a few areas you need to work on, and we will assume that you can't totally cut him or her out of your life.

But this brings up a question: would it be ok to just cut them out of your life if you can? Yes. You need no "moral doubts" about it. People who try to manipulate you not only are dangerous, but they also break ethical laws, which means that you have every right to keep them out of your life.

Is it feasible all the time though? It's hard… If we are talking about someone you meet freely, like a friend, an acquaintance etc., it is easier to say, "Bye bye, our roads part here." But with family members, colleagues or even friends within a group of friends, this is much harder to achieve.

Thankfully, there are strategies you can use, and fortunately you will get to know them right now!

Find Out What They Want

If you find out what the manipulator wants, you will start getting an advantage over him/her. Even if you don't get the exact idea, but a general one. It's like when parents know why their children are throwing a tantrum… They know they can turn the tables, don't they?

Let's go back to your colleague… What may s/he want? While it is possible that s/he may want a loan, or even to steal your partner or, even to propose to you. A deal which is actually a grift… But let us **start looking at what is most probable.** Being at work, it may have to do with his or her career, job, position or even clout in the workplace.

If where you work doesn't have many career prospects, maybe then it's not the promotion he or she wants. Maybe it's just clout, or looking good with the boss… or maybe it's a long term career prospect s/he is after. Still, there are those who seek the boss's approval, just for its own sake… Like there are those children who seek the teacher's "special approval" to be the teacher's favorite… Just as a reward in itself.

Of course, **you can use the manipulator's words, interest, frequent topics etc. to narrow down the options…** If she or he keeps talking about a particular person, area of the job, project etc., the chances are that his/her "hidden agenda" has to do with these.

Give Conflicting Signals

Yes, you got that right. It's not unethical, because you are doing it to protect yourself, and because these signals need to be about what s/he wants to know from you without your consent. If people ask you about your private business, is it ethical to lie? Absolutely yes! They have no right to know it and you could just tell them to mind their business. But that can be taken as rude and turned against you… So, what can you do? Tell them something wrong which in any case they should not be interested in, and should not have asked.

The same principle applies when manipulators are testing the ground… Let's see a couple of common examples. Imagine you work out that a colleague is testing your ability to say no and willingness to do favors. Let's say you are actually inclined to do favors, you like it. But you know that if s/he finds out how to get a favor from you, the manipulator may use it against you…

So, sometimes say, "Yes of course," as if it's what you'd love to do… Other times say, "No, I can't," maybe giving no explanation at all. Then spice it all up with, "Maybe, but why did you say you needed it?"

If you don't show the manipulator what makes you do things, she or he will not make the final move, the one that's meant to grift you, trap you, cheat you, trick you, whatever it is s/he wants…

Another example is when they seek your allegiance. You know those people who, maybe during meetings, or in any case in front of other people, call you into question to back them up? Manipulators do it a lot; only, they also use the people they involve this way as scapegoats if things go wrong…

Imagine the manipulator has a project, like selling a new brand of shoes (let's imagine we work in a store). S/he needs support when proposing it to the store manager. S/he talks to you about it. In front of the manager s/he calls on you and even makes you express an agreement which is beyond what you had told him/her... You may have noticed this tactic...

Then the manager says, "Ok, it looks good, let's try it!" The new brand of shoes come, they're poor quality, they don't sell, and... you find out that in a private meeting, the manipulator tells the manager that it was your idea and s/he only voiced your view because you are too shy... Thank you very much!

Here, then two things:

- ***Never allow the manipulator to claim the consent or agreement you actually did not give.*** Don't be shy and don't think about saving his/her face in front of the boss when s/he says that you "agreed fully" while you only mumbled a half-hearted "ok". S/he would not think twice about throwing you under the bus if necessary. Say it politely, but say, "Actually I only said it looked ok as a general idea/at first glance, but it needs looking into..."

- ***On a one-to-one basis, give positive and negative views over his or her plan.*** Sometimes say, "It could work," other times express doubts. Be critical, without being unreasonable. Do it especially as the manipulator is discussing the plan with you...

On this point, the conflicting signals can work on many levels. If s/he pays you a compliment, smile once and don't smile next time. If s/he says, "Can I get you a coffee," say yes once and, "No, coffee is bad for you," next time...

Without looking deranged ***you need to avoid giving him/her the certainty that you will react as s/he expects you to when the "moment" comes.***

In the end, keep this maxim in mind: ***manipulative people are also calculative people: muck up their calculations then!***

Don't Reward Flattery

One thing is a well-intentioned compliment, another is flattery. Manipulative people will flatter you till you are useful to their ends. And the more you respond positively, the more they will identify you as "an object to manipulate". So, cut it off as soon as possible.

When your now infamous colleague says, "You are the best in this office/store/job/class etc.," don't smile and blush shyly... Just say, "No, actually there are many great people here," or even better, ignore him/her... which leads me to the next point.

Ignore the Manipulator as Much as Possible

Giving no reply to manipulators means giving no feedback, which they cannot use either way. Imagine what Skinner would have done if the little mouse in the torture chamber (sorry, "Skinner box" as they call it) had not responded to the loudspeaker at all? Just because I know it was long ago, the loudspeaker told the mouse to pull the lever, the lights what the result would be, food or electric shock...

I don't know if he would have been disappointed, confused, upset... I know he could not have worked out how the little mouse thought and reacted to his stimuli. And manipulators see us a bit like mice to analyze and experiment with.

Plus, *the more you ignore manipulators, the sooner they leave you alone.*

Avoid Any Type of Confrontation with the Manipulator

You may wish to confront the manipulator, and tell him (her) in the face that you disagree with what s/he is doing... Don't! You will not really change the manipulator's mind, and you will obtain nothing – actually...

You may end up making things worse. Manipulators (and sociopaths and psychopaths) are usually very vindictive. They may play a role in front of you, they may even pretend to be coming towards you, to have changed their mind, they may even say "sorry." But many of them will start planning their revenge against you the moment you confront them.

This will be especially true if you do it in front of other people. Loss of face is something most of them cannot tolerate.

Alternatively, they may well use the incident to manipulate you even more. They may use it to gain your confidence, to show you that they are now reliable and then, when you least expect it... you've gotten yourself in a nightmare situation.

Get the Manipulator to Understand You Know What Sort of Person S/He Is

Having said this, there are ways of at least dropping the hint, even better, the doubt, that you know what they are up to. Avoid any direct confrontation, avoid any overt (and especially public) expression of what you know. And also avoid "teasing" sentences and words about it.

But just show, especially with behavior, that you have lost trust in the person. You may notice that the manipulator will start asking you probing questions aimed to ferret out what you know about him/her or his/her plans... And guess what?

Do not reply to them. Don't give anything away. Just leave the manipulator in doubt. That will be enough to find you "unsafe as a victim" and you should notice less ill intended "interest" in you.

Involve Significant Others and Get Their Viewpoint

Don't isolate yourself, never! While you should not "go public" at work about it, you should **talk to at least one friend or family member about it**. If you have a friend in the workplace, they would be fine too. But avoid the "colleague you know superficially" if possible.

You need to be quite honest about the manipulator with your confidant, and you need to **talk regularly about what the manipulator is doing.** At the very least every week.

Very importantly, **listen to what your friend or family member has to say; s/he may have a very insightful viewpoint, thanks to his/her internal perspective.** When you are in the middle of something, it's hard to see exactly what is happening to you, isn't it?

Also, **keep track of changes and improvements together.** It will be a developing situation, so it's easy to lose track of how things were, compared with now. Instead, you need to see if and how much the manipulator is giving up. But you also need to be aware of new, maybe intensified "heights"; the stronger and more frequent they are, the more likely it is that you are moving back into the core of his/her plan, or even that the plan is reaching a climax, reaching its "final sprint".

Don't Give the Manipulator Any Money

And finally, don't give manipulators any money. Even those who are not currently bothering you. Why? It's like an invitation to start manipulating you. Even if they ask for little loans etc.… Just say "no". They know that if you are willing to part with your money you are most likely a trusty person, and that plays in their hands.

What is more, in many cases, the final aim is money or money related, and, even if not all manipulators are sociopaths or psychopaths, loads of them see money as the ultimate reward, or a very pleasurable one anyway.

From Skinner's Box to "the Box"

Ok, I pushed it a bit… "The box" is an old-fashioned way of calling the television… But this is exactly what we are going to see next: how the television manipulates the masses, and how you can protect yourself from that "Big Brother" in your living room…

Chapter 9 – Mind Manipulation on Television

I switched off my TV in 2012, and I never regretted it. Actually, it's possibly one of the best things I have done in my life. "Don't you miss it," you may ask? Not at all! "How do you get the news?" I get it from other outlets, and I get more, better quality and a wider range.. I now actually get information on all the things that TV news doesn't tell you. In the end, you can change as many channels as you want, there will be different spins on the same news items. But the news items are basically always the same.

TV News and "Spin"

Do you know how much of what you get on TV is "commentary" or better "spin" on a news item and how much is the news item itself? The vast majority is all "commentary", depending on the item etc., but always far above 50%, usually more than 70% and in very controversial cases, like important topics, even past 90%.

But what is actually the function of commentary? Once upon a time it was meant to explain, and give different viewpoints. In a very small part, it is still so, but *most commentaries on TV are meant to "convince you" of a spin, of an opinion, of a point of view: they are mind manipulation.*

In the time you watch the TV news on TV you can actually get 2 to 4 times as many different items on other media! All you need to do is avoid all the "commentaries". But do you like actual commentaries? Have you noticed on TV that:

- *You cannot choose a commentary on a topic you want to develop,* they do it for you, they tell you what should matter to you.

- *Most commentaries are useless arguments between two so-called experts, or political rivals.* These don't actually add any in depth development or exploration of an issue or topic; they are just two people vying for your allegiance; this too is mind manipulation.

You can find in depth commentaries online, read them in the newspapers, on blogs etc. And you can *choose the ones that interest you.* This very choosing puts you *in control of what you read, listen to, or watch.* You see, a key *strategy to stop mind manipulation though the media is to become "free" from the media themselves.*

Now, most people watch more than one TV news bulletin a day… Do you? If you do, are the items different in the various bulletins over the day? Think about it.

…

You will see that part of the morning bulletin is repeated in the midday bulletin, then by far most of the dinnertime show is the same as the midday one, and at night there is virtually no change at all. So, what you get is **repetition of the same items with the same viewpoints, commentaries, and spin.** And as you will remember, repetition is a key mind manipulation strategy.

But then, how much do people actually remember of news bulletins? What do they remember most? Use your experience, think about friends, family, acquaintances, colleagues... what do you think?

...

The fact that people forget the news is common knowledge. Sometimes it goes too fast, sometimes people don't get it perfectly well to start with, very often the memory deceives us. You must have noticed the colleague or family member who gets the facts wrong when "repeating the news" to you...

But there is more... Here though, note that I am not advocating becoming addicted to social media, we will get to them soon, as promised.... But a recent study shows that people remember the news better if they read it online. And this is for the young and old alike.

It appeared in *Cognitive Research: Principles and Implications,* Nov 11, 2020, it's entitled 'Reading the News on Twitter: Source and item memory for social media in younger and older adults' and it's by a team of scholars, Kimberley A. Bourne, Sarah C. Boland, Grace C. Arnold, and Jennifer H. Coane.

It found out that young adults will recall the news *almost twice as well* if they read it online than if they watch on TV for example, while the difference is much lower for older adults. But here we are not advocating the use of social media as a source of news. There are many issues with this, for example, as it says, "the blending of news sources might make it harder to distinguish between news and social media". This phenomenon has reached worrying levels today; people confuse "gossip" with "fact".

What we are saying is that a significant part of what people see on the news gets lost... So... to recap:

- **Watching the news on TV is repetitive.**

- **Most of the time is spent on spin.**

- **We forget a large part of what we hear.**

Isn't it a waste of time? And why should you waste your time being told what to think and taught how to think?

But at this stage, **I am not suggesting to stop watching TV news all of a sudden.** That can actually be counterproductive. You see, lots, but really lots of what is online is mind manipulation too. Especially on some media, like "FateBook" etc. In fact, you will need to read the chapter on social media to understand how to avoid mind manipulation online. But...

You can start by watching the news only once a day, and choosing a "fairly reliable" channel. Plus...

After the news, make a (mental or written) list of the facts. This will help you remember them better, distinguish them from the spin and then you won't need "reminding" with another mind manipulating bulletin.

For the time being, stick to these two measures. We will look soon at what shows that media outlets are reliable or not... For now, I will trust your judgement.

An Alternative to TV News

The best alternative is newspapers, even online ones. Again, not all newspapers are reliable. ***By all means avoid sensationalist newspapers, magazines, posts and even news channels.***

Imagine a friend of yours runs to you, all sweated, panting, with a very worried face, arms in the air and says: "Hurry up! Something terrible has happened!" What would you do? You would start running with him/her, and maybe s/he will explain what's happened on the way. But you are already:

- Worried
- Irrational
- Running
- Doing something before you actually know what has really happened.

This is the exact effect of sensationalism. ***Sensationalism prevents rational thinking, creates a false sense of danger and urges you to act before you actually understand what is going on.***

Beware – I repeat – beware of anyone who uses this strategy: this is pure mind manipulation.

Choose newspapers that focus on facts, that avoid over-emphatic language, big titles with sensational and swiping statements. If you see that the article says something that then is different from the title, beware.

If you want to avoid being manipulated, you need to keep selective standards and expect very high standards when it comes to the outlets you choose.

It is possible to watch newsreels as well as in depth shows and insights online, but here too, you must choose very good ones, or you will end up from one form of manipulation to another. So, wait till we get to the social media and internet chapter.

TV and Social Media

There is a difference between what you get on TV and what you get on social media: some social media have no limits with their mind manipulation. There are people who shout like they are possessed, there are people who say the most unacceptable things, people who support the most unethical ideologies, people who give the most improbable thesis as "facts" and people who spread fake news.

So, I need to warn you: *swapping the TV for social media can be very risky; you may be exposed to forms of mind manipulation which are extreme.* But these are good sources, we will learn to recognize them soon (ok, we have started a bit already).

Some TV channels have become more and more similar to what you get on certain vlogs and online broadcasts: extreme, angry, extremist, ready to defend any untenable concept etc. But they still have a "modicum of restraint" compared with some of the things you get online.

On the other hand, the scientific studies I quote are not available on TV… I can't even find them in my local library; I can only find them online. You see, online you have both extremes: the hard facts, parliamentary records, scientific studies, etc.… And total and utter mind conditioning trash.

The latter appeals more easily and TV channels in general have moved that way, not towards the wealth of facts, figures, and beautiful ideas you can find on the net…

That's sad, and a change of tide will only happen when we, *the people,* expect better from broadcasters.

The Quality of TV Programs

There is general consensus that TV programs have worsened in the recent decades. We can take the oldest, the most influential, the "best quality" broadcaster in the world as an example: the "mother of all televisions": the BBC.

The BBC has reduced its world-famous documentaries, its comedy and satire production (world famous too), and it has cut its "world service" which was mainly fairly factual news. At the same time, other channels have proliferated, and are mostly based on really sensationalist and low-level programs.

The advent of so-called "reality TV" has lowered the quality of TV productions consistently, over time and significantly. I have no doubts in my view that there has been some intention behind this move towards sensationalism. Sensationalism costs less, in theory gets more views (even if that is not true – over time viewers all over the Western World have been decreasing in most counties as a proportion of the population). But sensationalism is also strong mind manipulation.

We just need to look at the history of tabloids (sensationalist "newspaper") to see that there is a scientific plan to manipulate people's minds behind them… And televisions followed the same pattern, at some distance.

So, most of the programs are really a waste of time. And the other programs? Like *documentaries, films etc.? You can get them somewhere else; choose a platform where you can choose (!!!) which ones you want to watch!*

By now you will have understood that *real choice, personal and free choice is an antidote against mind manipulation.*

Cutting Down on Time in Front of the TV

So, we have cut down from three TV news bulletins to one. We can replace most evening and night programs with movies, series etc. we can choose on another platform... And that is actually much better... Trust me; I watch the movies that I like, not the ones that some manager in a room hundreds of miles away chooses for me. And I am picky. But I am enjoying myself much more!

So... what are we left with? Maximum one hour of TV a day? Now, my question... How many hours do you spend in front of the TV? How many hours do people spend on average?

...

I spend none, I don't know how many hours you spend a day, but the average US adult spends *more than four hours a day watching TV.* That's a lot...

Now, what do you really get from those four hours apart from very little factual information you can get somewhere else? Ok, a good dose of mind manipulation free of charge (oops, no – they actually even charge you for it!)

Cutting down to one hour, how many things could you do instead? *With three extra hours at your disposal every day!* Make a little list please.

...

So, when I said, "Take up a sport or hobby" you might have thought, "I have no time though." Well now you have three hours a day, enough to become a professional agonist, or do other things, including having quality time with friends and family, having that famous "social life" we all complain we don't have, but then we don't give up a bit of TV trash to go out and have *real* fun...

By the way, as a note, US adults also spend another 3 hours and 18 minutes on social media... Can you see how much time we can free up if we break our TV and social media addiction? Can you see why I am by no means missing the old television?

But there is more...

TV Commercials

No need to say that *TV commercials are very effective,* because of the "moving picture" quality of the ads (and other reasons we will see). They are in fact much more effective than commercials in newspapers, magazines, etc. The very quality of the commercials makes them powerful means of mind manipulation. They look great at times, some, to be honest are actually very artistic. But remember that they are not "for you" they are "against your will" and their only function is to "bend your will and manipulate your mind". In fact, for those who commission them, sign them and broadcast them to you, who are not even a "customer", but a "target". Words do matter!

Anyway, we already said that **even if you are distracted, TV ads still have a powerful and subconscious effect on you.** In fact, starting a chat or putting the kettle on while watching commercials may well be even *worse than watching them intently.* Remember, your conscious mind is the one that defends you from mind manipulation!

But the big question is: how long do we actually spend watching commercials on TV? **On average, 25% of TV time is dedicated to commercials, that is 15 minutes every hour.** Good channels reduce this to 11 minutes. In some European countries, state channels go below this.

Considering the average US adult spends 4 hours in front of the TV every day, this means **one hour being repeatedly and insistently manipulated into being a consumer and buying something.** Then of course there are all the other aspects of mind conditioning in ads, like:

- **Conforming to some social "values", like being "cool", rich, slim, well dressed, showing off, being "masculine" ...** These are what we call "non values" or "false values"; real values are being good, being generous, helping others etc.... Not really promoted in commercials, are they?

- **Becoming dependent on having, not being.**

- **Feeling the social pressure of "keeping up with the Joneses" (peer pressure).**

Now, one hour a day is 365 hours a year, that is more than 15 full days (and nights) spent being mind conditioned. That's about the same as Alex DeLarge gets in terms of mind conditioning in *A Clockwise Orange!* Every year, to you, your family, your children!!!

And the worst is still to come!

Television and Alpha Waves

When was the last time you fell asleep in front of the television? I hope it was long ago, because you know quite well that it's not good for you. When you wake up, you feel hazed, tired (weird, you should be more relaxed and awake), sloppy, even "bloated", "feverish" and you may even have a headache...

That should ring a bell, and a worrying one at that! What's so special about the television that makes us feel so weird? Why do we fall asleep so easily in front of it, but we become more tired?

The answer is simple and scientific: **televisions send images in alpha waves.** This is a wavelength, and one that has an effect on our brain and our mind.

You see, we don't always function at the same wavelength... **When our minds are almost switched off, it works in alpha wavelength.** At this stage, we are at the **lowest level of thinking while still awake.** Below that, there is unconsciousness. But as you know, at this level, **rational and critical thinking are switched off, and we have no defenses against mind manipulation.**

Our mind in fact has different wavelengths according to the activity it needs to do:

- The higher is **gamma**: this is when we are very functional, rational, focused, in "problem solving" mode.

- Just below, there is **beta**: a mind in beta waves is busy and active, but it is not on a "mental high speed highway" ... like in gamma.

- The lowest waking wavelength is **alpha:** this is restful, when we are relaxing. In Nature, this is quite good; the problem starts when you receive *loads of stimuli (and reinforcement) during this phase.* You see, at alpha wave level our mind should have little or no focus and a calm, relaxing, "empty of stimuli" environment. Like if you are on a beach listening to the waves.

  It is not capable of dealing with many stimuli at this wavelength. You see then what television does? *It lowers your defenses, puts it in a wavelength where you cannot cope with much stimuli, with information etc. and then bombards you with instructions, ideas, opinions etc....* This is pure mind manipulation. At a very high level and on a colossally gargantuan scale!

- Lower than alpha waves there are *theta* waves; these are the ones we are in during periods of drowsiness, when we are falling to sleep, like during the hypnagogic phase.

- The lowest waves are **delta;** here we are sleeping and dreaming.

Now, if you fall asleep in front of the television, its alpha waves will also *prevent or refrain your mind from going into delta waves*; this is why then you wake up feeling tired and not relaxed. And we all understand that "TV sleeping" is not at all like "proper sleep".

People compare being under the influence of TV alpha waves to "being under hypnosis". In the "common" sense, the popular concept of hypnosis, it is fair to say so. You have no willpower, and they are telling you what to do.

From a psychological perspective however, it is different. But it is *worse!* Apart from the fact that hypnotists have deontological (ethical) rules, like doctors etc.... Then when you are hypnotized, you are in *theta waves...* just to be precise on technical issues.

So...

Cut Down on Television Time...

... and only select positive and good quality programs and channels! I think I have convinced you that it's a wise step, and that for almost a century now (70 years or so, depending on where you live) *television has been the biggest, most widespread and most powerful instrument of mass mind conditioning in the whole world.*

You will literally feel free, and you will feel like you are taking control of your life if you cut down on TV time, and your day will look like it has twice as many hours in it!

But careful, during those hours you will get back to yourself, be careful. Of course, don't take to social media as a replacement. But mind your door too! There are professional mind manipulators who go round ringing people's bells all day long! And no, I am not talking about some strange looking and oddly dressed "exotic" man... Most likely he will come in a suit and tie, wear a smile, and even a badge... I am talking about salespeople... next...

Chapter 10 – The Professional Salesperson

"Ring, riiiiiing!" the doorbell goes, you go to the door, open it and there he is, the professional salesman in a suit and tie and a new vacuum cleaner, better than the one you bought last year, and before you can say, "No thanks," he has started his spiel and…

…An hour later, you have bought this new wonder of technology that looks oddly similar to the one you got last year. But that one, despite all the promises showed some flaws that are getting on your nerves, long after you paid for it, of course, so, second time lucky?

Then last time it was a woman, now it's a man… And you already try justifying to yourself a choice that deep down, after the intoxication, you are starting to doubt.

Ok, no one rings doorbells with vacuum cleaners anymore. But I wanted to remind older readers of a classic door to door salesperson from years ago – "where it all started" sort of thing… To be correct, they were mostly men, few women actually did that job… Still…

From Old Fashioned Door to Door Salespeople to Today's Professionals

Things have changed. Of course they have, but in this field, there has been developments; there has been an evolution of the same techniques; they have become more powerful, more exact, but there has not been a "revolution" in the methods.

The revolution has come in the means, actually in the mediums (media, the Greek plural of medium, comes from this). *Face to face sales are now fewer, and when you finally meet the salesperson, it's often after a long process of mind manipulation that started, maybe, with an email, a post on social media, a commercial or a flyer…*

"Good," you may think, "fewer of them around!" From one point of view, true. From another point of view, it means that *you have already been pre-selected, and this makes the salesperson's job easier!*

Not so happy now? You see, the old-fashioned door to door salesperson had a tough job on her or his hands… But hold on, let's look at why most were men…

They were men because society was still broadly composed of families where the husband worked, and the wife stayed at home. That meant that most workers were men, but also that most potential customers were women…

What is more, they were always well groomed and dressed as we said, that already made them look "respectable" and "reliable". This makes a star contrast with many street and door to door salespeople from the past in many European countries: these were traveling salespeople, gypsies etc. They would not present themselves as "well adapted to the dominant society" even as "businesspeople", but as outsiders.

Now, look at the suit and tie... Would you expect that on a baker? On a fishmonger? On a grocer? No... They "dressed up" to look even more professional than other sellers...

And that's a clue; that's not changed. They look like members of the board of directors of the vacuum cleaner factory, instead they are hierarchically some of the lowest on the company's ladder...

And that's a first lie. But it also does mean that they will appeal more to people who trust the mainstream system. Unfortunately, we are all trained to do it; we are trained when we go to the shopping mall, we are trained when we watch TV etc. Few people now prefer someone dressed as a farmer to sell them grocers! And this is especially true in urban and "Westernized" societies.

Anyway, we have had a quick look at the looks, now, let's see how they speak... I used the word "spiel" but they would call it "pitch" now. Once it was basically a sentence they repeated by heart, and they still do it, especially with cold calls (which too derive from the old door to door salesperson). But experienced ones now change it a bit, they "pitch" it to you. **They will notice something you like and bring it into the conversation...**

And this leads us to a point, on how to recognize them and take control against them.

Look at Their Eyes

When professional manipulators are talking to you, **they will look around you and at what you are wearing, what you look like**. They will cast little glances here and there... Why? They are studying you. They are **looking for information about you and your life to use against you.**

They won't use it negatively; they won't blackmail you... But they will try to **endear you and win your trust by faking empathy with you.**

For example, if they see a picture of you and your children on the mantelpiece, they may use it to "soften your barriers" and talk about how children love their product. If they see you playing baseball, they will claim they love and play baseball too. So, you feel that they are "like you", the "sort of person you would be friends with".

This is only a **pitch**; they will say they love baseball even if they loathe it. But in order to use these clues to gain your trust, they need to analyze you and your environment.

But do not confuse the normal glance to the side to the inquisitive looking around. We normally look to the side when talking to others; it's very hard to hold eye contact for long periods of time. I personally look out of windows and look for green spaces when I talk... But you can notice a difference between the natural eye movement and the directed eye movement...

You need to be very experienced to read eye movements on people, but let's say that a salesperson or in any case a manipulator most likely looks away in search for details, not to release the intensity of eye contact.

If you look at the focus of their eyes, the friend who glances away is "receptive and unfocused" vaguely like staring in the distance, or at the emptiness as we say. You will on the other hand notice that the manipulator is in fact focusing quickly on an object, and actual physical detail... That's how you spot them...

But of course, there is another point that follows from this.

Don't Let Them into Your Home and Keep them in an Emotionally Neutral Place

You guessed it; if I came into your living room, how many details and facts about your life, your social relationships, what you like, your family, your jobs, etc. could I find? Look around you (even mentally if you are not there) and make a list in 30 seconds...

...

You are right, this was the shortest spot of gardening ever for me! Jokes aside... I bet you found loads. I didn't go out really, I glanced to the side and saw a little African wood statue; just from this detail, how many things can you find out about me? Try it...

...

Done? You can say a few things about me already, and yet you have not even seen my living room... For example:

- I love art
- I love handcrafts
- I love woodwork
- I like colors
- I appreciate cultures different from mine
- I am fine with helping street salespeople (that comes from a market stall, it's not something you find in stores and if you knew more about where I live you would know that there are poor people selling these things in the streets...)

All of these would not be far off the mark...

If you really have to talk to these people (maybe for work), then *choose an emotionally neutral place.* A street is fine, a public place, a bar or coffee bar etc. *The more they know about your life the more they will be able to manipulate you.*

And on this point...

Elude Questions

The manipulator will ask what seem like innocent questions; but they are not! "Did you watch the news last night?" or "Do you like traveling?" or "Did you like the last episode of Celebrity Window Cleaners?" ... Don't be fooled by them. They may look innocent, but the're not. The salesperson is trying to find out things about you to use them later to gain your trust.

Fend these questions off with no replies if possible, dismissive ones, or even ludicrous ones, like, "Let's stick to the business at hand," or "I don't care either way," or "No, but I had Marlon Brando round to mow my lawn!"

Show them that you are not willing to give them any insight into your life. This alone will tell them that you may not be worth the effort and deter them, at least partially...

Following this train of thought...

Keep Them at a Physical Distance

It's not just "keeping them out of your private life" that deters them. You can also **keep them out of your personal and social space.**

You won't need a measuring tape for this, but keep these distances in mind, and use these measures as rough guidelines:

- **Never allow the manipulator or salesperson closer to you than 1.5 feet (45 cm).** within that radius you have your **intimate zone.**

- **Try to push the manipulator to the margins of your personal zone (1.5 to 5 feet, or 45 cm to 150 cm).** Move away, move back, try to draw an "invisible demarcation line" between you two, and try to get as far as possible towards (and over) the 5 feet mark (1.5 meters).

- **If possible, push the manipulator over the 5-foot mark (1.5 meters); that is the so-called "social sphere".** If you manage this, the manipulator will feel "outside the negotiating zone", pushed back with the "general public and passersby's" then s/he will try to get back into your personal zone. Don't fall for it; resist and push back... After a while, the penny will drop, and the manipulator should understand that you "are not game".

Keeping physical distance is a powerful way of "deflecting" the manipulator's attempts at "gaining access to your personal space and trust".

But how about touching?

Be "Cruel" with Your Handshake

Usually, the only allowed form of touching between strangers is the handshake... Use it to "assert yourself" and to give a sign that you are "closed to business". How?

Simply:

- **Give a strong, firm handshake.** Avoid any softness and squeeze quite hard (without hurting). Pretend you are squeezing a lemon!

- **Be quick and leave the handshake before the manipulator does.** This will trick him or her quite badly... If you stop early the message you give is that you do not trust the person you are shaking hands with.

The manipulator will pick up these signs and signals. The better educated and experienced the manipulator may actually pick up these signals consciously and rationally. But even if s/he does not, you will still pass them on to his or her subconscious, and that can have great results in terms of demotivating him or her.

You do want to demotivate the manipulator, and one way of doing this is to show that you are not interested. But there are other ways too.

Demotivate the Manipulator

We have seen one way of demotivating, which then translates into many acts: *showing that you are not interested.* But there is another way: *indicate that you are not capable.* I'll give you an example...

A salesperson is trying to sell you a cable TV contract... Show this person that you simply cannot afford it. Complain about money if you wish. Say that you are facing sudden and unexpected expenses, whatever is necessary to give the signal that *whatever the manipulator says or does, you are simply in no position to comply.*

A salesperson is trying to sell you a holiday? Say you are not taking time off work this year! Someone is trying to get you an even cheaper utility contract? Say that you cannot do it without your partner. "And when will you be able to talk about it to your partner?" is the obvious question. "S/he is away at the moment; s/he won't be back for at least a week."

That means, "Call back if you care in 10 days, and you know that I won't answer..." Which leads us straight into another tactic you can use...

Kick It into the Long Grass

Say you cannot take any decision. The manipulator will ask you "when" of course, and you need to:

- **Be vague on the time.** Give an approximate number of days, weeks etc. There's a huge difference between saying, "On Friday," and "In at least a week." The first gives an appointment ready to schedule. The second says, "Not sure," and it also asks the manipulator to count the days. This shows that you are not collaborating… But there is more… If the manipulator calls and it's too soon, as you haven't given an exact number, s/he will know that s/he will have basically spoilt all her/his chances… Use it on them!

- **"I will not know until…"** This formula puts a condition in the future. "I will not know until I check with my boss," you could say at a business meeting. Or "I will not know until my daughter tells me which school she likes to go to…" You see, adding conditions that cannot be established now makes the manipulator understand that there is no chance of immediate success. It delays things but it also means that the manipulator needs to invest extra efforts for a result s/he thought s/he would get straight away… That may make them reconsider and realize that you are not worth their time…

- **Change medium…** "How will I know if your daughter has decided," asks the manipulator… "You can send me a text message," should be your answer, not, "Come and see me later…" Show that your preferred method is not face-to-face, but distant communication. That already is a massive blow to their plans. Then, of course, don't answer the text message and if you can, even block the number… That should pass the message on, and with the least possible risk and stress on your behalf.

Even this method follows the idea of **"putting a distance between you and the manipulator."** But there are even more ways you can use, including what comes next.

Ask for a Written Document, Agreement or Contract

This is also useful for cold phone calls and other marketing strategies. My father gets an awful lot of those. Excuse me the digression, but they know he is one of those who likes to change his utilities providers… That's a little trap by the way… The more often you change your electricity company, the more others know you do and try to contact you and get you to change again…

Anyway, my Mum always tells him, "Get them to send you a written proposal!" You know what, even with these "reliable official big companies" in most cases the proposal never comes through the post. Why? They know that **one thing is listening to, or even hearing terms and conditions, another is reading them…**

Manipulators will not usually like to put things down in writing because:

- **You can read a written document when you want, with calm and, above all, in their absence.**

- *You can read a written document with someone else, or show it to them.*

- *It is easier to pretend that they respect a contract if it is written.*

This does not mean that they will absolutely deny you a written document. I find that especially with online sales, the trend is that if you ask for one you get a very improper answer, however: "No, we can only make this offer on the phone," which to my knowledge is actually illegal in all the EU and many other countries.

They may even have a contract but avoid it at all costs.

Don't Allow Manipulators to Hurry You When Reading a Document

They will give you a text, which often is long, written in small print, hard to read, and **they will insist on you signing it as soon as possible, in a hurry. Absolutely never do this!**

Take the contract home, read it calmly, check every detail, discuss it with your partner, family, friends and for anything really worth a lot, show it to a lawyer! Take your time and beware of offers that expire soon... There will be others. One of the reasons for these offers (which look a bit like the offers at a department store, by the way... not by chance, we take them lightly because unfortunately we have been "trained" to do so).

Very often, these offers are perfectly fine at the beginning... They have written in big letters something like "99c a month!" and it's true. For the first few months. But in the small print, they have something that reads like "We reserve the right to alter the offer without notice". And guess what? You have 60 days to cancel the contract and on day 90 the 99c starts going up... First, it's $1.50, then $2.00 then $3.00 and at the end of the year the average is higher than the cellphone contract you had before.

In the end, ask yourself a question: **why would an honest negotiator hurry you into signing something?** If I am confident about the value of my offer, I would actually be happy for you to take your time and see how good it is, no?

There is a famous law in negotiations, well known by governments and big business: **in a negotiation, the negotiator who is pressed for time is at a serious disadvantage.** If a company has a strong need to clench a deal by a certain time, they will never want the company they are dealing with to know it. The reason is that this company would push the deal to the very end, and then get the hurried company to sign any bad deal.

Don't let manipulators put you into this position. Always claim all the time you need. What is more **beware of any words, sentences and signs that try to put you in a hurry.**

I usually say, "No, if you are trying to hurry me *by principle,* I stop all dealings immediately, sorry," at the very first sign of pressure.

Don't Lead Them On

And finally, don't be tempted to lead them on... I know the temptation... Sometimes we want to play, even play cat and mouse... But really, these are professionals, and they always have great advantages over you.

Think that your time will be better spent reading a book, watching a movie, playing with your children or even doing the washing up, really... *Any sign of interest will be taken as a sign of your weakness.*

So, while you may be thinking that you are playing the cat, you are actually the mouse. They are actually studying you systematically and, even if you don't buy the now notorious vacuum cleaners, they will still get something from you. Guess what?

You think it's just your time? No, have you got a picture of young children? Fine, you will get someone ringing the bell, and, Ring, riiiiing!" the doorbell goes, you go to the door, open it and there he is, the professional salesman in a suit and tie and a new *stroller for your baby*, better than the one you bought last year, and before you can say, "No thanks," he has started his spiel again.

You see, they can still make their time worthwhile by collecting information on you and literally selling it to another company, another salesperson that wants to sell you something, yet another manipulator...

Of course, the best option is always to "shut the door in their faces" and these are strategies to use if you can't do that (straight away). But there are ways of getting past your door anyway, and there are manipulators that you will find harder to shut out... And you will find them in hordes, on the various "InstaGross", "FootBook" and "TelePost" ... Yes, and now on the notorious social media, up next...

Chapter 11 – Social Media: The Last Frontier of Mass Manipulation

Take a mental picture of a busy street about 20 years ago. Then take another mental picture of the same street, with the same number of people, on a similar day – but recent. Take a picture of a table, at a café, or restaurant 20 years ago, with people having fun. Wind forward 20 years. What's the main difference you notice?

Clothes have changed little in 20 years (fashion has not moved much forward), hairdos have changed a bit more. But the big difference will definitely be smartphones. Loads of them. Virtually always in almost everybody's hand. And with smartphones come those tiny colorful icons of letters, birds, and other symbols: social media!

Do you remember a time when social media did not exist? Do you remember what you did instead? Do you remember how your life was different? Some of us do, the older generation. But younger people have been brought up in a world already "packaged" with social media. I'm not sure that the social media are actually the ones inside the package though… maybe it's us?

I don't need to tell you that *social media is very addictive.* Depending on your age, you will be either one of those who say that social media is taking over our lives or one of those who hear it all the time… And in fact, *on average, each US adult spends 3.5 hours on social media each day.*

This means that social media has become a major factor in our lives, and, in turn, of the way we think.

How Social Media Isolates You

3.5 hours a day are by far more than adults spend with their friends every day. And because of the nature of social media, that time may actually be subtracted from time spent with family members too. I will give you a little time lapse to show it to you.

Let's take a family from the lower or middle to lower class. Let's place this family, for example, at the beginning of the 20th Century. What would they be doing in the evenings? In many cases, you would have them all round a fire, some knitting, some reading if they had the knowledge and money (books did cost a lot at the time), and, in many cases, they were listening to stories, or, in some cases, reading was actually done aloud, for everybody (that was typical in centuries past in the middle class).

In any case, people sharing personal experiences, with stories etc., was the norm. You did have the night out at the local "public place" (whichever it was, according to the country, a pub, bar, etc.) for men, but when at home, nights were spent listening to older people (including parents, relatives and, especially, grandparents).

That went on till the television became very popular. It depends on the country, but in some cases, the TV only made it into almost everybody's home only in the 60s and 70s, and even then, most families only watched one program at night, often the news, at least at first.

But let's tele-transport our family into the 1980s of example. What would they be doing? To start with, in what were first basically extended families, even if not living under the same roof, by 1980, evenings were a "nuclear family" affair. Parents and children watching TV in their home, grandparents maybe just a few hundred yards away, but in front of their television…

Stories from the old days? Forget them. Some families kept their tradition, especially rural ones. But even then, these "old fashioned nights" were limited to summer nights when friends got together, maybe in the open air. In urban settings, this tradition virtually died out. If parents went out, once in a blue moon, they mostly went to places where children didn't fit in… So, going out became even rarer, as you would need a babysitter or, if you are lucky, a friendly relative.

But here notice how the circle is closing around the individual, especially around young people growing up in the different eras. A child grew up listening to the stories of his/her parents, relatives, grandparents, and family friends or neighbors once.

Then, by 1980, most children would grow up mostly talking to their nuclear family, but no longer at night (the time for fun and storytelling, not for practical talk, like "how did school go?"). At night, most of the time was either disconnected to the family, it was the TV that set the conversation (mostly done by short comments, soon followed by "sssssssh!").

Wind forward to recent years and watch! Most of the time is spent either watching TV, or on social media, and in other cases, there is also the time spent on video games to add. *How much do you interact with others around you, physical people, when on social media?* Very little. Maybe you will talk a bit more in front of television. When playing video games, isolation is complete.

Those 3.5 hours spent on social media is time subtracted from real, in person and meaningful relationships. This alone should convince you to cut down on them.

But remember that *one of the key strategies of mind manipulation is isolating the victim!*

When you are reading something on, for example "InstaTram", can your mother, brother, friend tell you if it's a lie? How often do you check with "real" people? In most times, very little, if not at all.

You can see how the ability to pass on an idea, a piece of information etc. without the risk of being contradicted is the perfect advantage for liars and mind manipulators. But you can say, "Ah, there you are, but I can check with my online friends!" True, but those online, many times, will not be able to give you a different point of view from yours… Why?

Internet and Social Media Bubbles

Have you heard of social media bubbles? Basically, *social media (and search engines) use algorithms to "suggest" what you should buy, what you should read, what you should watch and who you should be "friends" with.* Have you ever noticed how eager social media is to show you "suggested friends"? You will always find them in very visible positions on the page. And "making friends" (following etc.) is very easy…

But how do they select them? *They select people that the algorithm identifies as "similar to you".* This may look and sound innocent enough when "similar to you" means people who like cats, like you, or gardening, like me… But when it comes to deep rooted ideological ideas, like extremist groups, things become a bit more sinister.

And guess what? It's very easy for these algorithms to identify and match these ideas. In fact, you will be aware of the *radicalization of extremist groups on social media…*

Because you see, the *"group of people who think the same as you on a topic" is called a "bubble",* and some bubbles are fairly open (the gardening "bubble"), but the more the bubble is based on extremist views, the more the bubble itself becomes isolated (from other bubbles, or groups of people).

This is a very dangerous phenomenon, as you may well be aware of. These people basically end up in "sects" that have no contact with other groups of people online. Not only, but because they all think the same, *the bubble becomes a sounding chamber for their extremist ideas.* If you could look inside one of these bubbles, you would see that the people who shout the loudest, who are more extreme (even violent) are those who get most "likes" … This is *positive reinforcement of negative, extremist, intolerant and even violent behavior.*

And this makes them radicalized and very dangerous…

This is a very topical issue as you will know. It shows without a shadow of a doubt that *social media is capable of mind manipulating large masses, and can even push them to accomplish criminal acts on a vast scale.*

We know that *terrorist organizations use social media to radicalize and spur of action.* The question is, however, "Why do they use social media for this?" and the answer is, "Social media are powerful mind manipulators; they have perfect structures for it, and they create the perfect environments for it."

From a historical and psychological point of view, we had not yet solved the problem of mind manipulation on TV when a new, more isolating, more powerful system of mind manipulation came along: social media.

Social Media and Behaviorism

Let's start with a question: take any social media you know, what is the system of "rewards" it has? How important is it? How frequent and repeated is it?

...

The answer is of course that the "heart", "star", "thumbs up" is a system of rewards, and that it has become a very, very sought-after reward by social media users. It is repeated frequently too... That's perfect behaviorism, and that is mind conditioning at its purest state.

So, how many "likes" did your post get yesterday? Well, think that every like is positive reinforcement, think that you are like a mouse in a Skinner box... Maybe those "hearts", "stars" and "thumbs up" have a more sinister function than their lovely looks want us to believe...

We have already said this, but it's worth remembering that social media also has negative reinforcement, and that mainly comes from other users: **you get negative reinforcement when you say something unpopular.** Negative reinforcement comes in the form of negative (sometimes rude, offensive, and even threatening) comments from other users.

Now, imagine being inside an extremist bubble. What do you think is the effect of positive and negative reinforcement on the social medium used?

...

You will imagine that in an extremist bubble, the negative reinforcement can be very unpleasant indeed. So, this works to totally root out any form of dissent, any idea of "contradiction", and, in many cases, even of fact checking.

In a more open field, like in a public forum, there may be a different effect. But hold on, if you are a reasonable, polite person who likes to discuss things nicely, your reinforcement is **neutral.** If you are a vulgar and violent person, you actually can take part in mass mind conditioning.

So, **social media gives the power of negative reinforcement only to people who are aggressive, negative, vulgar, violent, and rude.** Whole, polite, and gentle people have no effect at all.

Where do you think this reinforcement will lead? There is a **huge, structural problem with social media.** The only solution is to change the very structure of these media platforms, and there are countries that are trying to do this. How?

Well, algorithms! Oddly enough, they can be used to promote positive messages. The EU is now discussing a law that would force social media to use an algorithm where insults, threats, and even fake news would be "depreciated", sent down the "feed". That would discourage negative behavior, as being aggressive would mean being "less visible" not "more visible" as is nowadays.

And, as we mentioned it, we might as well talk about fake news on social media.

Fake News on Social Media

Fake news is one of the latest additions to mass mind manipulation. There are now "fake news factories", basically "marketing agencies" of ill repute that systematically and scientifically produce fake news, so that people's minds can be manipulated. There is basically a big business of fake news.

The problem is when the fake news is circulated in a bubble; you see, there you have no one who is willing to fact check it, and even if you did, you would never dare say it is fake, because of the massive negative reinforcement you would get.

Oddly enough, people who receive fake news in bubbles are very often the same who then accuse others of "being asleep" or "being under mind control". It's a very interesting phenomenon. But in their bubbles, they're repeatedly being told that they're being given access to some repressed truth, while at the same time they are being fed loads of lies.

But don't get me wrong. There can be repressed news. Actually, there has always been repressed news in the modern world. A whole war between the then USSR and Japan was fought and the whole war was kept secret by both!

The point is that **you need to check the reliability of the news you see**. True, journalists are no longer good at that. They too spread fake news. They too have ideological bias. But to claim to be different only to do worse is somewhat ironic, no?

The vast majority of fake news comes from social media. But it is true that even mainstream TV channels and magazines and newspapers have increased their own publication of fake news in recent years.

How to Fact Check Fake News

"Fine, so fake news is everywhere," you can say, "but how can we free ourselves from it?" Good question, and this is one of the steps you will need to take to **choose your information sources correctly.** We touched on this topic when we were talking about the television, remember? We basically agreed that you would not jump from TV to internet immediately because the internet is as, if not more treacherous than the television itself!

To start with, and this is my main piece of advice, **keep your standards super mega ultra-high**. People are often very "forgiving" with internet news outlets. You see, you don't end up in an extremist bubble not having noticed some fake news in it, or from the main information sources within it. You end up in there having *forgiven* the source for some fake news... Maybe (mostly) because they were convenient...

"Well, it's not true (I suspect), but I'll repost it all the same," (consciously) and, "because it suits my world view, the version of the story that's convenient for me," (more or less subconsciously) are not simple "carelessness", they are self-delusional and they're self-damaging! These are the thoughts that open up the door to mind manipulation and mind manipulators.

Can you imagine a better victim than one who is willing to believe a lie? That's why you must make sure that you keep your standards super high.

So, what happens if a source that has been reliable but then passes on some fake news? This does happen by mistake, there is a sea of fake news nowadays... ***Check the willingness to correct it, and say, "We got it wrong, this is the real news".*** This is now even portrayed as "weak", (it's a way to undermine reliable sources), but in fact it's a basic standard, an ethical obligation... It was once called *"errata corrige"* and reputable newspapers and magazines always had them, with, "In the last issue we said [xyz] but in fact it is ["so and such"]. We're sorry about it."

So, ***the hallmark of a reliable information source is the willingness to admit its own mistakes.*** The exact opposite of what mind manipulators would like you to believe...

Primary and Secondary Sources

Sorry, I have been watching a famous historian's lectures these days... But if you studied history you know what I am talking about. When I studied the language of newspapers at university, in a course that was very much centered on language manipulation, I was amazed to find out that most articles are massive cut and paste jobs...

You see, articles "report" and "spin" news. Reporting means taking the information from somewhere (it used to be Reuters, the AP, etc., now a famous plastic blue bird online is a major source of "information" for newspapers). They "report" interviews, and very often they "report" even other newspaper articles.

For a historian, ***news outlets of most sorts are "secondary" sources.*** To say it in a simple and memorable way, they're mostly "second if not third hand". They are not the original source, which, instead, historians call ***"primary sources".***

For example, a newspaper tells you about a new law (say a stimulus check to be topical). Fine, that is not the original source of the information, is it? So, which one is the original source? The text of the law itself.

But this text has first passed through a government representative who has explained it to the media. Then this explanation has been written down and re-adapted by a journalist. Finally, an editor has checked it and even changed it to make it appear in the light of what the newspaper, site etc. actually wants it to have. By this time, you know how many spins the actual law has had? How many opinions have been added to it?

Odd that when you are writing an essay at school, they ask you to "quote" your sources and then reference them, but professionals only quote (misquote, even) opinions of experts or celebrities, hardly ever actually quote important sources and they almost never reference them.

I watch a news site on a famous platform. This is not a mainstream site, though it is quite in depth. In the description, it ***links all the primary sources of the show.*** I find this very reliable. Even written articles, blogs etc. often have links... Very often, however, these links are only a marketing tool. Why? They just link you to other pages of the same blog or newspaper!

Instead, trust those that, if they're talking about a law, for example, or some data, they link to the original source of the data. It's easy to write "200 billion birds fly over NY every year," without any actual source to prove it, isn't it? So, if you say it, at least if it's the main point of your article, do me a favor and give me the link to the statistics, the study, the data that proves to me you are not lying...

This is again, expecting that your source **does not claim to be the authority, but gives you a link to a true, reliable, and impartial source.**

It will take you a little to get into the habit of double-checking sources, but then, little by little, you will be able to select a set of reliable sources that are good for you. Once you have established which sources and news outlets you can trust, you will only need to do this sporadically, for extra safety or in case you have any doubts about maybe a particular item.

Could I suggest reliable news and information sources to you? Yes, of course I could. But I won't do it, because you need to trust yourself first, not me, I can only show you the way, tell you the tricks. Actually, beware of suggestions unless they come from trusted people you actually know or at least you really trust. Even then, double check the reliability of the channel, newspaper etc. Even trusted friends can make mistakes. Even trusted friends can be fooled by manipulating media...

Look for Consistency

We all change our mind every now and then. But if you are a person in the public eye, if you are an "influencer" of any sort, when you change your mind on a topic you need to say it, and explain why.

Instead, many outlets, channels, and influencers follow a double false line:

- They never admit they're wrong (especially if confronted).

- They change their mind often and they don't tell you they made a mistake, or they changed their mind "because" ... xyz ...

You see how the two things are contradictory? Also note the pattern of mind changing:

- *Do they change their mind every time general opinion changes, or worse, every time someone "higher up the influencer hierarchy" (a politician, some big, vested interest) changes tune?* In this case, "their minds are being changed for them", and in any case they are not reliable.

- *Do they change their opinions according to their convenience, or what is convenient for their narrative, or view?* These too are unreliable.

Finally, **expect consistency**; if they state a rule is valid for someone, a group of people, or an idea, then it must be valid for everybody, all groups of people and all ideas. Even major TV channels have "double standards". If someone on their political side does something wrong, they are very lenient, sometimes they try not to mention it altogether, or put a justifying spin on it.

When politicians "on the other side" do something wrong (or not even that!) they get on the moral high ground and pontificate or sometimes they become aggressive.

Instead…

Expect Correctness

Everybody has an ideological bias. There is no escaping it. Your values will always inform what you say, how you say it and how you interpret things. And you too may be looking for a news or information source with a specific perspective.

The fact is that **reliable information sources, news outlets etc. are correct even with people who oppose their views.** It's fine to disagree, but do they treat adversaries with respect? If they slander them, if they tell you lies about them, if they attack them "under the belt", for example with personal attacks, insults, insinuations on their personal life, comments on their looks etc. Then, for sure, they are not reliable.

Respecting adversaries does not mean liking them, nor agreeing with them. It means, for example, that if they are talking about a person, they give that person a chance to reply. Talking behind people's backs is not acceptable in real life. It does not become acceptable if you do it on social media either.

If they are news outlets, do they invite the people they criticize to speak their mind if possible? Do they stick to facts and actions when criticizing, or do they bring in a "character assassination" strategy? Do they overstate things, or do they keep a level head?

Expecting correctness from those who give us information is simply expecting a basic professional standard. It's like expecting professional behavior from a medical doctor… You see, **manipulators have only to gain if we lower our standards;** in fact, they willingly encourage us to do…

Very correct informers instead will want you to raise the standards you expect, even from themselves. At least they should not encourage you to lower them. There's a guy I used to watch on an online channel, he always closed (he still does) his shows with, "Never trust what you read and only half of what you see."

Why do I like it? It's reminding us to keep our critical minds active and keep very high standards. I won't make any "endorsement" to individual channels for ethical reasons; I am here to tell you that **you need to choose your sources well but also independently.** So, I can't be the first to go against it, can I? But his channel is an investigative journalism channel that deals a lot with mind manipulation and disinformation…

Finally, **how can you trust a channel, influencer, newspaper etc. which is not correct with adversaries to be correct with you?** This is a question that many people should ask themselves when they see their favorite vlogger attack their "enemies" ruthlessly and dishonestly… Most cheer them up… Instead, they should think, "Hold on, this guy passes on information to me. How in the world could I ever trust him?"

Understand Bias

Everybody has his or her ideological bias. Whenever we relate to something, we take a perspective on it. In fact, I would not even trust someone who told me, "What I say is completely unbiased," especially when it comes to hot topics, politics, world views, etc. Of course, no commercial could ever claim to be "impartial".

But **many influencers, channels, news outlets etc. claim to be free from bias, while in reality they are not.** That is a form of mind manipulation. You see, we bestow a lot of trust on "impartial people" like judges. And I have found fake accounts on social media that pretend to be "impartial" while passing sentences on a topic. Then you look at their timeline and you find that they always condemn what a particular side does, never the other side…

Imagine two drinks, two similar drinks, for example. Let's call them "Code" and "Popsy". Fine, they are not new but very popular and there are many people discussing them online – there is a lot at stake if you win or lose this match on which is better.

Would you put it past a CEO or marketing manager to hire a social media marketing company with false accounts that go round changing people's opinions? And which is the best position to change people's minds? One of perceived (faked) impartiality. Don't need to put it past CEOs. Many political organizations use these strategies all over the world. And that is manipulation on a massive scale.

But **bias does not necessarily need to be a negative trait.**

I'll give you an example. I love gardening, remember? But I actually like organic gardening. So, I will look for information on organic gardening sites, channels, look for organic gardening books and magazines etc. These all have an ideological perspective. They do not like chemical products.

You see, the fact is that these **sources are honest about their bias, and they treat adversaries with respect.** This is the bottom line. John cannot be unbiased about, for example, Human Rights, he will always advocate for them, but he says he does, fine? How about those who instead are against Human Rights, but they don't admit they are? They of course already start with an incorrect, dishonest and **hidden bias**. And it's very hard to get them to admit bias.

Very often, when you corner these people, rather than admitting their bias they block you and move onto the next discussion. Discussion in which they will pretend they have not learned anything from you… For them, blocking you and starting afresh is a "reset". They are interested in influencing you and those who read the thread, but even if you prove it to them that they're wrong, it just takes them a "click" and they can pretend you didn't say anything. And they will pretend!

Like me, like most people, you will want to find information sources with views that agree with yours. And you will find them. But **don't start from the premise that because their views are similar to yours, they will not want to manipulate you**… If they are not correct, open, or their facts don't check out, if they don't admit their mistakes, if they don't respect adversaries and so forth, they are not reliable.

It also happens that **groups of manipulators collect followers in one area and then slowly lead them to another.** So, they for example attract people with one political view and slowly lead them to another political position. So… When you find someone with a view like yours online, do not assume that this is their actual view, the view they hold away from the keyboard. They may well be "fishing" in your group to lead you slowly to their actual and real views.

I know, it all sounds so treacherous and in fact it is. For this very reason you need to **expect fair play.** It's easy to get caught up in cheering sprees for your team… But that can work against you in the end.

True, social media is a far more sinister world than people think. You have algorithms that control your freedom without you even noticing it, bubbles where you become isolated, you have marketing agencies that have accounts ready to manipulate you, you have groups of people who pretend they like you and then slowly convince you of what they actually believe etc…

Fake Accounts

… and then you have fake accounts. Loads of them! And even here things are much more complicated than most people know. There are different types of fake accounts.

Bots are **automated accounts**; these are literally remote-controlled accounts, often small, and they have a "crowd" function. They manipulate people's perception of reality by making it appear that a post, an idea etc., is popular or not. This is their main function.

They also have other functions, like amplifying a post's views (often with fake news or a very partial) and pushing it up the "charts" (trends, timelines, anyway to make posts more visible).

Sometimes these also post a little comment, or at times, they are automated so that they post a given sentence. They are used for "storms"; they all post the same hashtag or sentence in a short time, so people think it's popular.

It's the high tech and modern version of astroturfing!

How do they do it? They repost, they put "thumbs up" or "stars" etc. As simple as that. And there are apps that do it automatically on your profile. You just need to enter a handle or profile name in "always re-tweet this profile". And every post will automatically be re-posted, or liked if you want… Do you know how many "influencers" (including politicians and pop stars) use them?

But how many are these? In July 2018 Twitter shut down a whopping 70 million accounts (!!!) because they were clearly fake! This time I had to mention the company, sorry…

How can you recognize bots? It's fairly easy:

- **They are usually small accounts with few followers.**

- **They have a very limited scope;** they only deal with one topic, or one celebrity, or one politician... They basically are a "one trick pony".

- **They often have long numbers in their handles** (at the end of the name, on Twitter, there are 8 numbers in most bots).

- **The profiles are not convincing on closer scrutiny;** you will notice that they have no "real personality", that they are limited in their description etc.

- **They interact very little.**

Avoid these, or block them altogether. There is basically no point in talking to bots.

Then there are **sock puppets.** These are far more problematic. They are **anonymous accounts managed by someone behind the scenes.** These **look real, even with pretend pictures of themselves, clear interactions, and a "personality".**

You will see that the face pic is always then fake, like bought from a stock image company. Alternatively, they use catchy images. **They often have one or a series of symbols next to their profile** (frogs, flags, even ducklings can work as "codes"; they use them to recognize each other online; it's like saying, "I belong to this group").

They will interact a lot; actually, these are in some cases those that launch the big posts. In a marketing or propaganda team, basically you have a group of people. Each has many accounts, and none has the actual name of the user. They can have dozens each! The accounts these manage themselves are sock puppets. So, instead of a politician saying something bad against the adversary (which would look bad!) they get a sock puppet to do it, so it looks like some real person did it.

And then they pay for bots to like the post, to re-post it and make it look like many people think the same. Then, other, smaller sock puppets, will come in to defend the main post. These have very typical argumentative strategies...

They use things like **kettle logic** (they don't respond to a critic, but they relaunch with another point), or **red herrings** (if you say something, they will point out something different, like "squirrel!" so that you go down that path) ...

Why do they do that? Because if you go and argue against the posts of the sock puppets you play in their hands... The post will gain visibility according to the likes, the re-posts but also the interactions, the "comments". It does not matter if these are positive or negative. And how many people actually read the comments? And what do people do when there are loads of comments? They skim through quickly... And if they see the sock puppets' supportive replies they will think that (1) many people actually do back up the head post; (2) they actually have real points to back it up. Both are fake!

Sock puppets often have many followers; and sock puppets of the same group always follow each other. They too are easy to recognize to the experienced eye, but for many people they look real.

Sock puppets are often those profiles that "shift opinion"; so, they will follow you, ask for your friendship etc. because you are in a "target group". Then as "friends", they will start passing (dis)information to you that will slowly change your mind, and you will get new "friends" that follow the same information etc. until you end up in a bubble and where you have not even realized that your opinion has changed. And by then, you are surrounded with people who think the same and reinforce that (almost always false) belief, and no one contradicts them.

They basically "absorb people into a bubble" a bit like amoebas... It's a horrible image; but it's actually like this.

So, careful with sock puppets.

Don't trust accounts that don't actually show their real face.

"Catalogue faces" as I call them, are easy to recognize. They look professional, they often have a neutral background, they just look like models... And you will never find a second picture of them in the whole profile or timeline.

But how about people who want to have a social media account but don't want to show their faces?

Some people have found a way out. In the end, you only need to receive information from a small, trusted group of accounts. So, there are groups that privately share pictures, even regularly, so they all know who they are behind the scenes, and they all know they are real people, but they keep their anonymity in front of the whole wide world.

As you can see, people are very creative indeed, and ingenuity can save you a lot of problems...

What's in a Word? The Language of Social Media

We already touched on this point, once more, in the chapter on television. But I think it's worth reminding a few points and maybe looking into them in more depth. ***We use language to shape our ideas, and language manipulation is manipulation of ideas.*** One of the reasons why feminists around the world are particular about "taking control of language that describes them" is that if the language is freed from patriarchy, thought is freed from patriarchy.

We also looked at ***doublespeak***, a concept developed by George Orwell in *1984*. But there are more Orwellian traits on social media than this. There's a clear *Animal Farm* realization... Do you remember the dogs and the sheep in *Animal Farm?* Sock puppets and bots have very similar functions to these two allegorical animals respectively.

And these often push *intimidating language.* Note that they start slowly, by making simple, low level insults "acceptable". Like calling somebody "stupid" online is an insult, but the word is not too strong... So, they use it for some time till it is accepted, then they move on to a slightly stronger word...

You can see what this has led to: outright life threats and the like. **They slowly push the boundaries of what language is acceptable, and of what ideas (discrimination etc.) are acceptable...** By the time they have reached their objective, all sorts of horrible things have been normalized.

It's a Nazi technique, to be correct. But Orwell gave us a clear picture of how it can be used in less dramatic, tragic, and extremist contexts. So, **never trust any account, channel, blog, news source that is trying to "normalize" offensive language, insults, offensive ideas, personal attacks etc.** These are just the dogs and sheep of some propaganda machine.

P.S.: There are many propaganda machines at work on social media at the moment. Many political leaders have their own, as do political parties but also corporations, groups with hidden intents and many more...

Avoid "screamers and shouters". To start with, theirs is a show! They're not "outraged" by what they are talking about. They're just using an old **marketing technique.** You may remember TV salespeople who shouted all through their TV sale? They did it to pretend to care... It worked. People got a headache, but they bought their products.

Now many political, social and cultural commentators are shouting like deranged people all the time. **They want you to think that they care deeply about what they say. It's a lie.** Any professional notices how this is just an act. You can see how they decide which trigger to use to start their **performance,** and how they artificially wind themselves up...

You will also notice that some of them (especially those more into their careers) do it for virtually anything. It's like screaming mad over a drop of spilt water. **Many become excessive, even grotesque with their fake rage.** That's explained by their role. They are radicalizing people. And the more people follow them, the more they need to take them into a radical position. But these people, to be kept under the manipulation. Need more and more, stronger and stronger "doses" and reinforcements...

I compared it to a drug on purpose. Now, new waves and generations of disinformers come onto the social media stage regularly. They start more moderately and then they become extreme, even clownish... Till they are no longer useful, and they get replaced.

So, **careful with any signs, any tendency to convince you by just shouting, by winding you up instead of by explaining things clearly to you.** Think about it this way, **in the end, the job of an informer, journalist, newsreader, commentator etc. is not to use you as their emotional punch bag, is it? It is to inform you correctly, clearly and with a level head.**

People take exams about things they feel very deeply! I did... I never shouted my ideas at a professor... I doubt I would have passed. So why shout at an audience if not to hit their emotional response, but switch off their brains?

We have already talked about it. But please, keep it well in mind.

You want to get *ideas and opinions expressed in an honest, clear, and commensurate way. It's their job to be calm, not yours to be the emotional valve of their (fake) anger… A professional should be able to report even the most dramatic news in a fairly calm and collected way.*

It does happen every now and then that even the calmest and most collected person loses control. It happens especially in debates where the speakers are heavily pitched against each other, where the presenter does not get them to respect the rules or where the rules are not clear (or don't exist).

But careful; people who do it regularly and especially willingly are trying to manipulate you.

The Two Faces of Social Media

I shall close this chapter with the image of the Roman God Ianus, always depicted with a head with two faces… Social media offers you a wide range of sources. Some are wonderful. I listen to debates, speeches, documentaries, plays, etc. while I am writing… I watch the films I choose at night… I also find lots of data I need, and research papers… books!

And social media can be used to share these. But *avoid using social media as the platforms where you shape your ideas.* Reading a linked article from a reputable source is cool. But making up your mind according to what accounts scream is allowing someone behind a monitor to manipulate your mind. Ah, by the way, think of them as "accounts" and not people… It really helps.

So, again, *you need to take charge of your life, of which sources you allow to pass information and ideas on to you and which not, which types of arguments and language you allow into your world and which not, which type of influencers you listen to (professional or not) and which not.*

Now you know what to look for and what to avoid. You should feel empowered now. You can defend yourself from social media mind manipulation!

We are now coming towards the end of this book, and we have seen lots of strategies to defend yourself from manipulation of many types, online, on TV, face-to-face etc. The next chapter though will be full of light and hope. Why? Because we will look at the "aftercare" in a way, but also at the positive path you can start as soon as you decide to fight off manipulation…

Do you remember when we talked about Behaviorism that it "wires" your brain so that you respond in a certain way? Do you remember that we said that you can "rewire" your brain too? That's exactly what you are going to learn next…

Chapter 12 – Deconditioning and Rewiring Your Brain and Mind

Do you remember that time you had the flu, and you went straight back to work or school as soon as the main symptoms subsided? Or I'll give you a more pleasant example... Do you remember that mad weekend when you didn't even get home and went straight to school or work? In both cases, how did you feel?

Of course, you felt "groggy", "under the weather", "hazed" etc. Why? Your body and your mind were simply not ready to function at their best. Ok, the flu has gone, but everything we do to our mind and our body leaves traces, symptoms, and consequences long after the actual problem has ended.

In mental terms, the consequences can last for a very long time, even months, years, or a lifetime. Just think about how long it takes people to recover from a breakup... So, this leads us straight into the major point: it takes time to heal.

Understand Natural Time Cycles

"Time is the best healer," they say, and it's true in many ways. The main issue is that we live in a society that encourages us to "rush". Being fast, coming first, beating the competition etc. are all encouraged by this modern world, especially at school and in the workplace. This is the reason why most people have, at some stage, gone to work without having recovered fully.

When you see a medical doctor, s/he will sign you off work for longer than the actual symptoms of the complaint you have. But for mind conditioning symptoms, and many other problems that we don't see doctors about, you need to use a bit of DIY, don't you?

So, you will need to understand how our body and our mind work along *natural cycles of time.*

It makes a huge difference if you take an afternoon off or a full day off, doesn't it? If you take half a day off, you don't get half as well, half as relaxed, half as refreshed or half as re-energized as if you take a full day off. You receive fewer and lesser benefits in proportion...

Why? Because our mind and body need a full 24 hours to let go of some thoughts or problems completely. Imagine you are trying to push a big jelly blob out of a skylight... If you only do it partially, it will slide back into your room, won't it? This is why we have relapses. It's like we leave the "blob" in question (a virus, a mental problem, an ailment) half in and half out... It does not bother us too much at this stage, but as soon as you turn your back on it, it comes back.

Now I will give you another example. Think about when you have an argument, or someone says something that upsets you... If the person comes back to you after 5 minutes, are you ready to talk normally? The answer is, of course, "no"! The same applies to children when they have a tantrum. What happens if you bring up the topic again in a matter of minutes? They will start the tantrum again...

This is again because of a **natural unit of time in our mind,** one of the smallest we can use at this time. **The minimum time it takes us to calm down is 20 minutes.** So, if someone gets worked up, give her or him 20 minutes (be generous) to calm down...

Note that the media never gives people 20 minutes to unwind when they are trying to spur you up. Infuriating news follows each other fast and clashes come in quick succession...

So, we already have **two units of time to use: 24 hours and 20 minutes.** You need 24 full hours to get over any sort of significant damage. You need 20 minutes to calm yourself down.

Then again, if 20 minutes is one third of an hour, 8 hours is one third of a day... And you need **8 hours to sleep.** The 8-hour pattern is far more important than people think. We find it in nature, and even mind manipulation studies are aware of it. Most psychedelic "trips" have a basic 8-hour pattern too. Our mind is capable of "switching between realities" in this period of time.

All strong hallucinogenics have a basic 8-hour effect duration (it changes, it goes up and down, some have a very long "after", but this time crops up again and again as the basic duration). What can we understand from it? We can think that **it takes our Consciousness 8 hours to absorb a deep and significant experience.** It looks like we actually need a "change" for 8 hours a day, in fact.

Sleep and dreams have become central to many healing and self-development, even de-conditioning practices. We now understand them in a different way from the past. The practice of **lucid dreaming** can in fact have amazing results when it comes to rewiring the brain, deconditioning the mind and even expanding our Consciousness.

Then again, there is the **lunar cycle, 27 days.** For a full recovery from traumatic experiences, you will need a full **moon phase.** This has been studied in different contexts, including in molecular biology. Gabrielle Andreatta and Kristin Tessmar-Raible carried out an in-depth study on this, which appeared in the *Journal of Molecular Biology* on May 29, 2020 with the beautiful title 'The Still Dark Side of the Moon: Molecular Mechanisms of Lunar-Controlled Rhythms and Clocks'.

It gives us an insight into how deeply lunar cycles time deep processes in many species, and, though most is still to find out, they conclude that "the accumulated data from different species underline the importance and likely complexity of the processes involved." This is only to show that it has deep biological connections, but how about with our mind?

It appears that **moon phases have an impact on our sleep** for example. According to Csilla Zita Turányi et al. their research shows that "the results are consistent with a recent report and the widely held belief that sleep characteristics may be associated with the full moon", as stated in 'Association Between Lunar Phases and Sleep Characteristics', which was published in *Sleep Medicine, Vol.15, Issue 11,* November 2014.

In any case, if you want a practical suggestion, use this long cycle for important healing processes. For example, if you really need a big holiday, take 27 days off if you can (I know most people can't – but I am talking about that "big break" some people may need after serious crises, stress etc.).

If you need to get into a new habit, take 27 days of repeating it, and it will become natural to you...

Then of course, we have *seasons*; these have strong emotional connections, each season has its own mood, its "feeling" and its identity. Sometimes, we identify a whole experience with a season. For example, summer love stories take up the whole essence of a whole season.

Finally, of course, at least on the Human time scale, we have *years*. A full revolution of the Earth around the Sun is a very important time, both symbolically and psychologically. But don't take New Year's Eve as "the day everything changes". That's just a date like many others.

Understanding natural time and cycles means allowing each problem the necessary time scale to heal. You will not get over serious mind conditioning in a day or a week; even less when we talk about the "after effects". However, you can get over the direct influence of an advertisement in 20 minutes.

You see how it works? Serious damage will take more time. In fact, you will not get over the cumulative effects of commercials in one day, nor a week from when you stop watching them...

Neuroplasticity: The Brain and Its "Wiring"

There are different theories on how the mind and brain work. The mind is not as easy to "break into its individual components" and describe as the brain. Mind you, there is still a lot we do not understand about the brain, but...

The cells inside our brain are called neurons. You may have seen them. They look a bit like a spider or octopus, or a strange sea creature with a bulging head (called "soma") and then long tentacles (called "axons"). These axons have many terminals, a bit like the branches of trees, or the fingers on our hands.

These terminals get in touch with the terminals of other neurons forming *synapses* (or *synapsis* in the singular form). Basically, the axon terminals look a bit like receptacles (like shower heads, some may say). These face each other and exchange *electrochemical signals.*

It is with these electrochemical signals that neurons exchange information. On a mental level, this is *the way ideas travel inside the brain. The more a synapsis is used, the stronger it and the axon becomes.* This is why we find it easy to recall ideas, names, dates etc. that we use very often: the path is clear, large, and fully in use.

The more a synapse is abandoned, the more it and the axon become weak and ineffective. We may look at the process like branches drying up in a tree... Little by little that "through path" disappears... This is how we forget things.

If a stimulus is followed by something unpleasant, we will avoid that synapse in our mind, so that path will wither. If it is followed by pleasure, we will "walk that path" more willingly and often and that synapsis will strengthen.

You already knew this principle, but now you also understand it in a physical, neurological sense and dimension. It's like building up muscles or letting them go flaccid on many levels.

The ability of the brain of producing these links, and developing new pathways is called *neuroplasticity.*

Drugs and Brain Wiring

There is something few people are willing to say about psychedelic drugs. There are now many studies that say that psychedelics don't just "cause visions and hallucinations"; they actually have the power to develop many of those synapses we talked about, including in areas of the brain that we normally use little, or pathways that we usually do not follow.

We could say that they "make us think in new ways". Many people even within the creative, inventive, innovative and business world now use "microdosing" to help them think better. They take very small doses of substances like LSD; these do not make them "trip", but they still have the effect of facilitating new connections in the brain.

This is now a well known factor. As Dr. Lily Aleksandrova says in 'Food for Thought: Can Psychedelics Boost Brain Growth Factor Levels?', we now know that "research shows that BDNF (brain-derived neurotrophic factor) can help rewire and overwrite stubborn neutral pathways by creating new connections that facilitate more flexible and adaptive thoughts and behaviors. Psychedelics appear to tap into this mechanism."

Of course, I am not suggesting that you take psychedelics. But this explains why the CIA and others used them a lot in mind conditioning. Maybe, however, with studies coming in now, these psychedelics may be used in the near future by professionals to help the rewiring of manipulated minds. The progress in the health benefits of cannabis moves in that direction, and it appears that Ayahuasca in particular has impressive qualities in freeing up the brain from mind conditioning. For example, it makes people stop taking other, addictive drugs. And Ayahuasca assisted therapy for addiction is being developed by scientists as we speak.

It's in fact not a new type of therapy, already in 2013, its effects were being tested, and Gerald Thomas et al. from the Center of Addictions Research of British Columbia, Canada, state that "this form of Ayahuasca-assisted therapy appears to be associated with statistically significant improvements," and that "alcohol, tobacco, and cocaine use declined".

Can You Rewire Your Brain without Psychedelic Drugs?

"Shall I be waiting till these new therapies are available to everybody," you may wonder? The answer is a resounding no! Of course, you can still rewire your brain without "chemical assistance". Things will happen more slowly, and you will need a lot of determination to do this, but if you follow some guidelines, you will succeed. Many people have.

We already touched upon it, remember? We talked about vaping in depth for example.

Replacement therapy is in fact a way of rewiring your brain. And we have already seen that. But at the same time, you will want to *aid the neuroplasticity of your brain while you use the replacement therapy or other methods.*

And there are many tips I can give you to help you along the way.

Choose the Best Timing

Like with all therapies, if you start it at a good time, you are much more likely to succeed. Imagine starting to rewire your brain when you know you will have lots of practical problems…

You see, when we have to solve lots of problems, our brain tends to go down those paths it knows better because it can be quick. This means that, *in a problem-solving mode, you will tend to strengthen already developed synapses, and not develop new ones*.

There is more; think about when you have emotional problems, can you think properly?

…

I agree with you! You can't. There is no denying that when your heart is suffering, your brain does not work correctly. There are many physical explanations for it. Chemists will tell you that when we suffer, we produce substances and hormones that prevent us from thinking properly.

Other perspectives may simply tell you that when the neurons in your heart (or guts) are strained, they override those in your brain. A more holistic and mentalist approach will say that the heart and mind are two sides of the same experiential process, and that when one is strong, (e.g., the heart) the other allows it to express itself till it can rest and be peaceful.

It doesn't matter which approach you prefer; they all say the same thing: you can't think properly if your heart is suffering… or if your guts are in the grip of fear. We'll talk more about fear soon.

Choose a time when you are at peace, when you don't expect problems. Start at the weekend, not on Monday. Start when you are off work or off school. Start when you retire. Start when you have a stable relationship. Start when you move to a better home… Start in summer or spring, not winter (unless you live in Australia, New Zealand, South Africa etc., of course!)

Don't Let Fear Dominate You

Let's go to your guts… did you know that **we have more than 100 million nerve cells in our guts**? It's another brain. We actually have a few brains around our body. And this is **the brain that sprints into action when we are in danger.**

If you meet a lion in the savannah, you need to change your thinking mode from analytical or emotional to… "emergency". So, the brain in our head takes a back seat, and the one in our guts takes over. We go into a "safety mode", which, of course, does not allow us to think properly.

There is a reason why mind manipulators at high levels (I am thinking about politicians, here, especially tyrants and autocrats) keep talking about danger, risk and instill fear. Media that only cause fear in readers and viewers do the same. They talk to your guts. **If you feel fear, you cannot think rationally.**

But how can you practically achieve this?

- *Avoid (eliminate, if you can) all media that talk and shout about dangers and fear.*

- *Don't worry if you don't succeed. You can try again, and again.*

- *Take time off news and media every day.*

- *Take up calming and relaxing activities.*

- *Avoid violent noise and noisy places.*

- *Keep in touch with Nature.*

We will find the last one, keeping in touch with Nature is useful for quite a few points in rewiring the brain. As for noisy places, even if we get used to them, they provide a continuous stimulus for your gut neurons. They give a "background impression" and that is one of fear and danger.

Now, onto talking about taking "time off" from the news and media…

Prepare for Bed

Are you one of those who watch the news last thing at night? If you are, you will have to change that… Think about, for example, when you go to bed and suddenly a problem comes to your mind… what happens?

…

For most people, this will keep them awake, maybe for an extra 20 minutes, maybe an hour… maybe all night! Now, what happens to your dreams if you watch a horror movie at night?

…

It depends on the movie, true, and on how far you are used to them. But let's take really scary movies and more susceptible people. Why? Because the symptoms are more visible. It does not mean that other people don't have the same reaction. Their brain works in the same way... Only because they are more used to these stimuli it reacts less...

Ok, you know what I am hinting at... Many people literally have nightmares. But hold on... let me ask you a trick question: does our brain work when we sleep as well?

...

Of course it does! And it does wire and rewire even during those 8 hours... And it's not little...

It takes a minimum of 40 minutes to unwind before going to sleep. In this time:

- *Only watch, read, talk about positive and pleasant things.*

- *Get yourself comfortable.*

- *Take relaxing herbal teas, like chamomile.*

- *Use relaxing smells, like lavender incense sticks etc.*

- *Listen to relaxing music.*

- *Don't think about problems and work.*

Preparing for bed is very important indeed. You see, you *recover your mental and emotional strength*, and this will make a huge difference the day after, when you will need willpower, stamina, and strength to keep rewiring your brain.

What's more, is having 8 to 10 hours of calm makes rewiring the brain itself much easier and faster. It's like starting again the day after from a neutral or almost neutral state, if not positive, instead of a negative one. You are already "closer to your aim" when you wake up in the morning!

If you can spend even more time doing this, even better. I spend all nights, from when I have supper onwards unwinding from the day... Which leads me to the next tip...

Find a "Switch off Time"

On top of preparing for bed itself, you need a moment when you say, "This is my 'me' time," and not "work time" or "problem time". Work worries often linger on into the evening, then at night. And that weakens you, and makes rewiring far more difficult.

But to do this effectively, you can't just say, "Fine, it's all over with work," in most cases. You need to:

- *Unwind*

- *Get it off your chest*

This is why the "how did the day go" question and conversation with families, flatmates, friends etc. questions are very important. And it must be followed by good, honest and liberating conversations. I know, listening to other people's problems when you get back from work or school can be hard. But think about it this way: you are, in a way, counseling each other. You let your significant others get it off their chest, and they allow you to do the same. Just take turns and after a few times you'll have a well-oiled routine.

Try to **close this routine with positive points**. Follow the format "these things went wrong and upset me, then these things went well". You can even have a little **ritual to mark the transition into the "me time".** Many people have a glass of wine (red is far better, it relaxes, white wine makes you nervous) to unwind. It could be a good ritual. Tea, a walk in the park etc.… All will do, even singing a song!

I would suggest getting all these things off your chest, again, before the evening meal. **Keep the evening meal as a starting moment for "me time".** If you can earlier, even better. You see, the importance of **eating with a positive mindset (at least once a day) has amazing effects on your mind, brain, and mood.** It's, to start with, major positive reinforcement.

But eating also has very primordial, visceral, ancestral links. Doing this correctly at least once a day is very invigorating, it allows you to find a positive connection with your nature, even at the most basic levels. One of the problems of modern society is that we spend little time dealing with food. We spend too little cooking, eating, planning meals, etc. This is one of the most important relationships we have with our nature.

Eating a microwaved meal in front of the television in a hurry is not healthy at all. It allows all sorts of influences on you (while the food is giving your positive reinforcement). Instead, if you do it in a peaceful, natural way, **the positive reinforcement of the meal will go to your own nature, and feeling confident about your nature is key to rewiring.**

Rewiring Is Like Training

Think of rewiring as training, like for sports. Can you train equally well when you are feeling tired? After you have had a massive night out? When your mind is somewhere else? When your diet is not appropriate? Of course you can't. This is why **you need to have the right conditions to rewire your brain correctly and set yourself up to succeed.**

But there is more… Have you ever trained for some sport? How would you describe the progress you made? I don't mean, "How much progress did you make?" I mean how was it at first? Did it go in phases? Did your training change over time?

…

I think you will say what most people say... It was hard at first, then it got easier, then it became "second nature to you". And these, roughly are the same phases for everybody and for rewiring the brain too.

- *The first few days are the hardest.*

- *Success is slow at first.*

- *In this phase, you are "learning the ropes", the basics.*

- *After a couple of weeks, it becomes "challenging but feasible".* It still takes considerable effort, but at this stage you feel that you can manage it.

- *Results become more visible and faster.*

- *At this stage, you learn from your mistakes and you also work out what's best for you.*

- *Progress accelerates, and you tailor the training (rewiring) to your personal needs.*

- *Then, after a long time, it becomes "customary", "usual", "easy" and second nature.*

- *At this stage though, your progress actually slows down.*

- *What you are doing at this stage is mainly consolidating your achievements.*

This is what will happen, and remember that the consolidation phase is very important indeed. Reaching the top of a mountain once does not mean you can reach it again... But if you consolidate your climbing skills, you will do it again and again. Things become feasible even when you are not 100% if you consolidate your skills.

Mind Your Diet

Your brain consumes 20% of all the energy your body uses every day. That's an awful lot! And it does not even move a single muscle! But it's not just a matter of quantity... It's a matter of quality too.

It is now ascertained that a poor, unhealthy diet (especially early on in life) is responsible for decreased intelligence scores, even later in life. And it's now ascertained that *your diet and your lifestyle affect your neuroplasticity.* A study on elderly people with cognitive issues by Christy Phillips, finds out that there are three main "modifiable lifestyle factors" that affect neuroplasticity: "physical activity, cognitive engagement and diet."

No need to say the typical US diet is poison. We said it already. In particular, you need to *cut down on animal fats and sugar.* These literally slow down mental processes and even cause lots of health problems that will then affect our brain.

The ideal would be to have *a healthy, organic, varied plant-based lifestyle*. It does not mean that you have to become vegan, but that the bulk of your diet should be healthy, plant derived and rich in carbohydrates and vitamins, fatty acids and minerals. Of the carbohydrates you take, don't forget fiber.

Many of the "substances that oil our brain" are contained in vegetables, like vitamins, long chain omega-3 fatty acids, folic acid etc. A Mediterranean diet, as you know, would be ideal, and it's super tasty too!

Keep Your Brain Fit!

One of the three factors that make your brain more plastic, so more easily rewired, is *"cognitive engagement"*. You know when people look at old writers, scientists etc., maybe in their 90s and they say, "How lucid s/he still is!" Yes, people who use their brain regularly will keep it fit, and it will keep healthy into their old age. It's as simple as that.

The problem is that people think that watching the news is using your brain, you now know it's definitely not: it's in a passive mode. And we cannot train by being passive. So…

- *Read a lot.*

- *Listen to good music.*

- *Go to the theater.*

- *Have cultural conversations with friends, even debates if you can.*

- *Take on an artistic hobby (gardening included!)*

- *In short, engage your mind in active (!!!) mental activities each day, for at least a few hours a day.*

Even learning a new language, going to evening classes etc. are very good, like doing crosswords and so forth. You got the gist!

Mens Sana in Corpore Sano

I haven't had far too much to drink… *Mens sana in corpore sano* is a famous Latin saying which means "a healthy body in a healthy mind". And it's true! **We need to look at our body as a whole.** If your body is not working well, it will divert energy from mental activities to see to other problems. This is why when you have a temperature or when you are in pain you cannot think well.

Choose a Positive Setting for Your Rewiring

Re-wiring requires a positive, peaceful and healthy setting. Of course, this is not always possible. If you want to do a little rewiring exercise when you are queuing at the post office, fine. But if you have a decently long session in mind, say 15 or more minutes, choose a good place to do it. It will work far better.

- *Avoid places linked with work or negative activities or memories.* Your office is not the best place.

- *If possible, choose a place which is natural or with a window on a natural, green space.*

- *Choose a quiet place.*

- *Prepare the place of how you want.* People like to use perfumed candles or sticks, or even just sprinkle a few drops of some relaxing essential oils, like lavender, sandal etc. If you want, ***put on low volume relaxing music and have ambient lighting.*** This will really help you rewire your brain.

- *Tell people you don't want to be disturbed.*

- *Switch off all distractions: TV, radio, computer or that terrible cellphone!*

- *Make sure light, humidity and temperature are fine.*

- *Avoid artificial light!*

On the last point we need to say a bit more. Artificial light keeps you awake and alert; it does not allow you to relax. To start with, lower lights 40 minutes before bed. But in these sessions, if you can, use natural light or candlelight.

Do Meditation

Meditation is by far the best way to prepare your mind for rewiring. It's also, as we have seen, an outstanding way of de-conditioning your mind, and freeing yourself from manipulation.

A quiet mind stops the repetitive and even "automated" synaptic firing that reinforce those paths induced by manipulation. A meditative mind is the quietest we can have. Even quieter than when we sleep in fact!

"But meditation is hard," I can hear some of you say… Not really… There are many ways of meditating, you don't need to sit in the lotus position to do it. Actually, the lotus position is only for experienced meditators.

You can meditate when you walk in a park or on the beach. You can meditate at home, standing upright, sitting comfortably or laying down. The key to meditation is just to switch off that rational, talkative mind, that voice in our head we keep hearing...

To do it, the best way is to concentrate on your breath. Just breathe in slowly through your nose, hold your breath in for a little while, like a second, you should not feel uncomfortable with it. Then breathe out slowly. Focus on it till you hear no more "words in your head".

If you learn to belly breathe (or re-learn to belly breathe, as when we are children, we do it all the time, just watch a baby), even better. And if it does not work the first time, don't worry; try again. You don't get fired if you don't succeed!

Use Music to Rewire Your Brain

Of course, music too can put our mind in a peaceful state and make it "open to rewiring". Even more, *listening to pleasant music while rewiring is a form of positive reinforcement.* But while doing the exercises, you need to listen to "the music your brain likes, not you!"

No heavy metal, death metal, punk, rock or other high energy music while you are rewiring. But you can treat yourself to Metallica *after* you have done the exercise as positive reinforcement. The problem is that *some music waves soothe the brain into receiving information, others distract it.* High energy music distracts you.

While you are doing the exercises:

- *Prefer slow peaceful music, with maximum one beat per second.*

- *Prefer music with real, natural instruments.*

- *Classical music (especially Baroque) is believed to be good.*

- *Meditation music is excellent.*

But avoid binaural sounds. There are a lot of "binaural meditation music" tracks online. Just don't! The problem is that they can cause more damage than good. The reason is that it is almost impossible to time the binaural sound to the other track. And if it's not perfectly timed, it has a negative effect.

Talking About Exercises

"But hold on," you're thinking, "you keep talking about exercises, but you haven't given us a single one!" OMG you called me out! Ok, then, just because you have, I'm going to give you a full chapter of exercises!

Chapter 13 – Exercises to Rewire Your Brain

Are you ready for some practical exercises? Don't worry; you won't build up a sweat. You can do most of the activities in this chapter in the comfort of your home. But sometimes I will ask you to go out. Contact with Nature has amazing effects, as you know. One thing though I need to remind you of before we start: *keep it positive! The rewiring, like replacement therapy, can only use positive reinforcement, never negative!*

So, on your marks, get set, go!

Belly Breathing

Let's start with a basic exercise. This will not in itself rewire your brain, but if you learn it, many other exercises and activities will become easier and more effective. There's something strange about the way we breathe... When we are children, we belly breathe, just like singers, athletes etc. No one knows why but at some stage, we start pushing our chest out to fill our lungs instead of pushing the diaphragm down and belly out (belly breathing, in fact).

Nevertheless, when we sleep, we revert into what appears to be the natural way of breathing: belly breathing. Belly breathing has a few major advantages:

- *You breathe more air.*

- *You oxygenate your brain better.*

- *You give your heart a slow rhythm.*

- *It is ideal for a meditative and relaxed mood.*

Let's try. First, breathe in normally. The only thing I will ask you to do is focus on your breath and your lungs. What happens to it? You "suck it in" with your nose, then you push out your chest (even with discomfort at times) and fill your lungs.

Now, focus on the bottom of your lungs, where your bowels start. Now breathe in through your nose, but this time, push the air down, towards the bottom of your lungs. Your belly will push, allowing your lungs to extend downward.

It may take a few trials, but once you remember how to do it, that's it.

Draw Your Dreams

What did you want to become when you were a child? What were your childhood dreams?

Visualizing is an excellent way of rewiring the brain. But I will ask you more in this exercise... I will ask you to go back to "before" the mind manipulation started, and using your memory, "graft your future self on your past self".

Get a nice box of crayons, a big white coloring paper, take time off all sorts of engagement and get drawing! It does not matter if you are a new Leonardo or just a scribbler. Put colors (positive ones) in your dreams, and bathe in the beauty of your childhood dreams.

When you do this, focus on the great pleasure you get from this activity. And at the end, pause for a second to enjoy the happiness this exercise has given you.

Smell Flowers

Does it look and sound simple? Well, it is! Our modern world uses the sense of smell to condition us, but it actually discourages proper understanding and active use of our sense of smell. Instead, building "perfumed" pathways in our brain is a way of building long lasting synapses.

I say flowers, but it can be any smell you like. Re-engage with your sense of smell, and use it as positive reinforcement. When you smell something, rather than trying to describe it, just focus on its "presence" and on the feelings it arises in you.

Get used to making positive links with positive, especially natural smells in your life. This can become a major asset when you want to shift your mind from an unwanted brain path to one you wish to encourage and develop.

Flip Your Conditioned Behaviors

Take a piece of paper, make it a big one. Draw a line in the middle and on the left-hand side, write down all the behaviors you feel are being manipulated in you. Use bullet points.

Take a walk... Do something positive and fun. Come back, and for each negative behavior put a comparable positive one on the other side. For example: "I eat too many sweets," on one side with "I will eat more fruit," on the other side. Yes, sugar is addictive... Or if you want, "I buy too many useless things," can change into "I will give my useless junk away to charity every week."

Try to turn the negative into positive. Now, if you can't "counter" each negative behavior at first, don't worry. Go back to it later...

What do you have now? You basically have a "roadmap" to change all the behaviors that have been induced into your personality. Shopping changed to helping others is actually a very useful switch. People often become shopaholics for many reasons, but having a social activity, like talking to the charity people etc., as a replacement is quite good.

Mind Your Language

Every time you say something, you make it a "deeper part of your personality". This is how people develop *idiolects* (the individual languages of each person), how people develop those words and phrases that they use all the time.

That's fine, but may I ask, are there any phrases and words you use a lot and you do not like?

Fine, make a list, and then write an alternative phrase of words next to each. Cross out the one you don't want to use, and underline, highlight or circle the ones you want to use.

Now it is time to remember.... Every time you are about to use a crossed-out expression, try to replace it...

Use Positive Language

I had a friend who always started his sentences with "no". He wasn't very successful, no need to say. He also had many confidence issues. You see, when you use negative language, you do two things with it:

- *You externalize it.*

- *You internalize it.*

So, start your sentences with "well" instead of no. When you disagree, do it with a positive opening ("I can see what you are saying, but..."); avoid "I hate", "I can't stand" etc.

Now, I wouldn't go so far as some sticklers do... You know, there are people who say that you should never utter anything negative... Of course it happens, of course people have to get it off their chest. I actually think that "not using negative expressions at all costs" can be counterproductive if people need to release tension, pain, suffering, worries etc....

But *changing your language to a positive one will make following positive in your mind much easier.* Think about words as road signs... The more road signs leading to a good thought you have, the more easily you will find it...

Use Positive Affirmations

Positive affirmations are a way of teaching your subconscious to be positive, and follow paths you set for it. It is one of the most powerful rewiring exercises we have.

Basically, what you need to have is one or more sentences with these qualities:

- ***Positive affirmations are simple and clear.***

- ***Positive affirmations are short.***

- ***Positive affirmations express willpower.***

I will give you a few examples:

- "I will eat more fruit during the day."
- "I will be happier when I wake up in the morning."
- "I will smile more often."

Make them suitable to your aims, your plan etc. These are like the "good version of mind manipulation" in the sense that they work on the same level, the subconscious. But instead of making you do things someone else wants, **they teach your subconscious to recognize your real will.**

You will need to repeat them over and over again (like manipulators do). You will also need to say them when you are quiet, calm, and receptive. You can say them to yourself for a few minutes every day, maybe before going to bed. That, as you know, is a time when our mind is very "open to suggestions".

But another time in the day would be fine too if you wish. Once more, when queuing at the Post Office for example. Or driving instead of listening to music that plays negative lyrics. Those "dead moments" in the day are excellent to rewire your brain.

Repeat them slowly to yourself, with calm and peace. You can use music, like slow, meditative music, to give you a rhythm for them if you wish. This too, works very well.

Regardless, always try to remember to **connect the positive affirmations with positive reinforcement.** Something healthy, preferably.

You will see the results creeping in slowly after a couple of weeks. It may be earlier, it may be a tad later.

If I can be a bit insistent, do use positive affirmations in your rewiring; they work wonders.

Use Visualization

How do you want to change your life? Who do you want to become when you free yourself from mind manipulation? No – don't tell me! I want you to **picture it in your mind** instead!
And get used to it! Get used to visualizing your aims, your objectives, your dreams, your positive journeys. You should do it regularly, in a peaceful place. If you can go to a park or a beach. Otherwise, indoors will do too, but set up the room like we said for mediation.

Just close your eyes. If you can meditate, do it and add this level to the visualization. If you want to bring a radio with relaxing music, fine. But birds singing will do quite well. Sorry, we don't use radios any longer, I know, cell phones then! In any case, visualizing while meditating pushes the images deeper into your mind.

Use candles, naturally perfumed sticks etc., if you wish. Make sure you feel comfortable, and wear comfortable clothes. Take your time. Don't do this when you are in a hurry. Above all, make sure you are well hydrated. We think and visualize better when we are hydrated. It's like watercolors! Sorry, joke...

Ok, you can picture what you have in mind in front of you, or better still, you can put yourself in the middle of it.

You will notice that when you visualize, it's not like you are fully in control of the images. They tend to take on a "will of their own" and draw themselves. This is fine, but who is drawing them, then? There are many theories, and I will stick to a simple and easily accepted one: it's your subconscious and your unconscious that are painting the pictures in front of you...

Note here, that people who have suffered heavy mind manipulation will often see negative, unpleasant and even frightening pictures coming from their subconscious. But have no worries about this and above all **don't take them seriously!** Make fun of them! It's the only way to get rid of them.

If your mind is fairly in control, you can easily push negative images aside. But after string manipulation, if you push them aside but you respond emotionally (you are scared, disgusted etc.,) they will come back. That is the manipulation trying to force itself onto you.

So, if you can be neutral, fine. But even better, laugh at them. That literally breaks up the pathways in your brain that lead to the manipulated goal... A trick that victims of strong mind manipulation have invented is to turn them into stupid cartoons! You can do it fairly easily.

A cartoon is not taken seriously to start with, and then you can make something stupid happen and you laugh at it!

Anyway, this is only in serious cases... In most cases, you will simply be able to visualize beautiful things, and that will rewire your brain to positive ideas, pathways, thoughts, aims and behaviors...

Laugh!

This is not actually an exercise... But laugh a lot! Watch comedy, tell jokes, don't take yourself too seriously... Did you notice what we said just now? When you laugh, you "ease the synapses related to that topic", this means that you ease the pathways to certain thoughts.

It has told you that deconditioning could be fun... Well, it should be fun, actually, even better, the more fun it is, the better it works!

Conclusion

Isn't this a raving mad world we live in? When I was a child, I thought mind conditioning was something belonging to Japanese cartoons. I grew up to find out that not only is it possible... It is, if you forgive me the phrase, in full swing!

I grew up to learn psychology, and in my studies, I became interested in dark psychology... Finding out that experiments on how to condition minds started centuries ago was only the beginning... Coming into the de-classified documents in CIA experiments, their cruelty, their range, the weaponization of mind manipulation, to then use it against innocent citizens... - well, that was a massive shock.

But even more, seeing that low level, but all-pervasive types of mind manipulation that uses the very language we speak and write, the newspapers, movies, television and even social media to keep us under control... - well, that actually promoted me to write this book.

And I hope I have helped you.

I have avoided personal opinions in this book. It's a very "sensitive" topic already; I have cracked a few jokes, used metaphors and tried to make your reading pleasant – but correct and informative. But my opinions have stayed out of it. Till now. Now we reach the end of this journey, I will express a personal thought: in my view, **mind manipulation is a crime against Human Rights**. Why? It goes against the very **Article 1 of the Universal Declaration of Human Rights:**

> **"All human beings are born free and equal in dignity and rights. They are endowed with reason and conscience and should act towards one another in a spirit of brotherhood."**

What do I see in it? I see that conscience belongs to us; it belongs to the individual and no one else. Trying to change my, your, or anybody else's Conscience against my, your, their will, is in fact a crime against this very first article.

We need to **take back control of our Consciousness and conscience.** Only when that is guaranteed will we really make inroads against mind manipulation. So far, it remains a "crime that society tolerates", like rape, torture and murder were in the past...

I am sorry I have had to take you into the bowels of hell with the studies and experiments (and outright crimes) done to manipulate people's minds. But it was necessary for you to know about it and then fight against it.

I hope I have helped you.

I am glad, on the other hand that you have learned all the theory and psychology that is behind this appalling practice. And I'm glad that you **now have the means to counter and fight mind manipulation with confidence.**

It is not an easy battle, but remember, it must be a positive one, even a funny one! ***The more you enjoy yourself, the more you are happy with your life, the easier it is to get out of mind manipulation.*** You can now see the light at the end of the tunnel…

In a way, the journey out of mind manipulation reminds me a bit of Dante's *Divine Comedy*. It's a journey to hell and then out of it, into heaven… And when the poet gets out of hell, or gets out of purgatory, or even at the end of the whole poem, there is always the same word: "stars".

He comes out of the darkness of hell "to see again the stars" … We are living through dark times in terms of mind manipulation… But if I hope I have done something, well, I hope I have shown you a path out of this "dark forest" and that now, after reading this book, you feel more confident. That you will so, because you have so many ideas and techniques to push back mind conditioning moving forward.

You even know how to rewire your brain, and become the person you have always wanted to be.

So, in a way, I trust that now you too, after having read this book, can finally see the stars… Never lose sight of them, and your path will get brighter and brighter. As for me, I hope we will meet again, maybe on the pages of another book, and for now…

Cheers to gaining better control of mind manipulation.

Reference Page

There is so much to say on this topic that I can't tell you all in a single book. But if you are a curious mind, and if you wish to find out more, here is a list of books you may wish to check out!

✓ Baum, W. M. (2017). *Understanding Behaviorism: Behavior, Culture, and Evolution* (3rd ed.). Wiley-Blackwell.

✓ Browne, J. (2020). *Understanding the Human Mind: Why we need thinking time*. Independently published.

✓ Faber, K. (2019). *Mental Toughness - Unleash the Power Within: How to Develop the Mindset of a Warrior, Defy the Odds, and Become Unstoppable at Everything You Do*. Cac Publishing LLC.

✓ Goleman, D. J. & Press, TH. (2020). *REWIRE YOUR BRAIN: Understanding the Science and Revolution of Neuroplasticity. Rewire Your Brain, Body, and Soul to Change Your Mind, Develop a ... and Control your Anxiety Disorder*. Independently published.

✓ Green, E. (2020). *Proven Psychological Manipulation Techniques: Guiltless Guide into the Psychology of How Cunning People Get What They Want. How to Play Secret Dark Games to Seize Control and Always Win*. Modern Mind Media.

✓ Green, E. (2020a). *Dark Mind Control Techniques in NLP: The Secret Body of Knowledge in Psychology That Explores the Vulnerabilities of Being Human. Powerful Mindset, Language, Hypnosis, and Frame Control*. Modern Mind Media.

✓ Hollins, P. (2018). *Psychological Triggers: Human Nature, Irrationality, and Why We Do What We Do. The Hidden Influences Behind Our Actions, Thoughts, and Behaviors*. CreateSpace Independent Publishing Platform.

✓ Jones, M. D., & Flaxman, L. (2015). *Mind Wars: A History of Mind Control, Surveillance, and Social Engineering by the Government, Media, and Secret Societies* (First ed.). Weiser.

✓ Kahn, M. D. (2002). *Basic Freud* (1st ed.). Basic Books.

✓ Ph.D., C. B. (2015). *The Neurogenesis Diet and Lifestyle: Upgrade Your Brain, Upgrade Your Life* (1st ed.). Psyche Media.

✓ Ph.D., H. S. (2014). *The Power of Neuroplasticity* (1st ed.). CreateSpace Independent Publishing Platform.

✓ Ph.D., H. S. (2019). *Negative Self-Talk and How to Change It*. Park Avenue Press.

✓ S. (2017). *MK Ultra Dark Labs*. CreateSpace Independent Publishing Platform.

✓ Skinner, B. F. (1976). *About Behaviorism* (1st ed.). Vintage.

✓ Soh, J. (2019). *Mind Hacking: Unleash The Hidden Power Of Your Subconscious Mind & Achieve Anything That You Truly Desire!* Independently published.

✓ Winship, A. (2019). *Neuroplasticity: Exercises to Improve Cognitive Flexibility, Conquer Trauma and PTSD, Change Bad Habits, Eliminate Depression and So Much More!* Independently published.

How To Analyze People & Emotional Intelligence Mastery

33 Strategies & Secrets for Speed Reading People, Body Language, NLP, Positive Persuasion & Dark Psychology Protection

By: U.P.P.

Unlimited Potential Publications

Table of Contents

Introduction

Have you ever felt manipulated, perhaps by a salesman, a colleague, a boss, a friend, a family member, or a romantic partner? And whenever you call them out on their actions, they make you believe that you're crazy—that you're too sensitive, and that you have a problem. The more it happens, the more you start to believe them. You start to overthink, you start to doubt yourself and your ability to decide without their influence. You lose a bit of yourself every day as you give in to their manipulation. You start to lose confidence, esteem, and freedom. Other long-term effects of manipulation include:

1. Questioning yourself. Prolonged manipulation causes people to question themselves, causing them to doubt almost every decision they make. This is probably because of consistent blaming, gaslighting, and other techniques of manipulation. When a person is victimized, he/she feels less and less about themself to the point that they feel lowly about their decision-making skills. It's also probably the reason why the person sticks with a manipulator. Because to them, the manipulators are the only people who understand their situations and would know what to do.

2. Anxiety is the body's natural response to stress. It refers to the feeling of fear or apprehension about what is to come. It could be caused by sudden changes such as the first day of school, first day of a new job, giving a speech, and many more. While anxiety is a normal part of life, it could be dangerous when it turns into a disorder. Often, people who are victims of prolonged manipulation develop a generalized anxiety disorder, panic disorder, separation anxiety, and phobia. All of which are characterized by an extreme fear or worry about events that may not even have happened or are about to happen and/or objects that do not generally evoke fear. Anxiety disorders can be dangerous because they can cause people to make impulsive decisions that can get them hurt or into trouble.

3. Passivity. Another effect of long-term manipulation is passivity. This pertains to a person's lack of drive to become productive in life. When a person has been manipulated, chances are, they believe that they're stupid or worthless. Even when they cut ties with the manipulator, these thoughts remain and affect how they become productive in life.

4. Shame and guilt. I have seen many victims of manipulation blame themselves for letting other people control them. Because of this, they feel "dirty" and stupid. They think about "what-ifs" which could lead to self-hate and self-blame. Often, victims resort to self-harm, even suicide because of their intrusive thoughts.

5. Avoiding human contact. Another long-term effect of manipulation is avoidance. Some victims start to generalize people, claiming that the next person who shows kindness wants something in return. This makes people asocial which could affect their emotional and psychological health even further.

6. Being overly critical. Another common effect of manipulation is being too cautious with other people. They no longer want to experience pain and shame, so they assess every person they meet, often too critically, to the point where they look at every flaw and exaggerate it. Unfortunately, this could be really unhealthy in building long-term relationships.

7. Requiring approval. When a person is manipulated, chances are, everything he or she does require the approval of the manipulator otherwise they are subject to punishment or

abuse. So even after they cut ties with their manipulator, they carry this need for approval. In whatever they do, they need to be reassured that what they are doing is correct. Otherwise, they're unlikely to act on it. Sometimes, victims walk on eggshells around people to avoid hurting them or annoying them. Even when they are no longer controlled, they still have a need to comply with others' wishes even if it hurts them or even when it affects their overall wellbeing.

8. Depression. Long-term manipulation leads to depression. Despite what people think, depression is not the feeling of sadness. It is a psychological disorder characterized by extreme feelings of hopelessness, emptiness, and grief. People with depression do not only display sadness, but they also have anger outbursts. They get irritated and frustrated easily, and they start to lose interest in things that they usually love. Other signs of depression include sleep disturbances, lack of energy, reduced appetite or binge-eating, restlessness, feelings of worthlessness or guilt, trouble concentrating, recurrent thoughts of death, and unexplained physical problems.

If any of you feel the symptoms, do not take it for granted. It is important to seek the guidance of a psychologist to determine if you need professional help.

If you're reading this book, you may already feel these signs but are not sure if they root from manipulation. If you still have no clue, let's play the "Put a finger down" challenge. The following statements below are commonly spoken by manipulators. So, put a finger down or put a checkmark beside the statements if you've heard them. If you did, write who you heard it from.

Here are 15 of the most common phrases used by manipulators:

1. You're crazy.

2. Look what you made me do.

3. I said I'm sorry. Why are you still upset?

4. It's always my fault.

5. I don't understand what you mean.

6. You're too sensitive.

7. It's just a joke.

8. You're impossible to talk to.

9. I thought you loved me.

10. All you do is…

11. If you do this…

12. Why do you always think like that?

13. Sorry if I'm not perfect.

14. That's why people don't like you.

15. You always act like this.

How many of these statements have you heard from people around you? And how many times have you heard these before? You may think that these are just sentences that reflect their feelings but if you dig deeper, these statements affect you more. It makes you comply with their requests because you feel guilty for not being enough or for someone who has a faulty mind. If you've put your finger down to one or more of these statements and have heard them more than twice from one person, then you might be a victim of manipulation. You just didn't know it.

Unfortunately, using words is not the only face of manipulation. Some manipulators do not take responsibility for their actions. Instead, they thought of the situation to make you the bad guy. Others even deny their promises. They give the impression that they will do something only if you accomplish something first. In the end, you're the only one putting in any effort.

The most common form of manipulation is anger and aggression. If you do not comply with their wishes, manipulators often resort to physical or emotional abuse. It could also be in the form of threats just to make people come by to them.

This ends now! You're probably tired of being accused of things. You're probably sick of putting up with others' bull. It's time you learn more about manipulators and their techniques. This book focuses on the techniques of manipulation and how to avoid them by speed-reading people and analyzing them through body language. This way, you can protect yourself from Positive Persuasion and Dark Psychology.

And if you feel like you've already been broken by your manipulation, you can apply neuro-linguistic programming or NLP to recondition your mind for healing and self-improvement.

Speaking from personal experience, learning the techniques of manipulation and NLP helped me become more emotionally stable. It made me stronger to face challenges and be more discerning of people who plan to control me. Trust me, I played the "Put a finger down" challenge, and I put them down on each statement. It all came from one main person (aside from a few people in my life at the time). The worst part is, it was someone who I trusted and loved.

At that time, I was ready to do everything for that person. All I wanted was to see him happy. Even when I wasn't at fault, I was always the first one to say sorry. When something bothered me, I stayed quiet because I didn't want to start a fight. Even when I was already abused, broken, and torn apart, I stood by that person because a part of me believed that he could change. Every time I attempt to break my ties, that person would always make me feel bad because I "easily give up on challenges."

One time, he cheated on me with my best friend. When I found out and got mad about it, he said, "It was her fault and so thought you would understand because you love me and trust me."

From a normal person's perspective, the next thing to do should have been to cut him off completely. But from someone who is already manipulated and abused, I had no idea how to start a new life without him. He made me look so weak, fragile, and stupid that I couldn't make any decisions without him. Because of his manipulations, I stood beside him even when my friends and family were telling me to run. This time, it wasn't because of love. It was because of fear. Fear that no one will ever love me again and fear that no one but him will accept me because I was already a broken toy.

When I finally got out, I already had anxiety and depression. It took me months to recover from that abuse. And when I did, I said, "no more." Now, I know better.

You don't want any form of manipulation to go that far. It's best to be prepared than to be too late. And if it already has, that's okay because you aren't doomed. You can recover! So, it's important to learn how to discern its faces and techniques. If you think manipulation destroyed you already, NLP can help you recover and build emotional stability. Oprah Winfrey, Tony Robbins, Lily Allen, and Jim Carrey along with other celebrities can attest to the benefits of NLP.

These include:

- Confidence building
- Improved body language
- Improved mental and emotional stability
- Improved skills in managing people
- Improved decision making and problem-solving
- Breaking free from your mental limits.

Unfortunately, manipulation and NLP are more difficult to learn and apply. You need proper guidance and correct information. I know thousands of books have already been written about these topics but only a few offer reliable information. Without ample supplementation, learning NLP and the techniques of manipulation could do more harm than good. In this book, you will not only learn the basic information about these topics but how to apply them in real-life situations. You will also learn various myths and misconceptions about these topics that often lead people into making worse decisions. Are you ready for the first step to break free from manipulation? Let's start with body language and its psychological impact. What is body language and why is it a fundamental factor in reading and analyzing people?

Chapter 1 – Why Does the Body React the Way It Does?

Body language is an integral part of communication. Whether it's in school, counseling, public speaking, even at home, body language is always observed. Many people think that body language is a set of mere actions and gestures to help convey a point. And some say that these are mere acts that can be taught and learned. In public speaking, for example, speakers are trained to look at their audience, move their hands in relation to their points, and express their emotions through their eyes. In counseling, counselors need to display open body language so their clients would be comfortable to share their problems. Conversely, the counselors are trained to observe the body language of their clients to see if they are lying, nervous, or agitated. At home, we are instructed not to cross our legs or cross our arms, especially when talking to our parents, because it shows disrespect. The same lesson is taught in school so children would display proper decorum in the classroom.

Over the years, people have been preoccupied with calling out people displaying the wrong body language for the occasion. Only a few took time to notice its internal reasons and external implications. People neglected to understand what lies behind body language. Little did they know that behind a small gesture lies a million thoughts in one's subconscious. How is that so? First, let's learn more about body language.

Body language is a type of non-verbal communication that involves a person's facial expression, gestures, posture, head movements, and eye contact. Although human beings have been using body language since time immemorial, it was only in 1952 when an anthropologist studied how it works. During this time, Ray Birdwhistell made films of people and analyzed them to make out patterns of behavior in specific social situations. In his studies, he believed that body movements have meaning and that they could be interpreted as language. He called these basic groups of movements "kineme." In language, it's likened to us a phenome that represents the smallest speech sounds to construct words. Birdwhistell also emphasized that these groups of movements should always be analyzed and assimilated with verbal communication to reach meaningful conclusions. Over time, he coined the word body language.

Body language can be expressed consciously to convey a point. When you're saying a firm no, for example, you can disagree by shaking your head side to side so you can express your disagreement strongly. When you want to show annoyance or frustration towards a person, you roll your eyes when they speak or raise your eyebrows. It can also be applied for clarification. When pointing directions, for example, instead of merely saying "there," you can point your fingers to give more concise information.

Body language can also be expressed unconsciously, which to some people, is more important to assess. A person can say yes, but his body language could be saying "no." A person could tell you how amazing their products are, but their body language could show they are lying. Of course, when a person is trying to manipulate you, he or she would come off kind, safe, trustworthy, and reliable. They are taught to display only positive gestures. But when you learn how to look at their body language through a microscope, you can eventually see the slips they don't want you to notice.

You see, unconscious body language is brief and difficult to assess with the naked eye. This is why investigators and law enforcers replay interview videos in slow motion. This way, they can see sudden movements and determine whether the accused is lying when asked a question. Even the strongest poker players have body language slips. But you need to have a microscopic eye to catch them. Once you develop your ability to assess other people's body language, you can protect yourself from possible scams, harassment, and manipulation. Conversely, when you learn to control your body language, you can experience a variety of benefits as well.

Understanding what the Body is Telling You

Learning more about body language has various benefits. Aside from discerning manipulative people, it can also help you improve yourself, your career, and your relationships. How?

Non-verbal communication is culturally defined. While many cues are general, some could have different meanings for different cultures. When you understand more about body language, you can unlearn inappropriate and unfitting body language. When you attend a meeting, for example, and you are about to face people of different nationalities, there is body language that seems appropriate to you but is actually rude to other people. Crossing your legs could be a typical move for you but is a form of disrespect in Japan and China. The same is true when you make eye contact with your superiors. Furthermore, giving a handshake and the 'OK' sign is inappropriate to some countries. These are only some things you need to study if you want to build rapport in your career. You can imagine what can happen if you choose to ignore proper body language during formal interactions.

The same is true in building relationships. When you're on a date, you need to learn proper body language. Don't slouch or cross your arms. Otherwise, that person will think you are not interested in him or her. When you're talking to your friends or family, don't stare at your watch or they might assume that they are boring you.

You see, non-verbal cues are powerful. Sometimes, it's even more powerful than your words. This is why you need to be aware of your body language so you can unlearn what needs to be changed. By learning body language, you can create a lasting positive impression. Plus, you can convey your meanings strategically and effectively. These benefits are important in all aspects of life.

Don't worry! Body language can be practiced, much like what public speakers do to convey their messages effectively. The first is understanding body language to its core. This way, you will have proper guidance when you finally apply it in your daily interactions.

Human Reflex, Inevitable or Not?

In my journeys, I've often encountered the question, "Is reflex the same as body language?" or "Is human reflex connected to body language?" To answer this question, let us first understand the scientific explanation for a reflex.

Reflexes are automatic responses that do not require the brain to take any action. It is enacted by your body even without you thinking it. An example of this is dodging a ball or catching it. Or when you put your hand on a hot surface, and you immediately take it off. During these instances, you don't think, "The stove is hot. Do I take my hand off?" Of course, you should! Also, when you step on a thumbtack, you don't have to think about removing your feet from the ground. Your brain knows how painful it is. And in a split second, your mind knows what to do.

Another example is arm twitching or finger twitching. Remember when our phones had keypads? There were times when your thumb would just twitch as if it's texting without a phone. You're not consciously doing it, but your muscles do it anyway. That's another example of reflex.

There are two types of reflexes: natural and conditioned.

1. Natural reflex is also known as an inborn reflex. These are innate instantaneous movements that require no previous experience. These are often displayed to protect the body from different circumstances. Examples of natural reflexes include blinking, watering of eyes, sneezing, vomiting, and coughing. Other natural reflexes include salivation, swallowing, and peristalsis, which maintain body efficiency.

2. The second type of reflex is conditioned reflex. This is developed over time and can be unlearned. An example of this is typing on the keyboard of the computer, playing a musical instrument, catching a ball, and many more. These reflexes can be honed and improved. Conversely, these skills could also tarnish. An example is playing badminton. At the peak of a person's game, they can receive the shuttlecock in a split second. But as they lose practice, their reflexes become slower.

   These autonomic movements do not just happen out of spite. They are caused by the interplay of thoughts and stimuli. In the example of catching the ball, your eyes see the ball moving towards you. That's the stimuli. Now, this information will travel to your brain and will create a series of actions that will make you catch or dodge it. Your brain actually worked to create a reflex. Say you did catch the ball and it caused you pain. The next time that ball gets thrown at you, your brain will know better and will make you dodge it.

Now, do you think that your autonomic reflexes are related to your body language? Let's look at your natural reflexes. From personal experience, you can observe that controlling these inborn reflexes can be impossible.

How far can you go without blinking? 5? 10 seconds? Unless you're Michael Thomas, who set the Guinness World Record for the longest time without blinking at an hour and five seconds, it's almost impossible for you to control that reflex.

The average blink rate is at 22 blinks per minute. Its purpose is to spread your tears to the outer surface of your eyes to prevent drying and irritation. It also protects the eye from dust and other foreign bodies. Many people think that blinking is only good for protecting the body, but it can also shield the mind from unwanted stimuli. Science has proven that people blink more when they are nervous, stressed, agitated, or in pain.

Another natural reflex is swallowing. People do not only swallow when they're eating. They also swallow when they are anxious. A dry mouth and throat are some of the common symptoms of stress and anxiety. This pushes the body to swallow more frequently just to get some saliva to lubricate the esophagus. These examples tell you that autonomic reflexes could be part of non-verbal cues.

In the last section of this chapter, we discussed how body language can be conscious and unconscious where the former can be controlled and the latter cannot be. Seeing how reflexes are uncontrollable, these fall under unconscious body language. This includes eye twitching, blinking, eye movements, and many more.

There are instances when people try to control these natural reflexes by fostering awareness and consciously stopping themselves from performing the reflex. For example, a person is known for blinking too much when he's anxious. When someone becomes aware of this response, they try to limit their blinking to hide their emotions. So, how then can you read non-verbal cues if some people can control them? As good as people may think in controlling their urges to respond, there will always be slips in their actions that will give them away. Even the best poker players, the best liars, and most notorious criminals give off signals that will eventually give them away. We'll look more into it in the next chapters.

The Human Body

People do not randomly move. Behind every gesture and every expression, there is an underlying reason that stems from the unconscious. Sigmund Freud, the founder of psychoanalysis, taught us that the mind has three levels of awareness–the conscious, preconscious, and unconscious. He believed that each of these levels plays a role in a person's behavior. The conscious mind contains all the thoughts, feelings, and memories you have right now or those that can be easily retrieved and brought into awareness. For example, what you ate for lunch, what you are wearing now, what you need to do later, and many more. The preconscious mind, on the other hand, consists of everything that can be brought to the conscious mind but are not currently in use. For example, what you did last New Year, who you were with during Christmas, and many more.

Lastly, the deepest and most hidden level of the mind is the unconscious. This consists of a reservoir of thoughts, urges, feelings, and memories that are outside your conscious awareness. These contain a series of repressed or unacceptable feelings of pain, anxiety, conflict, embarrassment, or frustration. Say, you were emotionally and physically abused as a child, you did not want to remember what happened because it was too much for your conscious mind. So, you buried the memories and you locked them inside, so they never show in your conscious mind again.

Even if you have already "forgotten" the pain and anguish of the events, you cannot fully keep it inside your subconscious. It's like planting a seed. Once it roots, it grows and will start to stem into your conscious mind. Soon enough, it will affect your thoughts, words, and actions, including your body language.

Freud added to his theory that communication could happen from one's unconscious to the other without involving the conscious mind. Did you experience being distrustful of a person even if you haven't met them yet? Just looking at that person could make you say, "I don't trust him" or "Something's not right about him." Though your friend says, "He seems nice. Very active and gentleman-like," you can't shake that gut feeling telling you to stay away from him.

Later, you find out that your hunches were correct. That does not make you psychic. It means that you were able to catch the subtle body language that person was giving off. At that time, you could not explain why you didn't like him. You do not have solid proof that he is mischievous. But if you learn more about looking at people through a microscope, you can support your gut feeling with reliable body language readings.

Did you know that women can read body language better than men? Although men and women can intuitively read others' body language, men usually override their gut feelings because they tend to look at the world in a more logical sense, where everything is black and white with no shades of gray. Even if their intuition is not to trust a person, they are more likely to ignore their gut feelings because they prefer to judge the situation based on what's presented to them.

Women, on the other hand, are more cautious in reading other people's body language. Hence, the expression "woman's intuition" is born. According to experts, one of the possible reasons why women can read body language better than men is their maternal nature. Women have this innate nature to understand infants' and children's non-verbal communication. They can easily discern the meanings of specific body languages such as fist clenching, kicking, thumb-sucking, and many more. And they carry this skill with them even as the child grows.

Have you ever tried lying to your mom? Well, I know most of you attempted, but it didn't work out because your mom knows every single body language you have, and she can discern you're telling the truth. No matter how much you hide your urge to talk fast or to stay calm, your mom knows there's something wrong. Often, they just pretend to believe you. But in reality, they just let it slide. Still, they are one step ahead of you.

Even if women do not have children yet, they possess this innate nature to look at body language under a microscope. They do not only pay attention to other people's words but also their non-verbal cues. This is why you can hear them say, "She was saying sorry, but I didn't think it was sincere," or "He said he was with his guy friends, but I don't believe him."

Men usually get baffled when they hear these "assumptions" from women. But there's a reason why women think like this. And it's not because they are crazy or sensitive. Aside from other things you can consider, like a guilty conscience which is a real issue. But let's say that's not what is happening and stay on the topic of reading body language. Women do know enough to look closely at other's cues. Little do people know that most often than not, these "assumptions" are correct. Body language reveals more truth than words spoken.

According to experts, learning to read body language is the closest you'll ever be to mind reading. By mastering it, you can reveal other people's true intentions and prevent all forms of manipulation. You can detect signals and red flags which could be lifesaving in the future.

Types of Non-Verbal Cues

Psychology has proven that speech only makes up about 20% of communication. The rest is non-verbal cues. This is not limited to hand gestures and eye contact. In fact, non-verbal communication has many forms—kinesics, oculesics, haptics, and proxemics. Let's learn more about them one by one.

Kinesics

This includes one's body language such as gestures and posture. These are often used to reinforce what a person is saying. It also aids in conveying one's emotions during a conversation. There are different types of kinesics.

Gestures include all forms of body movements and are further categorized into four types.

1. Emblems. These are gestures that serve the same meaning as the word. An example of this is the 'OK' and 'Come here' sign. While these are general signals, you need to be cautious when using emblems in specific countries.

2. Illustrators. These are body languages that illustrate a verbal message. An example of this is the common circular movement of the hand, which accompanies the phrase, 'over again," are pointing to a specific direction accompanied by the words, 'over there."

3. Regulators, on the other hand, are gestures that give feedback during a conversation. These include nods, short sounds such as "uh-huh," even a raise of an eyebrow is

considered a regulator. It may show that you disagree, or that you're annoyed by the speaker.

4. Adaptors. These are non-verbal behaviors that satisfy some physical needs. This is commonly found in public speaking when the speaker is uncomfortable or is nervous. You may often see scratching, flicking their fingers, or pinching their arms. Be aware of some gestures that signal a weakness. Some of these include gaze aversion, hunching of the shoulders, pulling the arms towards the body, pressing the knees together, or dropping the chin to the throat.

Posture is the second type of body language that reflects emotions, intentions, and attitudes. According to researchers, there are two types of posture—open and closed posture. Open posture communicates interest and readiness to listen. When the body is in an open posture, the back of the body is engaged, signaling positive and expanding emotions. When the front of the body is open, it emancipates a balance in the sense of empowerment.

Closed posture, on the other hand, reflects discomfort or disinterest and lack of attention. However, closed posture can also be an indication of rest, safety, and comfort. When the human torso is curved, the body is in a cycle of emotional quieting with an enhanced feeling of protection. We'll discuss more on posture in the next chapters.

The last form of kinesics is mirroring. This is one of the most common techniques to establish trust with another person. Observe couples in the getting-to-know stage. It's as if they have the same pattern of movement and speaking. You can see that their postures and gestures match. This usually indicates interest and approval among people.

Proxemics
The next form of non-verbal communication is proxemics, also known as the study of personal space. In our society, there are different levels of physical closeness appropriate to different types of relationships. Generally, there are four main levels of physical closeness. The closest one is the intimate distance, which is shared by couples and lovers, where they can be as close as 45 cm apart. Personal distance, on the other hand, is shared between friends or family members where they can be as close as 45 cm to a meter. Next, social distance can be shared between acquaintances and colleagues. This is referred to as the normal distance where you are 1 m to 3 m apart. The last level of proximity is public distance, which could be 3.7 m to 4.5 m apart. This can be shared by a teacher to his students or a public speaker to his audience.

Understanding these distances is important to establish trust and rapport with people. If you know your level of relationship, you will know where to position yourself and to converse with a person to maintain a level of comfort and appropriateness.

Oculesics
Remember when you were kids, and you were misbehaving in front of guests, your parents could not scold you because it would be inappropriate to make a scene in front of visitors. But when they look at you with those sharp eyes, you immediately stop what you're doing and behave. It's as if they communicated with you what's going to happen if you continue misbehaving. It's the same in school. When teachers notice that you're not listening or paying attention, they give you this look that says, "there's a consequence for not listening while the

teacher is explaining." To your mind, you might get embarrassed in front of the class, or you might be asked to repeat what the teacher has just said. Whatever the consequences, you don't want it. That's why you stop misbehaving and you listen intently to your teacher. These eye behaviors are known as oculesics.

Oculesics, also known as the study of our eye behaviors, is a form of non-verbal communication that decodes eye movement. For example, when a person looks up then to the right, it usually means that he or she is lying or daydreaming. When they look up then to the left, it indicates remembering something. However, before you make a final conclusion, you need to be aware of that person's natural movements because this can be reversed if a person is left-handed.

Haptics
The last form of non-verbal communication is haptics, also known as the study of human touch. Like any other form of work, non-verbal communication, haptics is also important to understand so you can interpret how people touch you. Conversely, you can discern what inappropriate touching for other people is based on your age and culture.

When discerning manipulation, haptics is also an important factor in determining the true intentions of other people. If there is a disconnect between their non-verbal cues, it can mean that a person is lying to you or is bothered by something.

Here is a list of the types of haptic communication:

1. Professional. Some jobs require their employees to touch their clients, such as medical professions, caregiving jobs, salons, spa and treatments, and many more. These professions allow a certain degree of touch, all of which should be related to their objectives. Other than that, it could indicate a red flag.
2. Punishment. Touch could also be negative, especially when it is expressed through punishment. This includes slapping, punching, kicking, and many more.
3. Greeting. The next form of haptic communication is touching others to greet them. Examples are handshakes, cheek-kissing, and hugs. Again, these cues vary depending on your relationship with that person.
4. Guiding. Haptics could also be used to guide people when they move. This is evident when caregivers assist the blind to their destination. It could also be evident in dancing where one person leads and uses his grip to guide his or her partner.
5. Gaining attention. Haptics could also be used to draw the attention of other people. This is evident in schools and offices when people touch other's arms or shoulders.
6. Sympathy. When people are distressed, touching them could be a source of comfort. However, the degree of touch varies greatly with your relationship. The patch could range from a gentle touch on the arm to a full-body hug.
7. Intimacy. Whether it's with a friend, family, or lover, intimacy could also be conveyed through haptic communication. Kissing, hugging, and holding hands, portrays closeness and love.
8. Lastly, this form of non-verbal communication could also be used for arousal.

It's easier to determine the meanings of touch. But how can you use it to discern manipulation? The trick is to look at non-verbal cues as a group. A person can pat your back and roll his eyes at the same time. One could pat you on the shoulder but give you a frown. A person could hold you tightly to make a point, but you see them looking sideways, which would indicate that they're lying. A person could also be laughing with you but punching your arm painfully. All of these can show their true intentions.

Don't get too excited about reading people's body language! You need to learn more about the factors that affect them. Let's get into the factors that affect body language and the hidden meanings of non-verbal cues in the next chapters.

Chapter 2: Is What They're Saying the Same to What They're Actually Doing?

How Humans Communicate

Communication is one of the most fundamental processes of human beings. It is the process of sending and receiving information or ideas through speech, writing, visuals, or actions. While communication is an integral part of being human, there is a proper way of conveying information. This includes proper use of words, delivery of actions, and presentation of visual aids. Improper communication usually leads to confusion, incomplete instructions, and miscommunication. This is why it is important to learn how to communicate properly.

Generally, there are five types of communication: verbal, non-verbal, written, listening, and visual communication.

First, **verbal communication** from the term itself occurs when we engage by speaking with other people. It could be face-to-face, over the telephone, or through video conferencing platforms such as Zoom and Skype.

Also known as oral communication, its objective is to make people understand what you want to convey. At its very nature, verbal communication is more precise compared to other types. In this day and age, for people to rely on technology, many still prefer verbal communication.

The second type of communication is non-verbal communication which is a group of movements that deliver meaning. Most of the time, these nonverbal cues speak louder than words. It shows what a person is really feeling compared to what he or she is saying.

The third type is **written** communication. It can be in the form of emails, memos, texts, and many more. Written communication is then subdivided into formal and informal. Examples of formal communication are memorandums, contracts, subpoenas, and corporate letters. Informal communication, on the other hand, would include your strands of text message with a friend, a family, or a romantic partner.

The event age of written communication is it acts as a final word. In the case of subpoenas and memorandums, the details are already stated on that piece of paper, and nobody can argue with those. They just need to comply. Another advantage is it allows people to review the information to foster understanding and retention.

However, there is a disadvantage of using written communication. Have you ever heard the statement, "Do not be afraid of anything unless it is written in black and white?" When something has been written digitally or on paper, it can be accessed and used against you. This is usually observed in contracts. The contents of some contracts could be mind-blowing. Sometimes, because of our busy schedules, we neglect to read and completely understand what we sign. But what if it contains something that could incriminate you? If you affix your signature at the bottom, they could use this contract against you.

This gives us a lesson to be wary in affixing signatures. Read what the paper says. Because once you verify that document by affixing your signature, they could use that against you when something goes wrong.

Moving forward to the next type of communication, **listening**. An example of this is a teacher lecturing in front of students. Even though the teacher basically does all the talking, there is still communication by how the students respond. The same is true during talk therapy when the client talks to a psychologist. This is made possible through active listening, which is one of the most important communication skills that people should develop.

Active listening means listening with all senses. It involves giving your full attention to the speaker by focusing on their meaning. During active listening, interest can be conveyed through verbal and non-verbal messages such as nodding, eye contact, smiling, and simply agreeing. You can also display active listening by providing feedback or clarifying the message of the speaker.

There are various benefits of active listening. First, it can help you build connections. It makes people feel that they're comfortable in sharing information with you. It also makes them feel that you are attentive, interested, and accountable, which could benefit you during interviews, courtships, and meetings.

Another benefit of active listening is it can help you identify and solve problems. This is usually observed in the workplace, where teams are faced with challenging tasks. During these instances, it is important to listen to the inputs of your colleagues so you can derive an effective solution to your problems. This technique also helps to increase your knowledge so you can make better decisions. Active listening can help you avoid missing critical information, which could make or break your career.

The last but not the least type of communication is visual communication. People are wired differently from one another. Some are predisposed to understand verbal stimuli better, while others prefer visual presentations. These involve pictures, artwork, colors, and fashion. Pictures are often the easiest to interpret because the image could already be indicated in the photo. Artwork, colors, and fashion, on the other hand, can be more symbolic. And interpretation could vary from one person to another. Colors portray different meanings. The color white, for example, symbolizes purity or innocence. Red on the other hand, could mean aggression, assertiveness, romance, and danger.

Fashion is also a valuable form of communication. Wearing a blazer, for example, is a symbol of strength and willpower. That's probably the reason why it is recommended during meetings, summits, and interviews. Coco Chanel was the first one to impose the blazer on women. During the war, men were the only ones allowed to wear them. But when Chanel created high fashion blazers for women, it became a symbol of power.

Another example is wearing white blouses for women and white polos for men. There's a reason why agencies assign these uniforms to employees. It emancipates hospitality, precision, and goodness. It makes them approachable to clients, so they attract more prospects to inquire about their products or services.

So, you see, there are many ways by which people communicate with one another. Whether this is verbal, non-verbal, written, listening, or visual, it's important to have a clear picture of the information you are about to convey. This way, you can identify the right words, body language, and symbols to use to relay information and ideas effectively. How do you do that? Let's learn some strategies in exchanging information through verbal and non-verbal communication.

Exchanging Information with Verbal Communication

Verbal communication is the primary mode used by humans to relay ideas and information. However, as easy as it is to say words, it is difficult to convey a message effectively if you don't know how. Now, I'm not going to teach you grammar or proper word usage. You can learn this from school and other sources on the web. What's important for you to understand in verbal communication is the underlying factors that make communication effective. You can be excellent in grammar and word usage. But if you ignore specific factors, it could affect the delivery of your message. Here are some factors you need to consider in verbal communications.

1. The first factor to consider is the type of verbal communication. Generally, there are four types: intrapersonal communication, interpersonal communication, small group communication, and public communication.

    Intrapersonal communication refers to your private conversations with yourself. This usually happens when you meditate or when you think. Some people debate about this topic, saying that thinking is not a form of communicating. On the contrary, it is the process of talking to yourself. This is why psychology has coined the term "self-talk," which influences how you feel and how you respond to different events in your life.

    The second type of communication is interpersonal communication which occurs during one-on-one conversations. Here, two people swap the roles of being the sender and the receiver.

    The next type of communication is small group communication. This takes place when there are more than two people involved. In this setting, each participant is allowed to interact with the rest. Examples of this are press conferences, team meetings, and board meetings.

    The last but not the least type of communication is public communication. This takes place when the speaker addresses a large group of people—usually ten or more. Campaigns and public speeches are examples of this.

    You need to understand that type of verbal communication so you can manage your time and your scope. It is also important to adjust your tone, word usage, and strategy.
    1. Medium. As we all know, verbal communication can either be face-to-face or through online conference rooms. Before you speak to someone, it is important to understand the medium so you can set the tone. During face-to-face interactions, you can easily determine when people are getting bored by your presentation. But in online conference rooms, it is almost impossible to monitor the attentiveness of your audience. For all you know, your audience could be dozing off. This usually happens in virtual classrooms where teachers cannot monitor whether their students are paying attention or not. This is why it is important to adjust the tone based on your medium. Since you can share your screen in online meetings, you can utilize other forms of communication such as videos and pictures that can

pique the minds of your audience. To keep them awake, you can also facilitate activities or have them participate in your discussion.

2. Language. Another important factor to consider when interacting with people is the differences in language. Many people make the mistake of using highfalutin words when talking to people of different nationalities. It makes them feel intelligent and superior. But in reality, it makes them egotistical. If you were to speak to an audience of different professions and nationalities, it is important to use clear and simple words that they can understand. Refrain from using jargon and colloquialisms that could confuse your listeners. If you were to use some, make sure to explain it to them so they don't feel left out of the group.

3. Age. Before speakers present to an audience, the first thing that they ask is the ages of their participants. This way, they can adjust their manner of speaking and their word usage to their audience. People from different age brackets have different preferences. They like different types of music, movies, and art. Plus, their fads and hobbies are different. Knowing the age bracket of your audience will give you an idea of how to reach out to them. For example, when you're talking to baby boomers, those who were born from 1946 to 1964, you can talk about the post-war phenomenon and other major events after that. This could give you the platform to gain their trust. It makes them feel that you know where they are coming from.

It's different when talking to Millennials and Generation Z. When these people are your audience, you could talk about what's trending on social media like Facebook, Twitter, or TikTok. You can talk about their cancel culture and have them participate. Then, they'll know that you can be "in" with them.

Now that you know the factors you need to consider before engaging an audience, you need to learn how what to do while speaking to an audience. Here are some techniques that can improve your verbal communication skills.

a. Don't limit your knowledge to the script. "Never get into a gunfight without extra bullets," they say. It is also applicable in public speaking. You see, even if you prepare a script for the duration of your presentation, it is important to bag other information in case you need them. For example, as a baby boomer talking to Millennials and Generation Z students about suicide awareness, they could ask you questions about trending movies and series such as the famous Netflix original series, "13 Reasons Why." This series is a platform for most students because they might associate their life with the story. Some students may ask about your opinion on the show, if the portrayal of depression and suicide is correct. If you know about the series, it could give you a better chance of better relaying information to the students.

b. Speak with confidence. If you were to engage an audience, speaking with command will evoke respect and trust from your listeners. If you express your ideas confidently, your audience Is likely to listen to you and believe what you say. Don't look down! You will look like you doubt yourself and the information you're about to say. If this happens, your audience will get bored and you become inattentive. Instead, make direct eye contact with your audience to assert your position as a reliable speaker.

c. Be dynamic. Many public speakers make the mistake of having a monotonous tone throughout the presentation. If you keep this up, by the end of your presentation, your audience would have had gone home or dozed off.

This is why it is important to have a variety of tones when you speak in public. Use your voice to add emphasis to important points. You can also add variations to your pitch to express your emotions. This will keep your audience interested and engaged.

These are only some of the most important strategies you need to consider during public speaking. Remember, what you give is what you get. If you offer them confidence, reliability, and trust by communicating effectively, you will surely receive the same feedback from your audience. It's going to be fulfilling, don't you think?

Paying Attention to the Non-Verbal Communication

If you think effective communication ends there, you're wrong. There is another thing you need to consider to relay information and ideas effectively. And that is non-verbal communication. As discussed in the previous chapter, non-verbal communication refers to gestures, movements, and symbols that convey meaning. This goes hand-in-hand with verbal communication to effectively deliver a message. Unfortunately, it could be difficult to connect your words to your non-verbal cues. If this happens, it could cause a disconnect between you and your audience. This is why you need to learn how to match your words with your non-verbal cues. How?

Here are strategies that experts use to establish command while talking to people.

1. Power pose. According to social psychologists, holding a powerful pose has an impact on your self-esteem and self-confidence. In theory, holding a powerful pose can increase testosterone levels and reduce cortisol levels, also known as your stress hormones. If you have this confident body language, you're more likely to feel powerful and dominant wherever you are. And when you feel it, you can embody it. And when you embody it, your audience will listen and believe you for it.

   How do you embody the power pose?
   First, stand straight with your shoulders back and your feet shoulder-width apart. Imagine that your shoulders are opening up from one another, so they rest centrally on the body. The next thing you need to do is press your hands on either side of your body so you can easily make hand gestures to put emphasis on your words. When embodying the power pose, it is important to face the audience. If you're in a large room, tilt your body in all directions to include every audience.

2. Eye contact. Psychology has proven that eye contact with your audience can help you build the connection between them. Plus, it makes them feel valued. Another advantage of making eye contact is it's easier to receive feedback from your audience. You can see if they're interested or bored. If they feel detached, you can amp things up and strategize to gather their attention.

   How do you make eye contact when interacting with a large number of people? One of the most common techniques is to make eye contact with one member for four or more seconds before moving to the next. Make eye contact for at least 4 seconds, then proceed to another member of the group.

   The second technique is the Z formation. From the name itself, look at one person from the far-left corner, then to the back right. Move your eye focus diagonally to the front left portion, then to the front right. This is one of the most effective strategies to connect with as many people in the audience as possible.

In one-on-one settings, on the other hand, you can make eye contact for 9 to 10 seconds before you break away. This way, you won't come across as intense or weird. The same applies when you are talking to small groups.

3. Hand gestures. When used properly, hand and arm gestures can help emphasize your message and make you seem confident to your audience. Proper gestures can amplify your stories and make them seem genuine and believable. It can also help evoke feelings from the audience, especially when the topic is emotional.

   To use hand gestures, one technique you can use is to put verbs into action. When your storytelling, you can emphasize the actions by showing it with your hands. You can also use symbolic gestures for emphasizing numbers, shapes, lengths, and sizes. However, be careful not to overdo it. Gesture sparingly so you do not look like an awkward dance instructor in front of your audience.

4. Movement. Moving around the stage is another way to show the audience that you are confident and empowered. It makes them attentive and engaged by your presence. As a public speaker, it is your duty to control the crowd and lead them. Moving around the stage is an effective way to do so.

   Some tips in pacing:
   Wait at least 3 minutes before you pace to another area. Many speakers make the mistake of moving around every 30 seconds. This can be distracting to your audience. You can time your movement every time you change a topic. This way, you're assured that three or more minutes have passed after your last transition.

   When you move, do not turn your back on the audience. This could come off rude and unsettling to some. Instead, try to move forward or sideward, especially when the audience is asking a question or when you're making an important point.

   Another no-no in public speaking is swaying or rocking on the spot. Instead of coming off as a confident leader, this body language could make you seem awkward and unconfident. If you do not have enough space to move in another direction, do not move at all. Compensate with hand gestures instead.

5. Expressions. Another thing that you need to consider when speaking in front of an audience is your facial expressions. This is important to emphasize your points so the audience can interpret your meaning and your emotions. Try filming yourself while speaking so you can identify where to incorporate your facial expressions. See how you look when you are happy, sad, angry, and confused. In the process, make sure that your expressions are believable to the audience.

6. Mannerisms. These are nervous habits that can detract the audience from listening to your message. If you don't know if you have them, film yourself while speaking so you can see what they are and what triggers them. If you're made aware of these mannerisms, you can

practice eliminating them. Common mannerisms include putting your hands in your pockets, using filler words such as "um" and "so," and playing with your hair or clothing.

7. Breathing. Even if your audience cannot see or hear you breathe, it is still an integral factor in portraying confident body language. When you're in front of an audience, it is important to maintain a slow and steady breath so you can reduce your stress levels. This can also help you prevent your body to revert to nervous mannerisms, bad posture, and excessive gestures that could distract your audience from listening to your message.

It is important to warm up before speaking in public. Inhale for 3 seconds, then exhale for 4 seconds. Repeat this as often as you need until you feel calmer.

When you're finally in front of the audience, make sure that you're standing straight so your lungs can function at full capacity. This is important so you can utilize your voice and add dynamics to it.

As you can see, verbal and nonverbal communication go together to effectively relay information and ideas. Knowing this, it is important to learn the techniques in combining these two types of communication. Once you understand these concepts fully, it can help you succeed in all facets of life, including your career and your relationships. Aside from that, it gives you an idea of how people can control and manipulate the decisions of others. Who would have thought that understanding verbal and non-verbal communication can change your life and protect you from manipulation?

Avoiding Miscommunications

Exciting as it is to analyze people's body language, we should learn our limits in doing so. There are different factors that affect one's body language. This is why we shouldn't be hasty in jumping to conclusions. You might expect people to respond using specific body language. But because of their culture, it could be inappropriate for them to do so. You may interpret some non-verbal cues as a sign of lying. But if you consider their culture, their body language might be conveying a different meaning. This is why you need to learn five examples of non-verbal cues that have different meanings in specific countries.

a. Use of hands and fingers
The use of hands and fingers to strengthen or emphasize your point is important for clearer communication. However, some gestures could offend other people in a specific culture. For example, the OK sign, where you put your thumb and first finger together to create a circular shape, generally means a good thing. But it is offensive in some countries such as Greece, Spain, and Brazil. To them, showing the OK sign means you are calling them an a**hole. In Turkey, that sign is considered an insult towards gay people. Even the thumbs-up sign is offensive in Greece and the Middle East. To them, that thumbs-up sign means "up yours."

Next, curling your index finger with a palm facing up generally means to come closer. But in countries such as China, Malaysia, and Singapore, they consider this gesture impolite.

Another body language that could be offensive to other countries is the conflict where you brush the back of your hand underneath your chin in a flicking motion. In Belgium, northern Italy, and Tunisia, this means "get lost". In France, however, this gesture is equivalent to macho grandstanding.

Many people think that every country accepts a greeting with a handshake. However, in some eastern countries, they regard a firm handshake as aggressive, so they bow instead. In Turkey, for example, a firm handshake is considered rude and aggressive. In Islamic countries, it is inappropriate to shake the hands of women outside the family.

Other motions that could be offensive to other countries include clenching your fist, crossing your fingers, even nodding your head. In Greece and Bulgaria, the meaning of a head nod is the opposite. To them, it means no. Before you use these actions during your travels or when interacting with other races, it is important to understand their culture to avoid offending the residents and to prevent miscommunications. If you're unsure, the best thing to do is to ask them what a specific signal our body language means to them.

b. Sitting. Who would have thought that sitting could have different meanings in different cultures? When you're interacting with other people, be aware of your posture when you're dining or attending a meeting.

In the United States, crossing your legs is normal during meetings. But in Japan, it is a sign of disrespect, especially in the face of someone older or someone with a higher position than you.

Another thing that you need to watch out for is showing the soles of your shoes or your feet. In the Middle East, this body language is considered offensive. This is why in these countries, throwing shoes at someone is a form of insult, which the former U.S. president George bush discovered during his visit to Iraq in 2008.

c. Eye contact. Generally, when people look away or look down when they're being asked a question, it usually connotes lying or nervousness. But in some countries, such as China and Japan, it is rude to make eye contact, especially when he or she is older or has a higher position than you. In Latin America and Africa, extended eye contact could be seen as a challenge, while in the United States and Western Europe, eye contact shows interest or courtship. In the Middle East, extended looks between sexes are considered inappropriate.

d. Touch. The next non-verbal cue you need to watch out for is touch. While it is normal for some cultures to hug and cheek-touch people, it could be inappropriate to some. Michelle Obama, for example, broke the royal protocol during her visit to Britain in 2009 when she gave an innocent hug to the Queen. Furthermore, in many Arab, European, and Latin American countries, people are more reserved in terms of touching. So, be careful who you pat, hug, or shake hands with when dealing with other people. It might seem an innocent mistake for you, but it could greatly offend them.

e. Gender. The last but not the least factor to consider when assessing body language is gender. In some countries, what is appropriate for men might not be for women, and vice versa. In Muslim countries, for example, touching or shaking a woman's hand is inappropriate.

Another thing that you should know in terms of gender differences is their form of communication. Generally, people are taught that when a person has a high pitch, it usually means self-protection, denial, or guilt. However, you need to understand gender differences when assessing these cues. Women are allowed to have a higher pitch because of their vocal cords. Another non-verbal gender difference is facial expressions and emotions. Women tend to be more responsive when they are being talked to. They are likely to respond "uh-huh" or "mhmm..." Women also like to show that they acknowledge the speaker by tilting their head or by opening their bodies to make them feel receptive. When they disagree with you, they have no problem showing it. They could raise their eyebrows or roll their eyes.

Men, on the other hand, are more robotic when expressing their interest in conversations. They offer less feedback and encouragement. Men only nod a few times during a conversation. Generally, you might see that as disinterest. But actually, that's just how men are. They are the answer-question type of people without showing their emotions.

The same is true with eye contact. Women tend to show their interest by sharing eye contact with the speaker. Men, on the other hand, avoid it. Most prefer listening while looking down or by closing their eyes. Some people might regard this as a form of disconnect. But sometimes, it has something to do with their gender.

These are only some of the important factors to consider when you're reading one's body language. Before we move on to an integral part of reading one's body language, it is important to understand these cultural and gender differences. This way, you can generate a more accurate reading and prevent miscommunication and misjudgment. How can you make sure to avoid these mistakes?

Be aware of your bias. Often, psychological bias plays an important role in making decisions and judgments. Here are a few of them:

a. Expectation Bias. This is the process of ignoring facts and statistically relevant information when it conflicts with what you believe in. Sometimes, because of this bias, we judge people and events based on our preconceived notions about them and not the facts that were presented. For example, a person was brought in for questioning. Because of this, you already expect that they are the culprit. However, investigators have proven that they have nothing to do with the crime. But since you already believe they're the criminal, you don't care about the facts. You just want them convicted because it's what your expectation bias led you to believe.

b. Confirmation Bias. The next psychological bias is the confirmation bias, in which people seek information that will reinforce their beliefs. This is one of the most common forms of bias because of the availability of information from the web. Unfortunately, not everything you read is reliable. But because of confirmation bias, you gather every piece of information you see that verifies your point, even if the source of information is unreliable or invalid.

c. Anchoring. The last but not least psychological bias is anchoring which occurs when you're already influenced by earlier information presented to you. For example, you were taught that lack of eye contact indicates lying. Because of that, you easily judge others for it, even when facts say you should consider their culture and gender.

Chapter 3: Reading Body Movements

I'm sure most of you are looking forward to learning the different meanings of body movements. Don't fret! In this chapter, we'll talk about the most common body language and its possible meanings. You'll be surprised how these movements can reveal what a person is truly thinking and feeling. Let's start with facial expressions.

The Face

Name the universal facial expressions that you see: happiness, sadness, fear, disgust, anger, contempt, and shock. But did you know that the face can do 4000 more? People just do not notice them because they easily categorize these nonverbal cues based on these seven main expressions. If you confine yourself to this concept, it will be impossible for you to detect the real meaning of facial expressions. The mouth can smile but the eyes reveal the truth. The eyes could say, "You can trust me." But the eyebrows say a different thing. Why do you think investigators do not believe a criminal even when he says, "I didn't do it"? It all lies in their facial expressions. Even if they use a poker face, there will always be hints that give off their true intentions. Let's dig in.

Eyes and Eyebrows:

They say that the eyes are the windows to the soul and there's a reason why. The eyes give off more information than any part of the body. Every twitch, every move, every blink has meaning. Learning each of these could help you discern manipulation and lying.

Did you know that women are better at reading non-verbal cues than men? Dr. Simon Baron-Cohen from Cambridge University experimented by showing eye photos to participants. They were tasked to determine the messages that the expressions conveyed. Is it friendly, relaxed, worried, hostile, or desire? On average, men scored 19 out of 25 while women scored 22 out of 25. If you pay attention to the different eye gestures and their meanings, you could have a perfect score.

But before we discuss the different eye movements and their meanings, it's important to have a baseline. It means assessing the normal eye movements of people. This includes their blink rate, their eyebrow movements, and their eye direction. You also need to determine their culture. Are they likely to make eye contact? Furthermore, check if they have a favorite glance direction. Some people have a habit of looking at the right or at the left. This could give you cues when assessing their eye gestures later on.

Before you go straight to questioning, you can introduce yourself first and make a comfortable impression. Make them feel that they are safe and valued during the conversation. This way, they are likely to show their natural eye gestures. Once you have recorded enough information, let's move on to the eye gestures and their meanings.

When a person looks to the right, it could mean that they remember a song. If a person is looking to the left, it stimulates a visual thought. They probably remembered a color or a place.

Now pay attention if they looked down to the right. This means that they're creating a sensory memory as if imagining what it would be like to jump off a cliff. But if a person looks down to their left, it probably indicates that they're talking to themselves.

These eye gestures will help you detect a lie. If you ask a question and they look down to the right, it means that they're creating a memory instead of remembering what really happened.

You can strengthen your claim if you observe that there is a disconnect in someone's gestures. Remember your baseline. When you asked his or her name, how did their eyes move? How did their eyes react when they told you the truth? Based on this, you can tell if there's a disconnect when their eye movements suddenly change.

For example, in Bill Clinton's interview about his alleged sexual relations with Monica Lewinsky, there was a disconnect in his eye gesture and hand gestures. In his interview video, you can see that he's using his right hand to convey his point, but his eyes are looking to the left. You can also observe that when he is telling the truth, he shakes his head or nods along with the statement. But when he told the press that he didn't have sexual relations with Monica Lewinsky, he did not shake his head no. This could indicate that he's lying. It's interesting how such subtle movements can give someone away, isn't it?

There are other eye movements that give a deeper meaning.

For example, looking left or right could mean doubt, reluctance, suspicion, or contempt. But if it is matched by their eyebrows up, it could indicate courtship or a sign of interest.

Another eye movement is looking down. When someone looks down during a conversation it can mean insecurity, lack of confidence, or perhaps that person's just thinking. But before you jump to any conclusion, you need to determine the culture of the person you're talking to. In China and Japan, people are taught that making direct eye contact with someone with a higher position than you is rude. So, for them, looking down is normal.

Next is the sideways glance. The sideway glance is more common in women than men. It usually indicates interest, especially when it is matched by a slightly raised eyebrow or a smile. However, you need to keep watch on two common cues like a tilted head motion and eye-rolling. These may mean that the person you're talking to is not believe anything you're saying. It could also mean that you look suspicious and they feel uncertain, hostile, or critical.

Often, women use the sideway glance as a secretive signal. When a person of interest enters the room, they use the sideway glance to communicate with one another. Other people could also wink. In most cases, it generally means flirting or joking. However, if it is prolonged, it could be threatening and malicious.

The next eye movement you need to watch out for is when the person you are talking to keeps looking at their watch. This usually means that they are at a disconnect, that they are rushing, or they are spending too much time talking to you. If you see them look at the time repeatedly, it could mean that they have another appointment to get to. So, it's best to cut the conversation short.

Next, closed eyelids. This usually indicates disbelief or stress. This is one of the common signs that babies use to indicate pain. When you see your children squeeze their eyes shut, it could mean that they're uncomfortable or in pain. This gives you an idea of what to do to calm them down. In some cases, you will see stammering eyes, wherein the person you're talking to closes their eyes every several seconds. When you see someone close their eyelids slowly, it generally means that they're disappointed are upset about something. But during intimate conversations, closed eyes could mean a good thing. It could indicate that a person trusts you and that they're in a moment.

Eyelid touching, on the other hand, essentially means the same thing as eye blocking, but with tension relief. During your exams, you can see your classmates touch their eyes when they stumble upon a hard question. You can even see others rubbing their eyes to soothe themselves whenever they feel stress or fatigue. Other eye movements for stress include rubbing between the eyes, slow eye movements, and eyelid twitching.

Another common eye movement is increased blinking. This could indicate that someone is bored, disinterested, or is feeling superior to you. It could also be their way of telling you to go away. If people blink 2 to 3 times in less than a second, it can mean disbelief. If you do it faster, it could mean nervousness as well. But if you observe decreased blinking, it could indicate that the person is lying. In a study conducted in 2008, researchers found that people blinked less when they're lying compared to those who are telling the truth.

Aside from eye movements, you need to consider the length of the duration of eye contact. On average, studies show that the most comfortable eye contact lasts around 3 seconds. Longer than that, and it is enough to make someone uncomfortable.

You also need to learn how to measure the intensity of one's stare. This pertains to the construction or dilation of the pupils. If a person likes what they see, they are likely to allow more light to enter their eyes to have a better look. This causes the pupils to dilate or grow wider. But if a person sees something offensive because they are likely to constrict their eyes, much like what your eyes do when you stare at something bright.

These are only some of the most common eye movements you need to know that help you determine whether a person is lying or not. It can also give you cues whether they're nervous, bored, or stressed, which could be enough to know where you stand in a conversation.

Let's move on to eyebrow movements. The most common movement we see is raising eyebrows. This usually means surprise or receiving good news. However, they could also mean that someone is worried. In some instances, people raise their eyebrows when they're in disbelief. You can observe this among women. When they do not trust the people talking to them, they often raise one or two eyebrows. It is also partly the reason why women pluck their eyebrows, to make their eyebrows more expressive.

Men could also raise their eyebrows. This usually occurs when they feel protective of women. At a bar, for example, when other men are taking a pass at their girlfriend or wife, other men could raise their eyebrows to men to warn them about what they're doing.

This is different from the eyebrow flash. During this movement, the eyebrow is raised only at a split second. This is an emblem commonly used to greet other people. But then again, it varies from one country to another. People from China and Japan are not allowed to do this in front of their superiors because it is a sign of disrespect.

Another meaning of the eyebrow flash is thanking someone or giving emphasis to specific words. In some cases, it could also mean agreeing with someone. Other times, it's a form of approval and compliment, which is evident during social occasions.

Mouth

Mouth expressions are also essential in reading body language. Sometimes, even when the eyes are smiling, the mouth connotes a different thing. Once again, you need to consider your baseline in assessing body language to prevent miscommunication and false assumptions. Without further ado, here are some mouth expressions and their meanings.

A smile is one of the best body languages in the book. Not only can it make your mood brighter, but it could also mean respect, joy, adoration, and approval. While these are the most common meanings of a smile, it has many more meanings. Sometimes, it could also mean sarcasm and cynicism. So, you always need to make sure that you interpret other people's smile based on the conversation context. Matched with their eye expressions, you can see what they really want to convey.

You also need to consider how the mouth muscles are shaped. Pay attention when a person has a pursed lip. This usually means distaste, disapproval, or distrust. Next, lip biting usually means worry or stress. If a person's lips are parted, it could mean that he or she is flirting with you, particularly if that person is staring at you for a long time. This should not be confused when one's lips are protruding, wherein the upper lip moves over the bottom lip. This could mean guilt, anxiety, or doubt. Conversely, when you see people pout their lips, where the lower lip is jutting out, a person might be expressing their frustration in a child-like manner.

You may have seen people who pucker their lips wherein they form their lips into a kiss shape. This usually indicates desire. But oftentimes, it could also mean boredom, disapproval, or even distress.

Next, when the lips are sucked in, or when the person 'swallows' their lips, it could indicate that someone is thinking and doubting something. It could also mean that a person is suppressing their speech, wherein they are preventing themselves from speaking out. It could also mean that the person knows they should speak out but they are doubtful of how the receiver will react. This could mean disapproval, lying, or withholding the truth.

A flattened mouth where the lips are pressed horizontally to one another, also known as exaggerated closing of the mouth is another body language you need to observe. This can indicate disapproval, frustration, and sarcasm.

You also need to consider how the mouth moves. If it moves upward, it could indicate a positive meaning. But if it turns into a frown, it could either mean sadness, disapproval, or grimace. Knowing this, there are instances when people turn their lips up for a split second. This could mean boredom or sarcasm. On the other hand, when people move their lips down for a split second, it could either mean that the person gets your point or has a better opinion in mind.

Another mouth movement is retraction, this is when the lips expose the teeth, like showing a broad smile. While many people interpret this as positive body language, it could mean aggression or mockery. Look at the eyes to tell you which is which.

There are also instances when the mouth moves as if it is speaking. This means that a person is thinking. Also known as subvocalization, this process is often subconscious. You can see people do this before public speaking, while rehearsing a statement, or while problem-solving and decision-making. Another mouth movement is chewing, sometimes even without food inside the mouth. If this is the case, it usually means that a person is nervous about something.

The last but not least mouth movement you need to watch out for, especially if you plan on protecting yourself against manipulators, is the mouth twitch. This is a sudden mouth movement that people cannot avoid, not even poker players and expert liars. Sudden and subtle twitches, particularly on the side of the mouth, could be indicators of lying, doubt, and disapproval. If you learn how to keep an eye out for these twitches, stay tuned to the next chapter on how you can hone your skills in body language reading.

Breathing

One of the most common mistakes people make in reading body language is relying solely on facial expressions and arm gestures. Little do they know that they can watch someone's breathing to understand what that person wants to convey. But before we learn how to assess someone's message through breathing, we may need to consider if people have heart or lung problems that could make them breathe faster or slower. We also need to determine if a person is tired or feeling hot. If so, they will naturally have a faster breathing pattern. Considering these factors, let's look at some of the most common breathing patterns and their meaning.

The most common pattern is deep breathing. While this usually indicates that one is attempting to relax, it could also mean that a person is afraid, angry, excited, nervous, or attracted. If a person suddenly holds their breath, it could mean that they are angry, scared, or in pain. However, if a person holds their breath with a glimmer in their eyes, it could mean attraction or excitement.

Another common meaning of holding one's breath or deep breathing is a mating call. When a man or a woman is attracted, they usually breathe deeply. For men, the aim is to broaden their shoulders to make them look stronger and capable. For women, the aim is to make their breasts look bigger which, according to the theory of survival, is attractive because it indicates that women are capable of giving more milk to children.

The next thing you need to determine is heavy breathing. This usually indicates fatigue or anxiety. Look at an athlete who just finished a 5-kilometer jog. You can see them breathing heavily. This is because the lungs need more oxygen when the heart is beating more rapidly. Now, take note when the person gulps in air and blows it back out. It could indicate stress and anxiety. During this event, a person might hyperventilate and get dizzy. In this case, a paper bag is necessary to keep that person from collapsing.

Another thing to consider is sighing. This usually indicates relief, hopelessness, or sadness. You can see people take a deep sigh when a struggle is finally over or when receiving good news like passing the board exams, testing negative for a disease, and many more. However, a sigh could also indicate hopelessness, disappointment, and tiredness. You can assess the correct meaning of a sigh by looking at how their mouth moves. If it moves downward, it could mean a negative sign. And if the mouth moves upward, it could mean that a person is sighing of relief.

Arms

Aside from focusing on facial expressions to read body language, there is another way you can assess what other people really want to convey. The next cue we will be discussing is arm body language. The arm is one of the most interesting appendages that convey more meaning than you anticipated. But before you read them, you need to understand if a person has underlying muscle disorders or psychological disorders that may cause them to display unnecessary hand gestures such as tic disorders. You also need to consider the environment and the temperature, for it could cause people to act and move in a different way. Considering these factors, let us discuss some of the most important arm gestures.

The first one is expanding arms. This is a clever way that makes the body bigger or smaller. If the arms are cinched to the middle, it could indicate a lack of confidence, fear, and anxiety. It also aims to grab people's attention. You can see this in wrestling matches where competitors expand their arms to make people cheer for them. However, if the arms expand to make the body larger, it could mean that the person is asserting his or her dominance, confidence, or aggression in the event.

The arm is also a useful tool so people can reach out without having to move the rest of the body. This can be observed when a person reaches out for a handshake. In this case, it could mean that the person is hospitable and friendly. However, if a person holds back their arms moving them backward, it could mean hostility or fear. You can also observe people moving their arms slowly and in a curvy manner. This could mean that they're offering comfort.

The arms are also significant in shaping objects and conveying meanings. People can carve objects and emphasize how big or small they are using their arms. This is evident in public speaking when speakers emphasize their point using their arms.

Another gesture is arm raising in which the arms are lifted. If it is done rapidly, it could mean frustration or confusion. You can observe these during arguments when a person suddenly raises their arms saying, "forget it," or "I don't know."

The arms could also be used as weapons, literally and metaphorically. If you see a person's arms tighten, it usually symbolizes a spear for attacking. In communication, it usually means that a person is offended or getting angry. It could also indicate stress or pain, even discomfort. You can also observe people when they use their arms and make them look like a shield. This means that they are defensive and that they are hiding something. But other times, it could mean that they are just frustrated. This is most evident when people cross their arms. This symbolizes a defensive shield that attempts to block out the outside world. This shield acts in two ways: it either blocks incoming attacks or it attempts to hide what a person is thinking or feeling.

Thus, experts usually regard arm crossing as an indication of anxiety which could be driven by lack of trust, internal discomfort, and vulnerability. You can also see arm-crossing when people are getting impatient or when interacting with people that they don't like. This is evident when people are waiting in long queues in a restaurant or when they are waiting for someone to finish talking.

In this case, you need to identify the extent of crossing because this indicates how closed a person is. Some people display a light crossing of arms. But in severe cases, you can see how tight and closed their arms are that they even close their hands to make a fist. Common celebrities who use arm-crossing as a symbol of closeness are Gordon Ramsay with his one-arm cross and Joe Bastianich with the classic two-arm. Both gestures could mean doubt and speculation to people who are presenting.

There are also instances when folded arms could mean that a person is trying to keep themselves still to suppress any signal that indicates anger or aggression. However, you need to assess the culture of that individual. Because in some countries, when a person holds still, it means that they want to pay greater attention to you. Hence, you can take this as a compliment.

However, arm-crossing is not all negative. There are instances when arm crossing indicates that the person is ready to hug you or empathize with you. It could also mean that a person is just comfortable, especially when there is little tension in the environment. This type of comfort indicates a lack of fear which may be driven by friendship or intimacy with other people. This is evident when the arms are in a folded arm position or when the arms are wrapped around the torso. If the thumbs are pointing upward, it could indicate approval and agreement.

Arm-crossing could also indicate concentration. Take Jennifer Lopez as an example. Observe when she serves as a judge in the World of Dance and American Idol. She crosses her arms and rests them on the table.

The next arm body language is reaching forward. This could be scary to some people, especially when their culture doesn't permit others to blatantly approach them. If so, they could see reaching forward as a form of attack. So, you need to watch out who to reach out to.

If you're interacting with people and they reach forward, look at how their arms are positioned. If their palms are facing down, it could mean that they are asserting their dominance and they expect you to acknowledge it by receiving their hand. However, in some countries like the Philippines, it indicates respect. When the elderly offers their hand with their palm down, the receiver takes it and touches the back of the hand on their forehead. In other countries, lords and ladies offer their hands to their subjects so they can take it and kiss the back of the hand as a form of respect.

But if you see that a person reaches out with their arms tight and or with their hands shaped like a fist, it could indicate doubt and hostility. Other times, you'll see people reach forward gently. In this case, it means they are offering support or affection.

The next gesture is hiding the arms behind the back, so they're hidden from view. This usually indicates that a person has a hidden agenda. It could also mean that a person is hiding something, and they do not want their hands to give it away. This is why you show your hands first when interacting with others to show that they are welcoming and friendly. Otherwise, not showing your hands could make people think that you are a threat. On a brighter note, the hiding of arms could indicate vulnerability because it exposes the torso. This can signal submission or comfort.

The last but not the least arm gesture I'm sure you want to know is the amount of 'flow' the arms have. In a 2013 study, researchers found that facial body language is not the main factor that gives away a player's hand, but arm body language is. Researchers found that participants guessed the poker's standing by observing arm gestures. Are you curious about what gave it away?

According to the study, poker players that have a good hand move their arms more smoothly. But those who had a bad hand and were simply bluffing had more awkward arm movements. This could manifest in stiff arms which could cause jerky robotic movements as compared to people with smooth arms that show a natural rhythm to them. Interesting, isn't it? Now you know better than to focus only on facial expressions.

Hands and Fingers

Let's move forward to the extremities of your arms, your hands and fingers. Contrary to popular belief, there is a difference between arm gestures and hand and finger gestures. Arm gestures are broader and bigger, and these are very useful especially when the people you're talking to like to hide their hands and fingers. But if they are visible, here's your chance to determine what each hand and finger movement means.

Everyone, including you are born to speak with your hands. Ever since you were a child, you may not have been able to enunciate what you wanted but because of your hands, you could converse with other people about what you needed and what you wanted. Hand gestures are important to make people listen to you. This was proven by Spencer Kelly, an associate professor of psychology and co-director of the Center for Language and Brain at Colgate University. He found out that gestures make people pay attention to speech. In his words, these gestures are not merely add-ons to language. Rather, it is a fundamental part of it. This is why you can derive a lot of information just by looking at someone's hands. Now, let's look at some of the most interesting hand gestures that convey information.

The first one is touching the neck or face. Experts regard this as a low-power position that could indicate anxiety, lack of control, or fear. You can even see people covering their mouths. This may be a polite effort to cover someone's mouth when they cough or yawn. However, it can also be a sign of disapproval or shock. Other times, people cover their mouths when they want to smirk, but they don't want to show you. This could be a sign of disapproval or cynicism.

Another common hand gesture is touching the hands. Often, you can see people wringing their hands as if they're washing them. This could be a sign of discomfort, nervousness, or lack of preparation.

You can also see others put their hands in their pockets. This is a defensive gesture that indicates powerlessness and shyness.

There are also instances when people use the same hand gesture over and over again, even if it is not connected to what they are saying. This usually indicates self-doubt, anxiety, guilt, or lying. This is reinforced when you see the tension in their arms.

The next hand gesture is clasping the hands in front of the body. This could indicate discomfort, defensiveness, or shyness because it shows the need to protect the most sensitive and vulnerable parts of the body.

In school or at work, you can see people fidget with their fingers. This usually means that someone is thinking or that they're anxious. It could also indicate impatience and boredom.

You can also see public speakers rub their palms together. This is a way in which people communicate positive expectations. You can observe this when people rub the dice between their palms as a sign of positive expectancy. You can gather more information by assessing the speed at which a person rubs his or her palms together. When people rub their palms quickly, it could indicate excitement, anticipation, and assurance. This can be observed among salespeople when they claim that they have the right product for you. They are taught to use this gesture when describing products and services to prospective buyers to excite the buyers and make them feel a sense of urgency.

However, when you see people rub their palms slowly, it could indicate doubt and anxiety. Or it could also mean that a person is thinking.

Another gesture is the rubbing of fingers together, particularly rubbing your thumb against the index finger. This is usually used as a money expectancy gesture. It is often used by salespeople when they are asking for tips. This is also observed when people are trying to borrow money, or when they are expecting money.

The next gesture you need to consider is clenched hands. Remember when you were feeling scared, anxious, or when you were holding back a negative emotion. Chances are, you clenched your hands until your knuckles were bright white. The stronger your feelings are, the tighter your clench. Another thing you need to consider is the height at which the clenched hand is located. According to studies, the higher the location, the stronger the mood. You also need to note when the clenched hand is near his or her mouth. This usually indicates holding back what that person wants to say. Be careful not to push people too far in these cases. The results may not please you.

Another hand gesture is steepled hands. According to researchers, people who view themselves as reputable had minimalist gestures which make them use the steepled finger position to demonstrate their confident attitude. This is also known as the power position because it is used by superiors during subordinate interactions. It is also used by people with self-assured attitudes. You can observe this hand body language among lawyers, accountants, and anyone in a position of authority.

The steepled-finger position has two main versions: the raised steeple that people use when they're giving opinions or is the one doing the talking. If this is taken to extremes, it could indicate an arrogant know-it-all attitude. People who use this gesture usually convert it to a praying gesture to attempt to appear more god-like. If this is the case, people tend to be more intimidating. The second one is the lowered steeple in which that person is listening rather than speaking. In this position, you will tend to look more interested and ready to respond. Women usually use this position, especially when empathizing with their friends while listening.

The next hand gesture you need to learn is face-framing. This is a common gesture used in courtship that is often used by women to attract men. In this position, a woman will place one hand on top of the other and present her face to a man as if serving it on a platter for him to admire.

Next is gripping hands, wrists, and arms. This gesture usually indicates superiority and confidence. You can observe this in prominent royal members of royal families and senior military personnel. This shows that they are fearless by exposing their necks, hearts, and stomachs to potential threats and hazards.

But observe when the grip moves up the arm. In this case, the meaning changes. If a person is gripping their wrist behind their back, it could mean frustration. Gripping your wrist is a way to control yourself by holding your emotion in. The farther up the back this gesture goes, the greater the level of frustration.

The next one is the palm-in-palm-behind-the-back stance. This also indicates superiority, confidence, and power. According to researchers, if you take this position when you are stressed or anxious, you can observe how your mood changes and you will feel a more positive vibe.

Let's look forward to gesturing with your thumbs. A major contributing factor to human progress is the development of an opposable thumb—a thumb placed opposite to the fingers, and a willing to stretch only from the hand. Most primates like chimpanzees and gorillas have opposable thumbs but they cannot use them as efficiently as humans. Due to the superiority of the thumb, humans were able to create tools, weapons, and other complicated structures. It also enabled us to write. Hence, the development of language. Aside from these uses, thumbs are also essential to convey information. The meanings associated with showing the thumb include dominance, superiority, and in some cases, aggression. Given the history of the thumb, it's not a surprise that it denotes strength and ego.

The most common thumb gesture is the thumbs-up. This position denotes agreement. However, as we discussed in the previous chapters, be careful not to use it especially when interacting with other cultures because they might regard it as offensive.

You could also observe other people's thumbs protruding from their pockets. This usually demonstrates dominance and self-assurance. Although this can be used by men and women, it is more common among men.

Have you ever seen people point towards others using their thumbs? If so, it may mean that a person is being dismissive and disrespectful. It could also mean that the person is ridiculing others.

You can also see people fold their arms with their thumbs pointing upward. This usually indicates a defensive or negative attitude. Matched with the show of thumbs, it could mean that the person is showing that they are superior.

Legs and Feet

Aside from our arms and hands, our legs and feet also reveal our mind's intent. According to research, people are less aware of what a particular body zone is doing the further it is from the brain. It is for this reason that leg and feet gestures are very significant when reading body language. For one, the brain is less likely aware of what it's doing. Little do you know that it is revealing more than you anticipated.

This is proven by Dr. Paul Ekman and Willian Friesen in their study about deceptive behaviors. Their research has proven that when a person lies, they produce more signals associated with deceitfulness in the lower parts of their body than in the upper parts. This is applicable to both genders. People are more aware of their facial expressions because they are trained to control them, especially because it is visible to other people. While they can control the gestures on their lower body as well, they do not usually pay attention to it because it is not as visible as their face. This is why it is a powerhouse of information that you should not ignore.

There are four main standing points you need to be aware of when assessing leg and feet gestures. The first one is the parallel stance. This is a subordinate position where the legs are straight and the feet are placed closely together. It is a formal position that shows a neutral attitude. It is a common stance taught to children to show respect to their teachers.

The second stance is legs apart. This is a common male gesture that indicates a stable and immovable posture. It indicates that a person is standing their ground and is favored by those who wish to show their dominance. It requires a straight leg and your feet should be placed around shoulder-width apart with your weight equally distributed between them.

Compared to the parallel stance, the leg apart stance has a higher center of gravity to communicate authority. It is also used as a dominant signal because men use it to highlight their genitals, giving them a more virile look.

The third stance is posing with a foot forward. Since the middle ages, men of elevated position and high social status display a stance that displays the inner part of the leg. This usually indicates masculinity and appeal.

The last but not the least stance is the standing crossed legs. This is how people usually stand when they are among others whom they don't know well. You can observe this in seminars and workshops where people do not know each other. This stance is a closed gesture that indicates submissiveness or defensiveness.

Now, let's discuss the common leg gestures when people are seated. The first one is the leg cross. More than 70% of the world's population crosses left over right. This is commonly used by European and Asian cultures. Many people interpret this leg gesture as a closed body language. To most people, this usually means being emotionally withdrawn from the conversation. It could also mean disinterest and boredom. However, many people cross their legs as a sign of comfort and sometimes, habit.

The next seating position is the figure four crossed legs in which one leg crosses the other and forms a right angle to form a number four. This is commonly used by American men and other cultures who have been exposed to American entertainment. This gesture usually reflects a competitive and argumentative attitude. However, it could also indicate dominance, relaxation, or youthfulness. The downside to using this gesture, is it is offensive to other cultures like the Middle East and some parts of Asia. To them, this gesture is usually a form of disrespect especially when interacting with people with a higher position or social status.

Another gesture is the leg clamp. This usually indicates a competitive attitude. It is characterized when people lock their figure four crossed leg into a permanent position using their hands as clamps.

Locked ankles. According to studies by Gerard Nierenberg and Henry Calero, there is a higher chance that the person is withholding information if they are locking their ankles. Airline personnel are trained to spot passengers who like service but are too shy to ask for it. Attendants can also pinpoint apprehensive and anxious travelers when their ankles are locked, especially during takeoff. In another study, researchers found that out of 150 male patients observed, 128 people immediately lock their ankles when they sat on the dentist's chair. This could indicate that they're uncomfortable or they are anxious about the procedure. This is also evident when interviewing people during investigation. In recordings, law enforcers review how the interviewees lock their ankles. This usually indicates that they're uncomfortable, withholding information, scared, or guilty.

However, there is a woman variant of the locked ankles wherein the knees are held together, and their hands are resting side by side or on top of their leg. This usually has the same meaning such as anxiety or apprehension.

The next leg gesture is entwining the legs which is more common to women than men. One leg entwining the other and the top of the foot locking itself to the other leg is a classic gesture made by women. Despite what people think this leg body language usually indicates insecurity no matter how relaxed the legs are. It could also mean shyness and reservations. Studies show that people meeting in a group for the first time usually stand with their arms and legs crossed. But as rapport develops and people become more comfortable with one another, you can observe that they release their closed pose and resort to a more open body language.

Another body language you can observe in women is the seated parallel legs. Only a few men can do this position because they do not have the same bone structure which enables them to sit in this manner. When women assume this position, they're projecting a strong feminine signal. When one leg is pressed against the other, it gives the legs a healthier and more youthful look which makes the woman more appealing. Even modeling classes teach this posture to women.

Another body language is the high heels effect. Women instinctively know the effects of wearing high heels. They feel more powerful and more attractive. High heels make the legs look more toned, giving the illusion of better health and more fertility, which according to the theory of survival, is more attractive to men. Using high heels also accentuates the arch on the lower back and contracts that will use muscles to make to make the hips wider and more attractive. All of these characteristics are consistent with the increase in fertility which has a direct relationship with attractiveness.

Then there's putting your foot forward. When you're interested in the conversation or in a person, you usually put your best foot forward to shorten the distance between you and the person. But if you're disinterested or unmotivated by someone, you can observe yourself put a foot back.

You can also observe other people fidget their feet. This usually indicates impatience and boredom. It gives you the signal that they don't want to be there or that they are waiting for the conversation to be over so they can flee. In a standing position, you can observe people tapping their foot to indicate their impatience. But if they are seated with their legs crossed, the hanging foot could twitch up and down or back and forth.

There you have it. These are only some of the most important body languages that you need to learn for better communication and to avoid deception and miscommunication. Again, before you start reading other people's body language, you need to have a baseline. Learn as much as you can about them particularly their culture, their mannerisms, and habits. From this baseline, you can see what deviates from their normal actions.

In the next chapter, we will discuss seeing body language as a whole or as a cluster. If you think individual gestures are powerful, wait until you can read them as a whole. This way, you can have clearer information on what they really want to convey.

Chapter 4 – Seeing Body Language as a Whole

In the previous chapters, we have discussed how posture plays a role in nonverbal communication. It is a type of body language that reflects emotions, intentions, and attitudes. Having a good posture is advantageous particularly in communicating and interacting. It's safe to say that it can make or break your ability to make a good first impression on other people. This is evident among public speakers and people with authority. What do you think would happen if a public speaker was slouching and had hunched shoulders? You probably would not pay attention to what he or she had to say because you'd be under the impression that the speaker was unconfident about themselves and the information they are about to convey. But imagine if that speaker owned the stage confidently. I imagine that you would be in awe and you would be captivated by how he or she commanded the audience. That is one example that shows how posture is important in communicating with other people.

Conversely, when you're the public speaker and you show that you're timid by putting your hands in your pockets or putting your hands behind your back, you are giving your audience the impression that you're not believable. It means that you lack confidence in that you're doubting what you're about to say. If this happens, the audience is at a disconnect. It will be difficult for you to command the room. Because of this, you'll see people sleeping, eating, or going out which will make you feel very uncomfortable. This is why it is very important to learn about body language, particularly posture. This way, you can make people listen to you and you will earn the respect you deserve when conversing with others.

In this chapter, we will discuss how to read posture by reading body language from all body parts as a whole. This way, you can gather more precise information from other people. But before we discuss more about posture, let's understand what affects it. These factors will also contribute to your baseline in reading posture as a form of non-verbal communication.

According to research, there are four main factors that affect one's posture. The first one is habit. Notice how most office workers have a curved spine. This is usually because of sitting at the office all day. The spine can be molded by office chairs and the screens tend to draw the face in. This usually causes the habit of slouching.

Another reason is repetitive movements. Sometimes, how we use our muscles makes a difference in our posture. For example, laborers who overuse their trapezius and deltoid muscles tend to have a misaligned spine because of the load they carry for long periods of time.

Next is injury. When a person has experienced an injury, the tendency is you don't want to move the same muscle as you did before. It could be due to phantom pain or trauma. You just don't want to inflict the same pain on the same body part. Or it's possible that you are no longer used to using the same muscle because of the length of recovery time. This is evident when people break one leg. Even if it fully recovers, they are so used to moving more weight on the healthy leg and they keep on doing it even after recovery.

The next reason why some people have bad posture is past surgeries. Most surgeries cause permanent scar tissue, which affects the proper movement of muscles. This is why they use other muscles more, which could affect posture. In this case, chances are, people will need more hours of therapy. And unfortunately, some people carry on with this posture for a lifetime. If their posture gets too bad, it could lead to other physical complications like lack of bone and muscle support, obstructed blood flow, decreased flexibility, indigestion, decreased balance, and persistent body pains.

To many of us who did not have an injury or did not experience surgery, there is a greater chance for us to better our posture not only for communication but also for physical health. Knowing this, let's start with the two kinds of body posture: the dynamic posture and the static posture. How are they different from one another?

Expressing with Posture

Dynamic Posture

Dynamic posture refers to the position of the body while it is in motion like when you're walking, running, picking something up, or bending over. It is literally any motion. Did you know that when you are doing typical things, it is still important to maintain a good dynamic posture? Particularly when you are walking, it is important to watch the alignment of your neck, mid-back, and low-back and straighten it. This way, you can maintain a good posture.

Static Posture

On the other hand, a static posture is how you hold yourself together when you're not moving like when you're sitting, standing, or sleeping. Like the dynamic posture, it is important to align your body to maintain a good posture properly. How do you do that? Let's start by determining what makes a good posture.

What is the key to a good posture?

According to researchers, the key to a good posture is the positioning of the spine. A correct posture should maintain the curves on your neck, mid-back, and low-back. Your heart should be directly above your shoulders and the top of your shoulder should be directly over the hips.

If you want to have the ideal posture, the line of gravity should pass through specific points of the body. This can be evaluated using a plumb line to assess the midline of the body.

This line should pass through an ear lobe, then the shoulder joint, to the hip joint, and through the greater trochanter of the femur. Then, it should pass slightly through the anterior to the midline of your knee joint. And lastly, it passes through the anterior to the lateral malleolus.

When you view your posture from either the front or the back, the vertical line passing through the body's center of gravity should bisect the body into two equal halves. In the process, the body weight should be distributed evenly between the two feet.

When assessing posture, you should also consider head alignment, the cervical, thoracic, and lumbar curvature, the shoulder level symmetry, pelvic symmetry, and hip, knee, and ankle joints.

You can also assess posture while sitting. In this case, consider the following criteria:

- The person's ears should be aligned with the shoulders and the shoulders should align with the hips.
- The shoulders should be relaxed, especially when the elbows are close to the sides of your body.
- The angle of your hips, elbows, and knees should be approximately 90 degrees.
- The feet are flat on the floor.
- Your forearms are parallel to the floor and your wrists should be straight.
- The feet should rest comfortably on a surface.

Types of standing posture

If you saw that there is a misalignment of your posture, you could classify it into one of these examples of all the postures.

1. Lordotic posture. Lordosis is characterized by the normal inward curvature of the spine. When this curve is exaggerated, it is usually referred to as hyperlordosis wherein the pelvis is usually tilted anteriorly.
2. Sway Back Posture. In this posture, there is a forward head and the hyperextension of the cervical spine. You can also observe flexion of the thoracic spine, lumbar spine extension, posterior tilt of the pelvis, hip, and knee hyperextension, and the ankle slightly plantarflexed.
3. Flatback posture. If you have this posture, you can observe that there is a forward head and extension of the cervical spine. You can also see an extension of the thoracic spine, loss of lumbar lordosis and posterior pelvic tilt.
4. Forward head posture. This describes the shift of the head forward with the chin poking out. This posture is usually caused by increased flexion of the lower cervical spine and your upper thoracic spine with increased extension of the upper cervical spine and the extension of the occiput on C1.
5. Scoliosis. This is one of the most common posture faults. This is characterized by a deviation of the normal vertical line of the spine where you can observe a lateral curvature and rotation of the vertebrae. Doctors can diagnose scoliosis when there is at least 10° of spinal angulation on the posterior-anterior radiograph associated with vertebral rotation.
6. Kyphosis. The last but not the least type of faulty posture is Kyphosis. This is characterized by an increased convex curve observed in the thoracic or sacral regions of the spine.

Do not take any of these faulty posture types for granted for these can cause major disability in the body. If you observe that you have faulty posture, it is always best to consult your doctor about the best approaches to make it better.

Still, the best way you can prevent any of these faulty postures is to improve it as much as possible.

You might be thinking, "What if it's already a habit of mine to slouch while walking?"

Well, the answer lies in awareness. You need to be aware that you have that kind of posture so you can straighten it as much as you can. With practice, you will observe improvements in how your body stance changes over time. When you're washing the dishes, for example, be aware of your posture. When you feel like you're resorting back to a slouching position, correct your posture right away.

Another technique to improve your posture is to remain active. Even if your job allows you to sit in front of the computer all day, it is important to make time for other activities such as exercise, yoga, or tai chi. These exercises are helpful to keep your muscles strong enough to support your body.

The next thing you can do is to maintain a healthy weight. According to experts, extra weight can affect how your bone structure supports your body. It's partly the reason why people have poor posture. According to experts, men should not have a waistline exceeding 37 inches while women should not have a waistline exceeding 31.5 inches. If this happens, not only will you have poor posture but you'll also experience other disadvantages like diabetes, obesity, and heart problems. As much as possible, maintain a healthy diet and do regular exercise.

Also, consider wearing comfortable shoes rather than high heels. There are instances when high heels can throw you off your balance and can make you walk differently. This puts more stress on your muscles, and it can harm your posture. If you're wondering how you can improve your posture while standing or walking, here are strategies you can use.

The first one is to stand straight and tall. Always remember to keep your shoulders back. It also helps to pull your stomach in. Next, put your weight mostly on the balls of your feet then let your arms hang down your sides naturally. If you make this a habit, you can observe the improvement in your posture and your stature.

The last but not the least technique to improve your posture is to make your work surfaces suitable for your posture. When you're working in front of the computer all day, the height of your table should be just right for your shoulders and arms to relax. If not, it will affect your posture tremendously. You can adjust your table or your chair to reach that comfortable position. If you're at the office all day and you want to improve your posture, you can switch your sitting positions often. You can also take brief walks in between work to rest and straighten your spine. Also, as much as possible don't cross your legs because it can affect the curvature of your lower back. Lastly, make sure that your back is supported.

There are also specific techniques recommended when sleeping. You need to make your bed suitable for the improvement of your posture. If you are experiencing body pains, psychotherapists usually recommend a firmer mattress so you can lie down comfortably and so you can straighten your spine. The ideal posture when lying down is to let your legs roll outward while the pubis rises as high as the navel. Your lower back should also sink down to the floor. Next, your arms should roll inward with your palms back. Then, allow your neck to flatten so your throat shortens. Lastly, position your head down and forward to relax your neck and shoulders.

Now that we have established what the ideal posture is and how you can improve it, it's time to put it to work by making it a part of our body language. Both dynamic and static posture plays a role in establishing a connection with people. Matched with the movements and gestures made by other body parts such as your arms, legs, and head, you can identify if you are open or closed to people and their ideas. Let's start by identifying the two types of posture in relation to body language: closed and open.

2 Forms of Posture

Closed Posture

Despite what people think, closed posture does not merely indicate hostility, anxiety, or lack of confidence. Everyone resorts to a closed posture in which the body closes, and the back of the body opens. It is the default position for rest, nurturance, and safety. Aside from feeling anxious, it could indicate that a person is relaxed or comfortable. According to psychology, the C-curve shape of the torso in this position is effective for psycho-emotional quieting and enhanced feelings of protection.

When we feel afraid, threatened, angry, or sad, something in our mind triggers and starts a pre-program stress reflex toward a closed posture. When we feel these negative emotions, it triggers a stress response, which tightens the body and mind toward the C-curve to protect itself. This unconscious reflex is also commonly known as the "red light reflex" and the "startle response". It is also widely known as the "slumping reflex", common in all animals that signal a protective posture to danger, distress, and negativity. All somatic areas on the front of the body, such as the pelvic floor, belly, heart, mouth, and throat are shortened and closed when you are feeling emotions.

According to psychology, unresolved negative emotions like anger, bitterness, and resentment are strong emotional energies stuck in the past. In addition, fear and worry are emotions of the future where people have reduced control. Suppose negative emotions are not released healthily. In that case, they can stay buried in the cellular fabric of the body-mind as reverberating memories for many years. Unfortunately, if these remain unresolved, it could lead to various psychological illnesses such as depression, anxiety, eating disorders, posttraumatic stress disorders, phobia, and many more.

To prevent the body from feeling these emotions, physical contraction of the front of the body occurs to suppress painful feelings and thoughts. Wilhelm Reich named this phenomenon of emotional contraction "armoring." While this is effective to bury unwanted thoughts, it could lead to distorted memories.

The common form of a closed posture is the fetal position, also known as the most primal or default position of mankind. The more your back is disengaged, the more it is optimized for comfort and relaxation.

When the body is in a C-curve position, you can observe that the legs are bent in towards the torso, so the tail is tucked under and the belly is shortened. You can also observe the flattening of the lower back and the rounding of the upper back. In this position you can also see that the chest is drawn in and the arms are bent inward so the shoulders are drawn forward. Lastly, you can see the head bow so that the neck and the throat shorten and contracts into the shoulders.

Open Posture

Now that we have established the closed posture and its forms, let us discuss the open posture which is expressed during waking hours for optimal body functioning. When the body is in an open posture, it makes it ready for daily activities such as walking, running, and lifting. The open posture is activated when the back of the body is engaged, and the ribcage is fully expanded. It is a symbol of positivity, hospitality, and expression. It emancipates a sense of empowerment that allows people to take on tasks for the day.

When the body is in an open posture, you can often observe them extend their arms forward and up, their head rises up and back and releases the throat from constriction. You can also see that the chest and heart are wide open. Also, the belly is long and relaxed. In the lower body, you can see that the knees are slightly bent, and the pelvis is tipped forward, opening the pelvic floor.

This is also known as the Bowspring position. This is evident among babies around three to six months old when they love to lie on their bellies. During this position, they display a natural engagement of their extensor muscles on the entire back of the body, allowing the baby to lift his or her head upward, arch their back, and extend their arms and legs out like a skydiver during a freefall.

In this position, there is reduced emotional guarding or armoring in the body and mind. Hence, babies seem more vulnerable. In an open posture, one's vital energy flows without obstruction in waves throughout the entire body, from head to toe.
This is why psychologists often recommend combining a positive mindset with the Bowspring dynamic posture to clear negative emotional energies and replace it with harmonious and joyful emotional energies.

When determining one's posture, it is impossible to do it when you are so close to the person. This is the reason why experts recommend a specific distance to interact properly with body language and posture. So how far should we be?

How Far Should We Be?

As we have discussed in the previous chapters, and proxemics refers to the distance between two people as they interact. It also describes one's perception of and use of space—how much space they take up and how they distance themselves from other people. Proxemics is developed by anthropologist Edward T. Hall. He discussed that there are four main levels of distance depending on the relationship of the people interacting.

1. **Intimate distance shared by couples: 16-18 inches**
   Despite what people think, intimate distance is not only used by couples who are seeking love and affection from one another. It can also be used during interrogations. According to research, when law enforcers invade the privacy of their suspects, they can provoke anxiety and an adrenaline rush that pushes people to confess.

   Intimate distance is also used in sports. According to sports psychologists, teammates have much higher rates of touch than average friends. They pat each other on the head and sometimes on the back or shoulders to show congeniality. They also maintain smaller distances between each other. This can be observed when they stand close together and huddle on the sidelines.

There are also instances when intimate distance is used in men's urinals. Did you know that men have an unwritten rule not to speak to each other while they are in the urinal? An article published in Metro specifically states the number one rule is not to talk to others while peeing, no matter the location. It is because men need more security when they are using the urinal. They take longer to urinate when other people are standing close to them.

The same is true when riding an elevator. When people are close to one another, especially when the elevator is at full capacity, there are rules that you need to abide by. An example is avoiding eye contact with other people. It is also essential to maintain a poker face to avoid awkward scenarios. Some even recommend keeping an eye on the floor numbers as they change. If you have a phone or newspaper, it is recommended you focus on it rather than your surroundings.

Almost 70% of the population is unaware of these rules. However, others break them profusely just to irritate other people, which is completely uncomfortable on their end. The reason why these rules exist is to avoid invading each other's privacy.

An example of this is the 2000 presidential debate between George W. Bush and Al Gore when Gore invaded Bush's space by acting with what he thought was a power move. Unfortunately, his actions made him look like a bully and the situation became awkward very quickly.

Fortunately for Bush, his reactions were on fire. He stopped talking and nodded towards Gore's direction to acknowledge his action and it made people laugh.

2. **Personal distance shared by close friends and family: 1.5 to 4 feet**
   According to psychology, this is the best distance to build rapport. However, in using this distance, you need to consider gender differences. Females tend to talk more closely with other people while males prefer to have more distance.

   But did you know that females are approached more closely than men? This is because as boys, they're given toys that take up space such as balls, cars, and trains. Young girls, on the other hand, are given dolls and playhouses which take up less space.

   In considering personal space, height plays a role too. In a 2019 study, researchers have found that taller people are more likely to invade personal space than shorter people. In theory, taller people feel more dominant, especially when interacting with smaller individuals.

   If you're planning to use personal distance to build rapport but you are hesitant because you don't want to come off rude to other people, you can ask your client if you can sit near him or her. It's the safest way to determine how comfortable a person is while interacting with you. But whatever you do, always respect their personal space. Do not stand too close to them or they will feel very uncomfortable no matter how good your body language is.

However, if you stand too far, you could cause a disconnect which is also detrimental to your objective. Consider the 1992 presidential debate between George H.W. Bush and Bill Clinton, the latter was asked a question from a person who was far out in the audience.

He remedied the problem by going to the speaker to communicate with him better. This made a significant impact since she can see him closer and get a stronger emotional connection than when he was further away. George H.W. Bush didn't get the same significant effect since he remained away from the audience.

One of the best approaches to build rapport with other people is applying Navarro's "Shake and Wait" approach. This can help you determine the appropriate physical distance in a conversation in 4 steps:

The first one is to lean in, of course considering personal distance and its limits. Next, give an appropriate handshake. Third, make good eye contact and then take a step back and wait for their reaction.

If the person remains in place, it means that they are comfortable with the distance. But if they take a step back or turn slightly away, they might need more space from you. Lastly, if they take a step closer, it could mean that they're favorable toward you.

3. **Social distance shared by acquaintances: 4 to 12 feet**
   This is the distance where strangers stand with one another, and it is commonly observed during formal business and social events. This is a neutral approach that doesn't really work well in terms of building relations. If you are in this zone, as much as possible, try getting a little closer and gauging a person's reaction. Are they receptive and warm, or do they immediately close off?

4. **Lastly, public distance used in public speaking: 12 to 25 feet.**

You can use these guidelines to determine how to distance yourself while interacting with other people. When they assert themselves deep into your comfort zone it might be time to call for help or to stay away from that person.

An example of proxemics is how a therapist and a client position themselves. During these situations, it is important to consider proxemics, especially when a person has underlying psychological illnesses. If you observe the proper proxemics, it can make the client feel safer. Plus, it could also protect the therapist in case the client goes amuck. The therapist will then need to demonstrate a proper sitting position with the client to ensure a comfortable position for both parties.

According to Edward Hall, proxemics is influenced by cultural factors. Children usually learn proxemics from their parents the same way they learn how to speak. Therefore, when assessing proxemics, it is important to identify what culture the person comes from. This way, you will know how to give respect to their personal space and how to understand the idea and the belief behind the behavior. Being able to comprehend what is near and far to other people prevents miscommunication and promotes rapport and better business relationships.

No matter how good you are at showing body language, it is useless if you don't know how to distance yourself from other people. So how will you master the four zones of proxemics?

The first thing to remember is not everyone stands the same even if there is a guideline, that is the four zones. Some people regard the intimate distance as too far or too near. Some regard the personal distance as too far. For example, contact cultures such as Latin America prefer to be closer than noncontact countries like East Asian and American countries. Country farmers and other people belonging to rural areas prefer standing farther back from one another. This is in contrast with city dwellers who are so used to standing close to one another because there is less space. This is explained by Edward Hall when he said that proxemics is not only used in communication but also in how communities arrange their town and their houses. In rural areas, houses are further from each other hence there is much more space. This is why people are used to interacting farther away from each other. In the city, on the other hand, people are used to a crowded space. This is why they don't usually mind sitting or standing so close to one another especially inside trains or other crowded areas.

Hall also considered biometrics as a form to categorize, explain, and explore how people connect in space. He used kinesthetic factors, haptic code, visual code, thermal code, olfactory code, and voice loudness in his book. Let's discuss each one by one.

1. **Kinesthetic factors.**
   Kinesthetic communication is a basic form of language that human beings use to interact with one another. In relation to proxemics, this category deals with how close people are to touching.

2. **Haptic code**
   Next is the haptic code, a behavioral category concerning how participants touch one another, holding, feeling, prolonged holding, spot touching, pressing against, or not touching at all.

3. **Visual code.**

   This category indicates the amount of eye contact between participants. This ranges from eye-to-eye contact, to a prolonged gaze, or no eye contact at all.

4. **Thermal code**

   This category refers to the amount of body heat that each participant receives from another. It could refer to the conducted heat detected, radiant heat detected, heat probably detected, and no heat detection.

5. **Olfactory code**

   This category connotes the kind and degree of odor detected by each participant from the other.

6. **Voice loudness**

   This category deals with the vocal effort used in speech. Some of the categories of voice loudness include silent, very soft, soft, normal, normal (high), loud, and very loud. Loudness is one of the most important factors to consider when interacting with others.

   Aside from the loudness of your voice, your tone conveys a much deeper meaning. Let's learn more in the next section.

Listening Closely

Indeed, people listen to your words, but they react to your tone. According to Daniel Day-Lewis, the human voice is a deep reflection of character. He emphasized how impactful a person's tone can be. According to him, one's own voice and tone come from the depths of one's being. Hence, it is almost impossible to fake. This is why when interacting with other people, the tone is one of the number one factors to consider in deriving and conveying meaning.

According to the dictionary, tone refers to the motivation of pitch, vocal strength, and quality that can add meaning to a word, sentence, or phrase. This is a part of a person's paralanguage which constitutes pitch, amplitude, pauses, and hesitations between words. Don't underestimate the power of tone because it can make or break the rapport you are trying to build with other people. This usually reflects the attitude or the feelings that are associated with the message. It helps you build the tone of the event, which could help you communicate more effectively.

Aside from these advantages, focusing on your tone helps you build authority and command. Imagine going to the stage and speaking to the crowd with a soft voice. Much like having a closed posture, people are less likely to take you seriously. It will be difficult for you to establish your authority and to make people listen to what you're about to say. According to experts, it is important to own the stage with your presence in with your voice. As much as possible, do not speak in a monotonous tone. Maintain a fun and lively tone to keep your audience engaged.

Another advantage of studying tone is you can assess what other people really want to convey despite the words they say or the body language they show. However, before you study and assess one's tone, you need to consider cultural differences. In some countries, they talk loudly as if they are shouting. But in their culture, that is the normal way of interacting with other people. In contrast, some cultures have very soft tones. So, even if they're angry you cannot tell because of the softness and tenderness of their voice. Before you interact with people of different cultures, you need to have that baseline and determine the normal tone of their voice. This way, you can avoid miscommunication and misinterpretation.

Once you've created that baseline, it is time to assess the different meanings of a person's tone in public speaking. Let's start on one's pitch.

Pitch

Pitch is an important auditory attribute of sound ordered on a scale from low to high. Think about the notes on a melodic score. This will show you how pitch works. When observing one's pitch, you need to consider gender differences. Generally, females have a higher pitch than males.

Informational: When the pitch is in a normal spectrum, it usually means that a person is conveying information. This pitch is somewhat monotonous, but it goes down the spectrum from time to time.

Grammatical: This is observed by the rising pitch, which turns a statement into a yes-no question, such as "He's going ↗home?"

Illocution: The pitch pattern characterizes the intentional meaning, for example, "Why ↘don't you move to California?" which connotes a question, versus "Why don't you ↗move to California?" which signals a suggestion.

Attitudinal: A declining pitch signal characterizes this. Instead of "Good ↗morn↘ing" which indicates excitement or joy, versus "Good morn↘ing," which demonstrates attitude or superiority.

There are also instances when a person speaks in a higher pitch than usual. This usually means anxiety, nervousness, lying, denial, or withholding the truth. Sometimes you can also observe other people speak in a lower pitch than usual. This usually indicates sadness and fatigue. But it could also connote pent-up anger or frustration.

You can easily pinpoint people's real intentions by looking at their paralanguage and their body language as a whole. If you see that there is a disconnect between their pitch, their verbal message, and their body language, you can infer that something's wrong or that person is hiding something from you.

Volume

This refers to the loudness or softness of one's voice at any given time. If you're speaking in front of people at a distance you may need to project your voice louder. But if you are speaking with a person individually, you may want to soften your voice. When you are trying to find the appropriate volume in a specific event, consider two things:

1. Is what you're saying confidential? Will it make someone uncomfortable? Is it unnecessary for others to know? If the answer is yes, it is important to speak quietly. If possible, talk with that person in a quieter and more secluded place such as the corner of a lobby or a conference room. The other person will surely appreciate your approach in dealing with sensitive topics such as financial information.
2. The next thing to consider is how the person will speak back to you. Do they have a booming voice? Are they likely to ask for clarification? Do they have hearing problems? If so, it is important to speak up to match the volume needs of your client. However, you also need to make sure that you don't escalate your voice so much that your client receives it as a display of anger or frustration.

When you're assessing someone's posture, it is important to learn about the forms and kinds of posture for a clearer interpretation. Matched with your knowledge in proxemics, you will better see the positioning of other people's bodies and determine what they convey. In learning this information, not only can you assess other's true intentions, but you can also improve your posture and your ability to convey information using body language and paralanguage. In the next chapter, we will discuss more about positive and negative body language so you can assess how often you do it. Learning these will also help you read people's body language as a whole to determine if they are genuine or if they have hidden intentions.

Chapter 5 – Positive versus Negative

How Often Do You Show Positive and Negative Body Language?

In the previous chapters, we have discussed dynamic and static posture as well as closed and open posture. We identified closed posture as a person's way of protecting themselves from unwanted emotions such as fear, anger, frustration, sadness, or anxiety. Open posture, on the other hand, refers to a more positive outlook of the environment. This is characterized by one's readiness to take on another day. It is also characterized by one's willingness to learn, interest, excitement, and joy.

Before you get to assess the body language of other people, you need to understand positive and negative body language. If you understand it, you will have a better baseline of appropriate interaction strategies. You will also learn how to pinpoint disconnects in people's body language, which is essential if you want to reveal one's true intentions.

In this chapter, we will discuss positive and negative body language which is essential in reading people's intent and meaning.

Positive Body Language

Positive body language is often regarded as appealing, receptive, and approachable. It gives people a sense of comfort, dignity, and likability. Aside from these, it makes others open in interacting with people this is why it is important to display this type of body language to build rapport and trust with other people.

If you want to show positive body language, remember that you should not show defensiveness. Defensive body language usually discourages people from approaching you making it more difficult to build a relationship. It is also important not to display a sense of disinterest towards other people because it can lead to disconnect which will bode ill if you're planning to land a job or plan to convince more partners.

Another key factor in showing positive body language is having a neutral stance. You should not show authority nor submissiveness. But at the same time, you need to be able to assert or put forth your opinions confidently without giving offense to other people. Here are some strategies on how you can show positive body language.

1. Stand erect. The first rule in displaying positive body language is to stand straight. Your back must be erect, so you give the impression of being tall. According to psychology, a taller appearance usually connotes a good impression as compared to slouching or hunching.

   When you slouch, you give your audience the impression that you're lazy and that you are irresponsible. It also shows that you have a very passive personality and that you have low self-esteem.

2. The second rule you need to consider if you want to show positive body language is to face the person you're talking to. Do not face sideways, and most importantly, do not turn your back from the person you're talking to. When you stand sideways, it shows that you want to run from that person and that you want to discontinue the interaction. Conversely, you need to observe if the other person does this. This means that he or she is uninterested in what you're offering.

   According to experts, the best way to interact with your clients is to direct your heart towards the other person. This means that your heart is facing the heart of your client without any obstruction in between. I guess it's safe to say that you're speaking heart to heart. During this process, avoid crossing your arms over your chest. This is a big NO in the corporate world, especially when you're trying to land a job or trying to seal a deal. This is one of the most common turnoffs.

3. The third most important goal is to free your hands. Most people like to hide their hands in their pockets while they're talking to people. This is another big NO. It usually means that you're not confident about what you're offering or that you are withholding some information that could be suspicious to your clients. As much as possible, show your hands and use them to emphasize your points. This way, you can convey trust and reliability to the other party.

4. Another rule in the business world is to look people in the eyes. However, you need to determine the limit of the average time of gazing. On average, you can make direct eye contact for two to three seconds while conveying a point then break away from time to time. This will keep you from intimidating your client.

5. The last but not the least way to show positive body language is to move and show some limb movements. When you show that your extremities are too stiff, it could indicate that you are anxious or that you lack confidence. It could also mean that you are withholding information from the other party. So, from time to time, switch the position of your leg but as much as possible do not cross it so they don't get the impression that you are closed about their ideas.

Positive body language is not only important when building intimate relationships. It is also important in the workplace where people are trying to make deals and to convince clients to avail products and services.

Negative Body Language

If there is positive body language, there is also a negative counterpart. In this segment, we will discuss what negative body language is and how it shows from the people you interact with. Conversely, we will tackle some of the most common negative body languages you may be doing that can turn people off.

Negative body language expresses undesirable feelings through gestures, facial expressions, and paralanguage. It could be conscious or unconscious expressions that show what a person feels during an event.

Some of the most common negative body languages you can observe from people include folded arms and crossed legs. Both could indicate that they are not paying attention or that they are close-minded about your opinions. Another common body language is turning their head or body away from you. This could mean that they are uninterested, or they feel angry or frustrated towards you. Another thing you can observe from people with negative feelings is a lack of eye contact or looking down. It could mean that they are not truthful, shy, or afraid of you.

During public interactions, you can spot negative body language that expresses people's feelings. When your audience is bored, you can see them slouching, looking at their watches or phones, fidgeting, and fiddling with items. If you observe your audience with these body languages, it's time to check yourself. Maybe you're not coming off as commanding and interesting to your audience. It's also possible that you are embodying negative body language.

Here are some of the common body language mistakes that disconnect speakers from their audience:

1. **Lack of eye contact**.
   This tells your audience that your mind is elsewhere, that you are not present in the moment. If they see this, they too will divert their attention to something else. Remember that when you are speaking in public, you command the audience. Chances are that people will mirror what they see. So, if you make them see that you are inattentive while speaking, they will also lose their focus.

2. **Staring at your phone or your notes often.**
   This makes the audience feel that you are not confident with your speech. It even makes it seem like you doubt what you say, which makes the audience question your position to discuss specific topics.

3. **Talking too fast.**
   Another negative body language is talking too fast. This exudes nervousness and self-doubt that causes a disconnect between you and the audience. Remember that people have different ways of processing information. Some process it quickly, while some people need more time to digest ideas. So, you have to deliver your speech at an average rate, which according to the National Center for Voice and Speech, is around 150 words per minute. As the speaker, it is your responsibility to allow your audience to take in what you are saying. So, relax, breathe, and take your time so your audience can listen and understand your points.

4. **Using too many filler words.**
   Filler words such as "ah," "Uhm," "like," and many more are signs of nervousness and self-doubt. If you use too many of these filler words, it could mean that you are not prepared and that you are doubting what you are about to say. This can easily turn your audience off.

5. **Too much use of negative language**.
   During public speaking, one of the best turn-offs is using too much negative language. Especially when talking about sensitive subjects like gender, beliefs, religion, medicine, and psychology, it's best to approach topics lightly. Take a look at these examples,

"Stop believing in fairytales. It will not get you anywhere."
"You will not succeed if you keep doing this."
"If you are narcissistic, you are cunning and manipulative."

As you can see, there is too much use of negative language. If you hear people say this to you, will you not feel a bit offended or attacked? Especially when you have the same thinking, these statements will make you feel apprehended or upset. Instead of this approach, you can reword your statements to sound more positive.

"While fairytales give us hope that there is a happy ever after in every story, we still need to think realistically about our goals."
"There is a greater chance of succeeding if you adopt this approach."
"People with narcissism are usually cunning and manipulative."

6. Closed posture

We discussed in the previous chapter what a closed posture is. While it can give you comfort and protection from unwanted thoughts, you should control when to embody it. When you show a closed posture in front of an audience, they might think that you have low confidence. This leads them to believe that you are unreliable. So, as much as possible, be aware of your actions when you're speaking in public always portray a positive posture to your audience.

7. Folding arms

While speaking with other people, especially when there's a table to rest their arms on, people tend to cross their arms. This might be a way to relax your limbs and show that you are paying attention. But understand that people interpret events and actions in different ways. You may come off as uninterested or closed from their opinions which could affect your transaction. So, it's essential to free your hands and use them to emphasize your thoughts. If you're not speaking, you still need to show your hands and maintain an open position. This will help your client see that you are open to their opinions.

8. Scrunched face

Ever heard the term "resting bitch face"? It's where people look naturally fierce and intimidating, which can be off-putting, especially in social interactions. Most people are not aware that they have a resting bitch face which affects how they interact with others. It makes the audience fear you instead of approach you. It also makes them feel intimidated by you, which could make your presentation ineffective and uninteresting.

If you suspect you have this look, record yourself while speaking. This way, you will see if you show a scrunched or frowning face while presenting. If so, practice smiling more and showing diverse facial expressions that match your opinions. This way, you can emphasize your point and show your audience that you are approachable. And remember, if you want to convince people and seal deals, your default facial expression should be a smile.

9. Being too stiff

The next negative body language that can break deals is being too stiff. This usually happens when a person is shy or anxious. If a speaker is too stiff, all other movements can seem like awkward twitches. It makes the audience doubt your ability to command the crowd, and so, they might take your presentation for granted.

One of the techniques to keep this from happening is to loosen up before you go and stage. You might have seen performers shake their bodies before the event? You can do this too, if you want to calm your nerves. You can also do mindful breathing. This process helps you clear your mind from unwanted thoughts. It also allows you to convince your mind that there's nothing to be afraid of. With practice, you can manipulate your brain to let go of that nervousness and go all-in when presenting in front of an audience. You'll be surprised how impactful these techniques are in exuding confidence and captivating the crowd.

10. Lack of dynamism while speaking

The last but not the least form of negative body language is having a stagnant presentation. Either one is standing so still rather than moving around and engaging the crowd, or one is speaking in a monotonous tone. Whatever the case is, it shows the audience that a person is not confident.

To keep this from happening, it is important to own the stage as discussed in the previous chapters. When it comes to your voice, apply some dynamism to it. Instead of speaking to your audience in one note, add variations to your tone.

Imagine a person saying, "I've got exciting news!" in a monotonous voice. Hearing this, it's almost impossible to believe that the speaker will deliver good news. Chances are, you don't want to listen to what he or she is about to say. But if you hear them add flair to the words by adding quirkiness or eccentricity, you will feel their excitement, and you will feel eager to listen.

These negative body languages are very common. So, it is important to check yourself and determine which negative body language you use. Record yourself while you practice and tally how many times you show negative gestures and facial expressions. After which, you know better to be aware of your actions whenever you're interacting with people.

Aside from determining whether people are bored or inattentive, you can also use negative body language to assess when one is lying. In the next chapter, let's discuss one of the most controversial issues in society—lying and deception. Is lying always intentional? How do you determine when a person is truthful or not? Let's find out!

Chapter 6 – Liar, Liar, Pants on Fire

Why do we lie? Is it always intentional?

Almost everyone has   lied at one point in their lives, be it intentionally or unintentionally. Sometimes, it's a spur-of-the-moment decision out of panic or urgency. Whatever the case is, n obody   can deny that   lying and deception are not a   decent practice. Unfortunately, people have become so good at lying that they don't feel guilty anymore or they neglect to think about the problems and catastrophes it can create. Sure, you may have gained something from deceiving others like discounts, promotions, sales, or commission. But at the end of the day, there is damage being inflicted on the system.

When we say system, it affects all the facets that an event or a scenario encompasses. It includes the one being lied to, the liar, the environment, and probably everyone who is involved in a specific case.

Let's take this scenario. In XYZ Company, three people are up for a promotion. During their interviews, person A and B were honest about their contributions to the company. In contrast, person C took the liberty of adding and editing their performance in the past year. This made the manager choose employee C over A and B. While this is beneficial for the employee, it affected the career, self-esteem, and probably even the personal lives of employee A and B. The company will also suffer from this lie because their new assistant director could not deliver the results expected from them. This could lead to bankruptcy or low productivity. As a result, employee C will either get fired or be demoted.

So, you see, even if you get the most out of a lie, there will always be a consequence waiting to happen. This leaves the question, is lying always intentional?

Most people agree that lying is intentional wherein people are fully aware of their actions. This is why most victims of lying feel frustrated, deceived, and angry at people who lied or withheld the truth. Often, when they spot an excessive liar, they immediately cut their ties out of fear or annoyance. Little do they know that lying can be automatic to some people, especially those with psychological disorders. Although this does not make lying acceptable, it gives you a deeper understanding as to why they lie. It also allows you to alleviate your feelings of frustration and anger and it will help you heal and move on.

Research has proven that humans have the innate need to protect themselves from unwanted feelings and events. In spur-of-the-moment decisions, people tend to choose their self-interest without considering the consequences. This happens when people panic. Even if it's not their intention to lie, somehow, they manage to withhold the truth for self-preservation. This is usually observed among children who grew up in a hostile environment. Because they already know the consequences of their actions, their immediate response is denial when they are being accused. The same is true among adults. Research has proven that people lie without deliberating about the consequences as long as the lie contributes to their self-interest. For example, during job interviews, the human resource personnel can ask if a person is willing to work long hours. Because most are taught to say yes with whatever job requirement, the initial response to any of their questions is "yes" even if the applicant does not really want to travel as much. In his or her mind, the initial goal is to land the job and they'll figure it out from there. So, it's possible that employee C from the previous example lied automatically to land the promotion because of their needs.

Another possible reason why people lie is the fact that memories can change over time as a product of new learning. Sometimes, the thoughts and memories in our brains assimilate with one another, forming a new story that the mind believes is the truth. So, even if the person does not intend to lie, there is an inconsistency in their stories because of "retrieval-enhanced suggestibility."

In research conducted, participants watched a film then they were asked to come back for a memory test a few days later. In between watching the movie and the memory test, other events happened. Half of the participants were given a practice memory test while the other half were given a description of the film to read which included some incorrect details.

Come the memory test, the researchers found that people added the false details to their description of the movie. You'll be surprised that the people who took the practice test reproduced the false information more than those who read an incorrect description. In this study, the researchers have inferred that when it comes to memory, practice makes imperfect. This is proven by another theory that rehearsing memories can make them more malleable. It is likened to taking the ice cream out from the freezer and putting it under the sun. By the time the ice cream goes back to the freezer, it would have become misshapen. It's probably one of the reasons why people lie unintentionally, it is a result of the malleability of memories.

The last but not the least reason why lying can be automatic is habit. There are instances when people have lied so many times that it has become their second nature. Although they do not have psychological disorders, lying is just inherent to them, which makes them lie even when they don't need to.   If you know someone who lies a lot, this is probably caused by the Pinocchio problem.

You all know the story of Pinocchio, written by Italian author Carlo Collodi. In the story portrayed by Disney, Pinocchio was carved by a woodcarver named Gepetto in a Tuscan village. Pinocchio was created as a puppet, but he dreamed of becoming a real boy. However, he is known for his frequent tendency to lie. And it's not because of any psychological disorder. He just likes to lie without any apparent reason. So, psychologists coined the Pinocchio problem to describe people who lied a lot but do not fit the criteria of becoming pathological, sociopathic, or compulsive liars. What is the reason people have this problem? Here are some of the most common reasons why:

Fear

Tad Williams, an American fantasy and science fiction writer, said that people tell lies when they're afraid. It could be what other people might think or do when they find out the truth. Many people believe that when they tell a lie, fear is alleviated but it only gets stronger because then people know the need to keep up with the lie. And often, they're afraid that people might find out the truth from others which will only worsen the situation.

This reason for lying is commonly observed in people who have experienced abuse. When a child grows up in a physically or emotionally abusive household, they are afraid to speak up. They're afraid to be honest because they already know the consequences. Unfortunately, some people carry this behavior outside a household and lie to other people as well even if the consequences are not as fearful as they anticipated it to be.

Manipulation

Another reason why people lie is the desire to manipulate the situation. Either people want to get away with negative behavior, or they want to get something out of people like sex, status, money, power, love, and many more. Unfortunately, the most common approach that people do to get what they want is saying the words, "I love you." This eight-letter sentence could be the most wonderful to hear, or it could also be the most dangerous. You never know if the people closest to you are lying and manipulating you until you find out the truth. This is why it is important to protect yourself by learning more.

Lying to manipulate also happens when people feel like they're losing control. They often lie to control people and situations around them to regain a sense of control and somehow alleviate their anxiety.

If you're a victim of manipulation and emotional abuse, you can break free from those harmful relationships and redevelop healthy connections that affirm your sense of worth. Part of the resolution is to identify if you are manipulated. You either call them out or cut the relationship completely. It all helps by talking to a therapist, confiding in a friend, and spending time in places and communities that nourish you are great first steps.

Shame

This is one of the most common reasons for lying. When people do something wrong and they are embarrassed by it, they tend to make up stories to cover what they did. They either blame it on someone else or they deny the reason and put others in front of the bus. One example of this is making stories to hide the shame of damaging intimate relationships by cheating. The downside is instead of coming clean and rebuilding the relationship, they hide the behavior until their partner finds out through slips of the tongue, uncovered tracks, and gossip. This will further ruin the relationship, and it could make it unfixable.

Hiding Addiction

A person who has an addictive behavior feels both fear and shame. This is the result of the standards and laws in society. An example is drug addiction. Because it is illegal in countries, people lie about it to their friends and family. At first, it's all fun and games. Still, when the addiction gets a hold of your psyche, it could lead to a dysfunctional life affecting your relationships, career, and overall productivity.

Another example is alcohol addiction. People pay less attention to drinking as a form of addiction, but it is as harmful as drug addiction. In no time, people will prioritize drinking over other priorities, which could lead to lying and deception. You can only imagine the lengths that people go through just to get a sip of alcohol.

Pride

Another common reason for lying is to boost one's pride and self-confidence. It could be in the form of exaggerating your accomplishments or minimizing the threats and problems—any approach that makes them look better to other people. They want to feel the grandiosity and superiority among people because they want to be adored and complimented.

In some cases, this type of lying seems harmless. But like alcohol and drugs, the feeling of grandiosity and superiority are addictive. If this happens, people could develop narcissistic personality disorder. This is characterized by an exaggerated sense of superiority and an uncontrollable preoccupation with success and power.

These are only some of the most common reasons why people lie. And as you can see, it is not as uncommon as you think. It's actually pretty typical because people are constantly protecting their egos from unwanted thoughts and pain.

In fact, in a study conducted by Robert Feldman in 2002 at the University of Massachusetts Amherst, he found that 60% of people lied during a 10-minute conversation. And in that span, the participants told an average of two to three lies. Suppose people can lie in a controlled environment. What can stop them from lying in their natural environment where they can say whatever they want?

A forensic psychologist at the Haas School of Business at the University of California, Dr. Leanne ten Brinke noted that people have good instincts in detecting lies. Still, our conscious minds usually fail us by seeing facts first before gut-feels. This is why people have moments when they say, "I knew it! He was lying!"

At the moment, the conscious mind only processed what the person was doing and how they acted. Even when the subconscious screamed, "He's a manipulator," the conscious mind battled this notion and said, "We have no facts to prove that." This is why people are easily manipulated and lied to and it stops now. You cannot control people and you cannot stop them from lying. What you can do is equip yourself with the knowledge you need to determine whether or not a person is lying to you. This will serve as your protection from unwanted advances and circumstances in relation to lying and deception.

Dr. Lillian Glass, a behavioral analyst, body language expert, and author of "The Body Language of Liars" worked with the FBI. She imposed that one should understand how people react in specific situations to catch a liar. Along with her techniques in observing facial reactions and emotions, body language, and speech patterns. Let's take a look at the seven interesting ways to spot a liar.

7 Ways to Spot a Liar

Before we discuss the signs of lying, it is crucial to establish a baseline, as we have discussed in the previous chapters. This is necessary to create a more accurate assumption in determining the possibility of someone lying. So, without further ado, here are seven signs you need to watch out for to figure out if someone is lying.

1. **They change their head position quickly.**

According to FBI agents, this is one of the most common signs that a person is not being truthful. The idea behind this is, when someone is scared, nervous, or hiding something, their body intensifies and stiffens because they're trying to prevent any unwanted body language that can throw them off.

So, when they're asked the question, they change their head position quickly. They either bow or tilt their head to the side. And if this happens, you can observe a jerkiness to their movements. When someone is relaxed, even if they move, you can see a natural and smooth movement. But when someone is nervous and possibly lying, there is a stiffness in their actions that can give them away.

2. **Their breathing may also change.**

Someone's breathing may become heavier when lying. It's a reflex that comes along with the increase of heart rate. You can observe this through the sound of their breathing or when their shoulders rise, and their voice gets shallow.

3. **They don't blink.**

This is a tough sign to spot, especially without knowledge about body language. As we discussed in the previous chapters, liars have perfected their confidence when interacting with other people. Because of this, they have learned not to break eye contact even if they are lying. Instead, they will stare at their interrogator to make them seem genuine. But if you look closely, you can observe that there is a decreased rate of blinking. It means that they can control their eye movements, to the point that they are disrupting the natural reflex of their eyes to blink. This gives you a clue that they might not be telling the truth.

In contrast, some liars usually have an increased blinking rate which could indicate that they are nervous, or they are withholding something. This is why it is important to create a baseline before interrogating someone. This way, you can determine when their thinking rate decreases or increases when you ask a question.

4. **They pause before answering.**
This refers to a long pause before someone answers a question. It means that people are either thinking about an alternative answer or simply withholding the truth. Sometimes, people forgot what they said moments before, and they're trying to remember it, so their next statement matches. You can observe this in their gestures and facial expressions.

5. **They touch their face, mouth, or throat.**

Another common sign that a person is lying is touching vulnerable parts of their body such as their face, mouth, abdomen, chest, neck, or head. According to psychologists, this form of behavior is a way of shielding the mind from unwanted stimuli. A person automatically does this when he or she does not want to deal with an issue or answer a question. Instead of explaining, they are closing off communication by covering specific body parts.

When the hands touch the throat for example, it could mean that they have an increased rate of swallowing, which is another sign of lying. When the hands cover the eyes, it could mean that they have increased blinking or that they are looking down.

6. They provide too much information.

There is a very high probability that a person is not telling you the truth when someone rambles on, giving too much information. Even when specific information is not requested, they tell it anyway, possibly because of nervousness. In a liars' mind, when they give too much information, they can make people believe that what they are saying is true. By giving the whole story, they think that the people surrounding them will no longer ask questions because every piece of information they need to know is already in their made-up story.

This is also a strategy to derail and distract the interrogator from his or her trail of questions. Instead of focusing on the main issue, the interrogator will then delve into the pertinent details. But then again, if you're a skilled interrogator and an active listener, you can see that some of the information does not match. There is incoherence. Plus, most of what has been said is not related to the main topic or issue. It's your responsibility to funnel the important details and ask them more about it. Don't hesitate to cut them off and ask follow-up questions because this can derail them from their train of thought.

7. They tend to resort to hostility and defensiveness

The last but not the least sign of lying is hostility and defensiveness. And with good reason! Most liars resort to negative behavior by raising their voices and exaggerating their movements to hide the fact that they are nervous. They tend to turn the situation around to make the interrogator feel like they are a bad person for accusing an innocent person. Often, you can hear them say that they are respected by the community and that they have a couple of accomplishments. But if you think of it, what does this information have to do with the main issue? This gives you a red flag that the person you're talking to might be lying.

Another strategy that people do when they lie is they blame other people for the situation. And when you ask more about it, you can see that they know more about the issue even if you haven't given any information yet. Out of the nervousness they feel, they are already telling pieces of the truth but putting someone else's name on the line. It's a classic move and unfortunately, many people fall for it.

Identifying the Kind of Liar You are Facing

Lying is such a controversial topic in society. When you ask people around you if lying is wrong and if they are likely to do it, you'll be surprised about their responses. Most people will say that lying is good or bad, depending on the situation. And if you ask them if they are likely to do it, many will say yes. This is proven by Dr. Feldman, author of the most recent Journal of Basic and Applied Social Psychology. In his studies, he found that 60% of people lie every day and the average is around two to three lies. This is backed by a study conducted by DePaulo and his colleagues about Lying in Everyday Life. They interviewed a number of college students and community members. During the process, 77 students admitted to telling an average of two lies a day. In addition, 70 community members told the researchers that they lie at least once a day.

This leaves the question, "What types of lies do people tell every day?" and "Are all liars the same?"

According to research, the type of lie people tell depends on the kind of liar they are. Did you know that there are five types of liars? Let's discuss them one by one.

Pathological liar

This is a person who lies incessantly to get what they want with little awareness. Because they have been lying for so long, lying has become their nature. These people may not even be conscious that they just told a lie. This is viewed by experts as a coping mechanism developed in early childhood. And usually, it is associated with mental health disorders like antisocial personality disorder. It's possible that these people have become so good at lying because they're protecting themselves from traumatic experiences such as abuse. Chances are, they will continue to lie to protect themselves from harm.

Pathological liars are usually goal-oriented. They lie to get what they want, often to exaggerate their worth. When they talk about their accomplishments, they make it seem like they are heroes, the people wouldn't have survived without them. But if they fail or they do something embarrassing, they play the victim to gain sympathy and acceptance from others. As a skilled lie detector, you can easily observe when one is a pathological liar when their stories are overly dramatic and complicated. They make their stories seem so detailed and colorful in hopes to make people adore them. Plus, they exude this confidence using their body language as a conduit for people to believe that they are telling the truth.

The worst part about pathological liars is their lies have become their truth. This is why they have a weaker grip on reality. If people attempt to make them realize what is real, it is enough to cause breakdown and hostility.

Compulsive Liar

This is different from being a compulsive liar. These are people who lie is out of habit. Compulsive liars tell lies even when they don't have to, and they bend the truth about everything. According to psychologists, compulsive lying is a common behavior that develops in early childhood due to being raised in an environment where lying is necessary and routine. Many of these people find it difficult to manage confrontations and tackle consequences head-on. Hence, they resort to lying. This behavior is usually observed in people who have attention-deficit/hyperactivity disorder (ADHD), bipolar disorder, and borderline personality disorder.

The difference between compulsive liars and pathological liars is that the former is not manipulative. They just lie out of habit. It just became an automatic response that is very difficult to break. In addition, their lies are easier to point out because their stories usually do not add up. Plus, they're very obvious in displaying lying behaviors such as avoiding eye contact, sweating, stuttering, or rambling. They also lie out of spite, even if they don't necessarily get anything from it. And when you confront them, they're more likely to admit to lying, but this does not stop them from telling more lies.

Does this mean that if someone lies a lot, they are considered a pathological or compulsive liar? Note that people need to be assessed by professionals for them to classify into these disorders. So, be careful when making assumptions about people who lie a lot. They need to meet specific criteria before they are considered pathological or compulsive liars. Although these are formally included in the Diagnostic and Statistical Manual of Mental Disorders, psychologists can recognize these behaviors as a sign of an underlying psychological disorder.

Sociopathic liar

These types of liars are very difficult to deal with because they lack empathy. They don't care if their lies cause harm to people and their careers, relationships, and health. This is probably the reason why they're called the most dangerous liars. They can make you doubt yourself and question your morals. And they will not even feel guilt for the harm they caused. These people like to play mind games to control everyone in their environment including their loved ones. And because they're charming, most people believe their lies and are likely to give them what they want.

Compared to compulsive and pathological liars, sociopathic liars do not respect the law or the norms. They can use false identities and nicknames to get what they want. Plus, they consistently display aggressive or aggravated behavior especially when they're called out. They are known for lashing out at people trying to help them or for calling out their behaviors.

White Liars

Next are white liars. These people often mix the truth with lies either to protect themselves or to avoid insulting and hurting other people. White lies could be in the form of making excuses. For example, a person you don't like is asking you to attend their birthday party. Instead of saying, "No, thanks because I don't like you," you often come up with a reason why you can't come. This is a more polite way to turn people down and avoid hurting their feelings.

White lies also arise when people attempt to hide parts of the truth because they believe that this will hurt other people. A very common example is when somebody asks if their dish is delicious. Of course, even if you didn't like it, you will pretend that you did so the chef will not get hurt.

Another reason why people tell white lies is to protect themselves from confrontation. This usually happens in job interviews, particularly when the human resource personnel asks why people left their old jobs. Some people would emphasize the negative factors that affected their work and productivity and leave out that they were fired because of their offenses.

Many people believe that this type of lie is harmless. To the liars maybe, but it can be detrimental to other people. The chef's dish, for example, what if they served the same dish to more critical people? The chef could receive insults that could lower his self-esteem and lead to then feeling demotivated in pursuing their career. Had you been more honest in the beginning, they could have improved the dish to get more praise from other customers.

This is why lying is controversial. Most people often experience a dilemma between telling the truth or hurting other's feelings. In this case, it's probably better to always tell the truth even when it hurts. When people believe that you're honest, you can establish trust and reliability. It will help you build relationships with the people close to you.

Another reason why truthfulness is important is you don't have to bear the guilt of withholding information. You know what they say, "The truth shall set you free." It can also help you keep your sanity. Even if you cannot control the reaction of other people, you can keep a clean conscience and you can let go and heal from the situation.

Occasional liars

The last but not the least category of liars is occasional liars. You cannot deny that most people lie occasionally for various reasons. Still, this should not be applauded or accepted. These statements, whether big or small can still cause an impact on the environment and the people in it. Although these people seldomly lie, many believe them because they are so used to hearing the truth. And when these people lie, they don't know if the statement is correct or not.

The upside is, once you study their body language and create a baseline, you can determine when they are lying. If you suspect so, there's no harm in confronting them because these people will usually feel guilty and will admit to their lies. If you call out an occasional liar, chances are, they will feel genuinely sorry and will work on their behavior.

Those Who Lie Behind the Safety of a Screen

If you think liars can only present themselves personally, some liars exist behind the safety of a screen. This means that they lie through various blogs, news, online applications, and social media platforms like Facebook, Twitter, Instagram, and many more.

Browsing through these platforms, you can see interesting information from news, blogs, and stories. Unfortunately, only a few of them are factual and correct. In most cases, even if the headline is correct, the article consists of fabrications and hear-say. Other times, people omit important information to make one party look worse than the other. This is more common in politics. Fans and advocates of each party write news and articles that exaggerate the accomplishments of a candidate. During debates and issues, they highlight the positive information about that person and neglect adding what they did wrong. The worst part is media platforms use the strength of their network to show credibility. This is why millions of people are deceived.

Other forms of deception that liars use are e-mails and chats. These are evident in mailing applications, dating platforms, and social media. Often, scammers use these tools to engage their victims and get them to disclose enough information to use their names to initiate a scam. Here are some of the most common types of scams you need to watch out for:

1. **Advance fee fraud**
   Advance fee fraud. This is the process in which scammers request fees or information upfront in exchange for goods, services, money, or rewards. But upon payment, the scammers will cut all forms of interaction, leaving the victims at a loss. The most common

victims of advance fee fraud are people who are new to the internet. Sometimes, because they lack guidance, they seek help from any person on the web. Some are also easily captivated by discounts and freebies. Little do they know that these people are about to take their money.

2. Sweepstakes and competition scams

This is another technique that scammers use to get money from victims. Scammers will communicate with you via chat or email claiming to be agents of sweepstakes and lottery companies. They will say that you have won fantastic prizes like a house lot, money, or car. But before you claim them, you need to give money upfront for "delivery fees" or "service fees." So unless you did join the lottery or any raffle, be wary when interacting with people who claim that you've won a prize.

3. Dating and romance scams

This next form of scam is no longer new to people. These scams occur when scammers create fake profiles on legitimate dating websites. They can use other people's names and identity to get you to believe that they're legit. Then, they will try to build a relationship with you so they can siphon money using "love" or "affection."

They will tell stories, making you believe that they badly need the money. These scammers can tell you that they or their family member is sick, that they need to travel, or they need to pay for tuition. Chances are, because they already got you to fall for them, you will not hesitate to give them money. After this, either these people will give "proof" of their expenditures to you so they can exploit more resources. It's also possible that upon payment, these people will permanently cut their ties. Note how cunning and patient these people are. They will spend months, even years, to convince you. They will take time to earn your trust. That's when they will hit jackpot.

4. Computer Hacking

Many scammers will attempt to access your computer and gather as much information about you. This includes your name, address, passwords, bank account numbers, even ID numbers.

Why do criminals want to access your personal information? It's simple. They want to sell your personal data to criminals so they can use it on the dark web. Once they get access to your most pertinent details, you are now subject to identity theft. They can use your profile to avail credit cards and loans and will spend this money however they want. In the end, your name is at stake answering to the expenses they made.

Another reason why scammers want your personal information is they want to frame you for their acts. Aside from stealing, they can initiate other crimes and make you liable for them. They can take control of your social media account and emails to commit more scams and extortions. It can be used for spying and manipulation.

It's also possible that they want to harm companies. They can wipe out your data or falsify your documents which can be detrimental to people and their companies.

To achieve this, most scammers use phishing through social media and email. They will trick you to open links or attachments. When you do, a malicious software will be installed on your device and the hacker will gather as much data as they can.

5. Auction shopping and online shopping

Many scammers use legitimate selling platforms to scam people. Typically, they offer several products and they will convince you to avail them. But before they deliver, they will require you to give money upfront or to key in your bank account details, usually outside the selling platform. When they get what they want, they either deliver an inferior item, a faulty item, or nothing at all. This is what online sellers call nowadays bogus sellers.

6. Banking and credit card scams

One strategy where scammers can exploit money from you is hacking your bank account. Typically, they will send you an e-mail or text, saying that there are anomalies in your bank account. They can even call you, pretending to be professionals and agents of your bank. These scammers will make you feel the urgency of the situation. And to fix this, you will need to disclose your name, phone number, and bank details for "verification." When they get enough information, it is enough to duplicate copies of your ATM card and exploit your account.

Another way that scammers can get your bank details is by putting a discreet attachment like cameras to ATMs or EFTPOS machines. This way, they can capture your account details, including your pin and CVV. When this happens, they can use your account for online purchases and other transactions.

7. Small business scams

Next on the list is using small business scams to extort money from people using small businesses. Scammers usually issue fake listings and products for free to trick you into signing up. Little do you know that there is a hidden subscription in the fine print. You may not be paying for the main product, but they will make you pay for the other items associated with the "free" product.

An example of this is scammers offering an application for free. But once you avail, they will get you to pay for monthly serial codes.

Another modus that scammers use is pretending to be small business owners. They will entice you to sign up to their website for free to enjoy freebies, updates, and prizes. Some will even initiate raffles just to get you to disclose your personal information. When you do, they will claim that you ordered products from them and they will make you pay for it. If you hesitate, they will threaten to sue you or report you to the authorities. This is why many people are scammed by these people.

8. Employment scams

This scam is very common among third world and developing countries because scammers will disguise themselves as employment agents. Seeing the difficulty of landing a job in some areas, many people are desperate in trusting these opportunities. These scammers will offer a job with a high salary. They even promise opportunities to work overseas on one condition. You need to give upfront payments for training, software, uniforms, service fees, clearances, and many more.

Be wary of these scams as they can present themselves legally and enticingly.

9. Gambling scams

This is much like small business scams, but they offer investment in real estate stocks, or foreign currency trading. Some will even offer lottery tickets, betting in horse races, and other sports events. They will claim to be professionals who can handle your investments strategically. But once you give them your money, you'll soon find that the people or the company does not exist at all.

10. Charity scams

Charity or medical scams are the most common on social media because it is the easiest way to convince people. The scammers will make up stories that they or their families are sick, and they need medical assistance. Other times, they can use other people's identities, real sick people and collect money for a cause. At the end of the day, the ill do not receive the donations but the scammers.

Lying online has become easier, don't you think? Especially with the lack of guidance, people can fall for these tricks easily. This is why it is important to learn when to trust people and how to detect online liars.

According to law enforcers, there are signs when scammers are trying to phish personal information to commit fraud or theft. Be vigilant when you observe the following signs:

Scammers will attempt to communicate with you with a sense of urgency, especially when committing bank theft, identity theft, or small business scams. You will receive an e-mail or a text. Some even receive phone calls out of the blue. They will ask your name and address, along with your bank account number to verify your information. Usually, these messages are poorly written, or they contain grammatical errors. Often, they also do not use the correct symbols and format as formal companies would use. Some of the main headlines or content they use include:

"Your mailbox has been hacked!"

"Your Facebook account has been compromised!"

"There have been unusual transactions using your account. Verify it's you."

Some victims also reported to receive pop-ups on their phones or computers, asking if they wanted to allow a specific software to run. If you receive these notifications but did not download any new application, you need to be wary.

How do you know if your accounts have already been compromised? First, you're unable to log into your accounts or someone logged in from an unusual location. You will notice unusual conversations or activities in your account. Your money will also go missing from your bank account. Often, your credit card will reach its limit, so it keeps getting declined.

Another sign of being compromised is financial institutions refuse to give you service because your credit score is low or because you already have a criminal record. In turn, you will receive bills and invoices for goods or services you didn't purchase. People will also start contacting you because they believe that they have been dealing with you. But in reality, someone has been using your identity to interact with them.

Seeing how dangerous and verifying scams are, it is important to protect yourself. As much as possible, do not pull them suspicious emails or texts, even when they have a sense of urgency. Delete these immediately to keep yourself safe.

When someone calls and they claim to be representatives of your bank account, do not disclose any personal information. Some will even pretend to be friends with your family members. They will make up a story saying that your brother, sister, spouse, or parent is in the hospital and in dire need of financial help. Before you believe any of these calls, verify it with the specific people or company.

It's also important to decline whenever you're being asked to download a suspicious file or to click on a suspicious link. Delete these immediately to prevent scammers from hacking your devices.

Another important way to protect yourself against scams is to choose strong passwords. Many people take this precautionary measure for granted. They usually claim that they have no money to offer anyway, so why make their passwords difficult to remember? In most cases, hackers who want to commit identity theft will choose accounts with the easiest passwords. So, even if you don't have money to offer, they can steal your identity and use it to commit fraud.

Law enforcement agencies warn people never to use names or birthdays as passwords. It's also important to mix complex characters such as capital letters and numbers. This way, it almost impossible to guess.

Another technique to prevent scams and hacks is to secure your networks and devices with reliable antivirus and firewall software. As much as possible, do not connect to public servers or Wi-Fi hot spots when trying to access personal information such as bank details.

How to Assess Lies in Texts and E-mails

According to a recent study, workers receive an average of 121 emails a day. With this number, some emails are phishing strategies while others contain fake news.

Hackers and scammers are cunning and highly deceiving. So, even if they appear to be legitimate companies and professionals in texts or emails, you still need to be vigilant before clicking on any links or disclosing any information. Luckily, there are signs that can give you clues as to when a person is being truthful or not. In a recent study performed in Austin, Texas, the researchers found that it is possible to predict lies based on phrases and sentence constructions. How? Here are major red flags:

1. Lack of first-person pronouns

When people are being truthful, chances are they will use first-person pronouns such as I, me, we, and us. One way you can assess when an e-mail or a text is a scam is too much use of second-person pronouns like 'you,' and third-person pronouns such as him, her, it, they, and many more. Researchers have proven that this is a common pattern across chronic liars. In their studies, they ran e-mails filled with lies on a lie-detecting software program. And they found out that 67% of e-mails using second and third-person pronouns consisted of lies.

When people use "you" too much, it is a strategy to give a sense of urgency. This will pique your interest, making you feel as if you are missing out. But as you read through the text or e-mail, you do not see them talking much about themselves and what they can do for you. Chances are, they also lack a concise but thorough introduction about their company. This gives you the idea that they do not have enough details to support their offer.

Also, when people use too many third-person pronouns, this could be a strategy to absolve themselves from the responsibility. It is a trick to get you to blame others just in case the transaction goes wrong.

2. Use of present tense

It has been proven that when liars fabricate information, they rehearse their stories in the present tense. It helps them believe in the characters they create, and it allows their minds to believe in the lies they are about to say. After which, liars will translate their stories into past tense to make them look plausible to listeners and readers. It can even evoke emotion, especially to people who do not know how to determine deception.

But as you read their message, you can see inconsistencies in their writing. It's possible that there is an unnecessary combination of past and present tenses, which gives you the impression that it's all made up. This is proven and tested by psychologists when they found that deceptive people combine present tense with past tense. This is because their brains are making up information, it has no clear definition of whether an event happened in the past or the present. From here, you can see inconsistencies with how people tell stories personally or online.

Observe when people tell the truth, there is consistency in their verb tenses. You may observe them using present tense, but only when they describe how they feel about their experiences. This usually happens to people who were traumatized because they keep reliving the events as they tell the story.

3. The use of concrete information

When people tell the truth, the mind does not put much effort into remembering the details because it already happened. You can observe truthful people share their stories smoothly without delving in too much about the details. This means that they are more abstract in describing their experience.

But when a person is being untruthful, you can observe them disclosing every detail about the situation. This could make reading their stories more difficult because the details are cramped in their sentences or paragraphs. They even include information you don't need to know. It seems to them that the more information they disclose, the easier for you to believe them. But it's quite the opposite. You can see it in their writing when stories and information are not incorporated smoothly. It could mean that they are making things up.

In contrast, you also need to watch out when people disclose too little information. It could mean that they are not prepared for an interrogation or they know that if they tell you more, they can give themselves away.

4. They overemphasize trustworthiness

Ironically, when people add words or phrases that supposedly will make you trust them more, you shouldn't. It's a classic strategy used by liars to make them look convincing. Some of the most common phrases they say are as follows:

- To be honest
- To tell you the truth
- Believe me
- Let's be clear
- The fact is
- Truthfully

Chronic liars use these when they know that they are not as believable. They hope that by overemphasizing their truthfulness, they can convince you of their honesty. It works often, especially for people who do not know these signs.

5. Generalizing

Another common technique that chronic liars use to make people believe them is using general statements such as those starting with "I always" and "I never." These people want to cover their tracks as efficiently as possible. So, they want you to believe that they could never do anything they are accused of. These statements are too good to be true, considering that as humans, no one is perfect. Mistakes, mishaps, and accidents can happen so it's impossible to have a perfect track record.

If someone is being truthful, that person will own up to their mistakes. And they will not generalize their actions. Take a look at the statements below:

A. I've never cheated in my life.
B. I didn't cheat on this one.

Without experience and knowledge, you might think that person A is telling the truth. But no matter how good a person is, there is no such thing as a perfect track record. In this case, person B might just be telling the truth.

6. Deflecting and evading

The next technique you need to know is evading important questions. When interacting personally or online, asking questions is inevitable. And when a person is being truthful, he or she has no problem disclosing what you need to know, especially if it's a matter of urgency. Chronic liars, on the other hand, will avoid difficult questions. Some of the replies you might get include:

- Why do you want to know that?
- That's not important
- What are you talking about?
- Are you accusing me of something?

If people are hesitant to answer your questions, it could be a sign that they're not being truthful.

7. Getting defensive and attacking

Getting defensive is a normal reaction especially when you get blamed for something you didn't do. But it's a different story when you get defensive and attack the people questioning you. Many chronic liars resort to anger and frustration when they get confronted about their actions. They get overly emotional and they tend to make the interrogator look bad. Some of the common sentences or phrases they use are:

- Why don't you believe me?
- How can you doubt me?
- You're wasting my time
- You of all people should understand

Other times, these people will even mention names just to deflect the blame. But when asked why they did it, they make up stories that do not add up.

While these are the most common strategies liars use to get what they want, you should not rely on these red flags alone. Remember, these people are cunning and most of them are highly intelligent. They can upgrade and build new techniques just to get people to believe them.

So, even if they do not meet any of the criteria, it's still best to verify their message by knowing more about the company, the people, and the message. Thankfully, search engines are powerful tools. One-click, and you can find pertinent details about people. But if you do not see matching sources and information, it could be another sign that the person who sent you the text or e-mail is a scammer.

It also does not hurt to crossmatch the information found in their emails with legal files, interviews and direct quotes, including press releases. This will help you verify helpful pieces of information.

Look at the timestamps! The news they are telling you today may not even be updated, which is a major giveaway.

Now you know! Not everything you hear from people is the truth. Even when they seem emotional about the situation, it does not mean that they are being truthful. You still need to watch how they speak through their paralanguage and body language to avoid deception. Always find the nose! Remember Pinocchio? Whenever he lies, his nose grows. Every person has a "nose." This is the body part that acts differently when people lie. It could be their hands, eyes, or feet. That's why you need to find your baseline!

You also need to take into account the accuracy of the things you hear or read on the web. Even if people seem legit, you still need to cross-check information and emails for any sign of deception. You would not want to be the next victim of a scam.

Do you want more strategies to read people and assess when they are being truthful or not? Read on to the next chapter on speed-reading people and its importance. What do you think is speed-reading and how do you apply it in various situations?

Chapter 7 – Speed-Reading People

How to Read People

There are instances when we are caught off guard by people who mean us harm. We might not be in the mood, or we may feel depressed, or we're just too busy that we neglect to assess people's intentions. Because of this, there is a higher chance we believe what other people are saying, and so, we are easily deceived. This is one of the reasons why we need to learn how to speed-read people.

Speed-reading is a new revolutionary system for communicating. It allows people to instantly grasp other's intentions so one can tailor their approach towards them. Seeing how cunning liars these days are, they use other people's weaknesses to get people's attention and deceive them. They could use one's feelings of sadness, anger, love, and stress just to get people to believe them. Other times, liars also use urgency to deceive people. They could take advantage of one's workload or schedule to get what they want. In these situations, you're more focused on what you're feeling or doing at the moment without paying attention to others' intentions. Chances are, you might only focus on their tone or the movement of their eyes. You neglect to check some of the major giveaways, such as their hands, feet, paralanguage, and many more.

In this chapter, we will discuss how to improve your speed-reading ability further. This way, you can assess when someone is being truthful or not in a shorter period. With the ability to speed-read people, you can tailor your reactions faster, and you will no longer waste your time hearing reasons and propositions from deceivers.

Developing Your Speed-Reading

Almost everyone, at some point in our lives, has tried speed-reading people. Remember when you were a kid, and you were trying to assess if your mom or dad was in a good mood so you can ask for something? Or when you're looking at your teacher's face to see if he or she is likely to give a quiz or not? These are examples of speed-reading people. It is the process of assessing one's temperament, mood, or intentions by looking at their body language, paralanguage, and tone.

When you're trying to assess your parents, teachers, or bosses, you already have a baseline on what they look like when they feel happy or stressed based on experience. But it's a different story when you're dealing with strangers. You have no baseline for their body language and their tone. You may end up victimized by deceivers. Thankfully, experts created the Five C's of Body Language.

This concept consists of cautionary areas that you should consider before ascribing meaning to body language. Apart from the customary meanings of individual body language, you need to consider contexts, clusters, congruence, consistency, and culture. These will help you achieve more accurate information about other's feelings and intentions regardless of the body language they are showing. Let's look into these factors one by one.

1. Context

The first C, context, refers to the external environment. When a stranger walks to you, consider what is going on around you. Where are you located? What happened before that? Where was the person located? What were they doing? Who were they with? What can you infer from their interaction with other people? And what are the reactions of people around you? All of these will give you insight into one's intentions before their approach.

For example, if a person scratched their nose in a restaurant, it could mean that their nose is itchy. But if they do the same thing in court upon being asked a question, it could indicate that they're lying.

Another example is when a person keeps looking at their watch or the door. When they approach you, you already have an idea about what they might say. They are probably going to borrow your phone to call who he's waiting for. But if the same person does the same body language in a meeting, you can infer that they might be anxious or that they are eager to leave the room.

2. Clusters

The next C is cluster. This refers to the combination of body language. Instead of focusing on one act and ascribing a heavy meaning to it, consider looking for clusters to give you a more accurate read. Experts recommend looking for more than three body language signs when speed-reading people.

For example, when you see someone sweating, blinking rapidly, shifting weight from one foot to the other, fidgeting, or breathing heavily, you can infer that a person is anxious. But if you put a heavy meaning to only one or two body language, such as sweating or breathing heavily, you might infer that a person may only be tired.

3. Congruence

The next factor you need to consider is congruence. This refers to the correspondence of one's body movements. It means that what they say corresponds to their non-verbal cues. For example, if they say they are happy, their eyes, hands, and posture should show the same. If not, it could indicate that they're lying.

For this aspect, you need to review the meanings of each body language. This will give you a better understanding of others' feelings and intentions.

When you see one's body language and posture, you already have an idea about what others are feeling. However, if it is matched by a contradicting non-verbal cue coming from their arms, legs, plus facial expressions, it could indicate a different meaning. Let's take a look at some of the incongruent body language that people make that can give their feelings and thoughts away.

We already discussed the meaning of arm-crossing and leg-crossing. Now, if you match this with a closed spine position, it could indicate boredom, disinterest, and disconnection. This also connotes hostility which could discourage discussion. But if you match arm-crossing and leg-crossing with an open posture, it could assert dominance and authority. It could also mean concentration and thinking.

Putting your hands in your pockets is also a sign of a closed posture. It could mean that you are doubtful and that you lack confidence. Matched with an open posture, it could mean arrogance or over-confidence, which could either make or break your first impression with other people.

We also discussed how putting your hands at the front or at the back has different meanings. If you match it with a closed spine, it could mean submissiveness, guilt, respect, or anxiety. But if you match it with an open spine position, it can indicate authority and dominance.

They also discuss the meaning of fidgeting hands and legs. Its negative meaning could be exaggerated when you match it with a closed posture. It could mean that you're eager for the conversation to be over and that you have somewhere else to be.

Now let's pair up facial expressions with posture.

In the last chapter, we discussed eye gaze in which a person looks directly into your eyes while having a conversation. Normally, this would indicate that they're interested and are paying attention. However, when it is matched with a closed spine position, and the person is leaning towards you, it could be threatening and distracting. This is commonly used by con artists when they want to distract you from your thoughts. Instead of letting you think properly, they use this body language to distract you and hinder you from making a good decision. Conversely, if eye gazing is matched with an open spine position, it could mean that a person is undermining you or is feeling superior over you.

We also discussed blinking, which is a natural reflex of people. However, increased blinking could indicate anxiety or lying. But if it is matched by a closed spine position, it could mean that a person is tired or is guilty of something. But when he or she starts to lean towards you and blink at your profusely, it could mean mockery or ridicule.

The next is lip-biting which is usually a symbol of interest or flirting. But if it is matched with a closed posture, it could indicate doubt, guilt, or lack of self-confidence. If it is matched with an open posture, it could mean excitement or anticipation.

Another gesture is covering the mouth. Usually, this means that a person is in shock or is respectfully covering their cough or yawn. But if it is matched with a closed posture, it could indicate that a person may be in pain physically or emotionally. Conversely, if the person does this with an open position, it could indicate relief or joy.

We also discussed the meaning when a person places their hands on their hips. When this is matched with a closed position and the person is leaning towards you, it could be an attempt to hear you better when you're explaining or that person is trying to intimidate you more. However, if it is matched with an open posture, it could indicate that a person is showing that they are dominant and superior over you.

There are many other combinations you need to watch out for. This is why it is important to review the meanings of body language and other non-verbal cues.

4. Consistency

The fourth C you need to know when reading people's body language is consistency. It is important to look for patterns of behavior to create a baseline. For example, when you observe someone holding their head in their hands, you might think they're bored or sleepy. This usually happens in the classroom, and many teachers see this as a sign of disrespect. But as you get to know the student, you can see that this is just a way for them to concentrate on the discussion.

The same is true when you observe people who cross their arms often. At first, you may think that they have a closed mindset or that they are asserting dominance. But as you interact with them, you see that it is their habit.

5. Culture

The last but not the least factor to consider when speed-reading people is culture. We reiterated in the previous chapters that culture plays an important role in how one acts, speaks, and thinks. So, before you ascribe any meaning to someone's body language, understand their culture.

Techniques to Speed-Read People

Now that we have established the five factors that could affect the meaning of body language, we can now delve into five of the most effective techniques to speed-read people. Luckily, an FBI agent, LaRae Quy, was willing to share his secrets in speed-reading people after 23 years in service. According to him, learning how to read others will greatly affect how you deal with them. You can adapt your communication style to make sure your message is received in the best way possible.

Some of you might be thinking, "I don't have what it takes to become an interrogator, much less to figure out what someone is thinking in an instant." But according to our FBI agent, people do not need to be top-notch interrogators to figure out what's on others' minds. There will always be signs but you need to know what you're looking for. So here are his techniques for speed-reading people:

1. Creating a baseline
   The technique that they have been discussing since the beginning of the book is actually proven and tested by FBI agents. This is why before you read people, you need to have a clear picture of how they act when they're relaxed. This way, you can pinpoint changes in their behavior when the context changes.

2. Mirroring
   Everyone has mirror neurons. These are built-in monitors inside our brains that reflect what others are thinking or feeling. This is why when we see someone we like, we smile at each other to show our fondness. Conversely, when you see someone you hate, you will frown, and the person in front of you is likely to mimic your reaction.

   When you're trying to assess when someone is being truthful or not, use your mirror neurons. Try to smile at them. If they reciprocate your facial expression, it could mean that they're sincere and genuine. But if they don't reciprocate, it could mean that there is a disconnect or disinterest between you.

3. Identify the strong voice
Despite what people think, the most powerful person in the room is not always seated at the head of the table. They are the most confident people. Observe when you're in a conference room. The most confident and outspoken one catches your attention above all else, including the leader or the head of the company.

This could mean that the leader has a weaker personality and may not even be open to your suggestions. If you're trying to pitch in ideas, the best person to share this with is the most confident for the most powerful person in the room. While this person may not have the position of power, he or she has the people power which comes from the support of their colleagues. In most cases, this supersedes position power.

4. Observing how they walk
This may come as a shock but observing how people walk makes a difference in assessing what's on their mind. Consider their posture. Is their spine in a C-shaped position? If so, they might not be confident, or they might have a weaker personality. You can also observe that they lack a flowing motion. Meaning, their body language is limited and hidden so their movements look stiff and jerky. But if they embody an open posture, it means that they are confident, powerful, and have a strong personality.

If you're in a meeting or conference, watch out for people who embody a confident posture. It could mean that they have lots of ideas in mind, but they're just waiting for the right moment to speak up. If you're the head of the meeting, consider asking them direct questions to pique their mind and pull great ideas out into the open.

5. Pinpointing action words
According to FBI agents, words are the best way to get into someone's head. Words represent thoughts, so it would help to pinpoint action words or verbs to get clues about one's personality.

For example, your boss said, "We decided to merge."

From this statement, the action word is "decided." This single word could indicate that your boss is not impulsive, thinks things through, and weighs their choices. And the fact that they used "we" could mean that they are team-oriented.

Compare it to this statement: "We want to merge." From this statement, you can infer assertiveness and arrogance.

It may seem that these action words are just part of the sentence. Little do you know the difference it makes when interacting with other people.

6. Look for personality clues
Each of us have different personalities. You may think that these do not show at first glance. But in reality, a person is overflowing with clues that give away parts of their personality.

Posture alone will give you an insight into whether a person is introverted or extroverted. You can also derive someone's personality based on their makeup, clothing, hairdo,

207

phone case, bag, and many more. Although these are superficial signs, they can give you clues about the person you are dealing with.

7. Listen intently

The last but not the least technique you can use to speed-read people is listening intently. Consider what they say and how they say it. How fast and loud do they talk? Sometimes, when a person speaks loudly, it could mean that they want to catch your attention, to feel more important, or to emphasize or prove something. It could also be that they are anxious and shy. But often, it's how they are raised, or it's in their biology to have a loud voice.

But what about if a person talks too fast? It could mean that they are thinking too fast that they are trying to keep up with their thoughts. They feel that if they don't talk quickly, they might lose their train of thought. Another reason why people speak fast is nervousness and anxiety. Some people want the conversation to be over with. But sadly, it is at the expense of clarity and understanding.

These are only some of the proven and tested ways to speed-read people in various situations. But what about if a person is wearing a mask and wearing a thick coat or jacket. In this case, it's difficult to assess what's on other people's minds because you cannot see their facial expressions or their body gestures.

There is a trending meme where people claim to have mastered the fake smile underneath their masks. They can squint their eyes to show smiling and welcoming eyes but inside the mask, there is a frown. So, how do you determine when a person is being truthful or when they are being friendly or not? Here are some tips to speed-read people behind a mask.

1. Watch out for squinted eyes

When you see people squinting to show that they are smiling, watch the creases around their eyes. If a person is truly smiling, you can see wrinkles around the eyes. But if a person is merely squinting, you can see a smoother appearance around the eyes. This could mean that a person doesn't like you or doesn't like what's going on. It could also mean that they disagree with what you're saying.

2. Another sign is touching the neck.

This is a macro-activity that gives people away even if they're wearing masks or thick clothes. It could mean that they are struggling with something or that they are stressed and concerned about the situation.

If you see someone touching their neck dimple or the visible indentation at the front of the neck, it could mean that a person is distressed or insecure. If you notice this, try communicating with them with more empathy to help ease their anxiety.

3. Rubbing the chest.

This is another sign that a person is stressed or anxious. If a person is rubbing the upper part of their chest with a palm or their fingers, it could indicate concern or discomfort. It could also mean a lack of confidence.

4. Watch the brows

Since you can't see their lips, one way to assess when a person is welcoming or not is through their eyebrows. When someone arches their eyebrows, it means that they are happy to see you or that they are pleasantly surprised.

But if you see them raising one eyebrow, it could mean disinterest, discomfort, disbelief, or disapproval.

5. Tilted head

The last but not the least body language to check when someone's wearing a mask is head positioning. If people tilt their heads, it could mean that they are interested in what's going on and that they are fully present. It could also mean that they agree with what you're saying.

There are so many ways to speed-read people. The signs are already there. But you have to let your subconscious play its part. As we have discussed in the previous chapters, it is important to trust your gut. Even when there is no visible proof, chances are, your gut is correct.

So, even if you're not going to act on it, listen to what your instinct has to say. Because this means that your subconscious already did prior research about the person you are reading.

It is also important to sense emotional energy. This refers to the vied that people give off. Although there is no solid proof or outcome of this vibe, you can feel your body tingling with it. Feel your goosebumps, and don't shy them away. If you feel like your energy is being drained by a person, it signals you to break the connection.

Lastly, consider flashes of insight or "aha" moments. Stay alert of any sign and red flag. Don't discount them just because someone apologizes or makes it up to you. This includes their handshake, hug, or touch. They may claim it's accidental, but it might actually be giving you the information you need about that person. Speed-reading is so interesting, don't you think? You can use all of your senses, including your emotional radar. This leaves us to think, "Can you use your emotional intelligence to speed-read people? Read on to the next chapter about emotional intelligence, its importance, and how you can improve it.

Chapter 8 – Are You Emotionally Intelligent?

What Does it Mean to be Emotionally Intelligent?

When reading people's behavior and intentions, you are not only focusing on the physical movements they show. You also focus on the emotions they exude. This is the reason why you get "vibes" from other people. It is a manifestation of their feelings at that moment. Mostly, you can detect when a vibe is negative or positive. But you can never fully interpret what they mean unless you have emotional intelligence.

Emotional intelligence refers to the ability to recognize the emotions of oneself and other people. EQ also refers to one's ability to understand, use, and manage their emotions to relieve stress, communicate effectively, empathize with others, and overcome challenges. It is an important aspect of mankind that helps achieve goals career-wise, relationship-wise, and other personal aspects.

Besides, emotional intelligence also helps you connect with your emotions, put your intentions into action, and make educated choices about what matters to you. According to experts, emotional intelligence has four attributes:

1. **Self-Management**
   If one is emotionally intelligent, they can display self-management skills which is the ability to control impulsive feelings and behavior in any given situation. Self-control is a vital part of this because it makes people control their impulses and temperament even when they are faced with difficulties.

2. **Self-Awareness**
   Next is self-awareness, which is the process of acknowledging your weaknesses and strengths along with the strategies you can employ for improvement. With self-awareness, you also understand who you are, taking into account your personality, values, and principles. It helps you clarify your thoughts and intentions, allowing you to make sound decisions in taking a course of action.

3. **Social Awareness**
   Another attribute of emotional intelligence is social awareness. This entails showing empathy to other people. With social awareness, a person can understand other people's emotions, needs, concerns, and intentions. If you have this skill, it makes it easier for you to pick up emotional cues or "vibes" and interpret them accurately, which is one of the most important aspects of speed-reading.

4. **Relationship Management**
   The last but not the least attribute of emotional intelligence is relationship management. This is the ability to form mutually beneficial relationships with others. With this skill, you understand how to build and sustain positive relationships, connect effectively, empower and influence others, collaborate effectively, and resolve conflict.

Emotional intelligence should not be mistaken for positive traits such as calmness and motivation. These characteristics are only some of the traits that an emotionally intelligent person will exude. According to studies, emotional intelligence is a skill. It's an ability acquired over time due to one's age and experience. It allows people to be wiser in dealing with their emotions as they mature.

Many people discount emotional intelligence as an important aspect of achieving success. Most are too preoccupied with improving their intelligence quotient or IQ, and they neglect to enhance their ability to manage their emotions. But in real life, it doesn't matter how intelligent you are. What matters, in the end, is how you deal with people.

This is evident in the hiring and selection process in many organizations. Most companies hire people with high emotional quotients rather than those with high intelligent quotients. According to them, you can teach skill, but you cannot impart personality, which, to them, is very important in teamwork. This is but one of the advantages of having a high emotional IQ.

Aside from that, this ability can also help people excel in school and work. With emotional intelligence, you can easily deal with narcissistic and arrogant people and prevent them from getting under your skin.

With high EQ, a person can easily get along with others, giving them more opportunities to learn from the experiences of other people.

Another benefit of having a high EQ is physical health. Believe it or not, this skill can affect several diseases such as heart ailments, diabetes, and many more. The body and mind are a system. What affects one will reflect on the other. When someone is anxious, they can experience physiological manifestations such as butterflies in the stomach, sweating, and shaking. Conversely, when one is depressed, they also experience heartache. This is proven by doctors when they found that people with depression have uncommonly sticky platelets. This accelerates atherosclerosis or the hardening of arteries, which increases the chance of heart attack.

The inability to cope with stress is also correlated to diabetes. It's no surprise that people resort to binge eating whenever they're upset, stressed, or apprehended. Without exercise, this can lead to obesity, and over time, diabetes.

People with high emotional intelligence also have a lower risk of psychological disorders such as depression and anxiety. According to experts, prolonged stress and the inability to cope with it can lead to mental health issues. Without intervention, it could lead to severe disorders that cause dysfunctionality in someone's life.

Raising Your Emotional Intelligence

Seeing how important emotional intelligence is, it is your obligation to yourself to raise your EQ. Not only will this help you manage your emotions, but it will also allow you to break free from all your emotional and psychological limits that keep you from achieving your goals.

Luckily, psychologist Marc Brackett, the founder of Yale Center for Emotional Intelligence found that there are ways to increase one's emotional intelligence. He developed a system around the acronym RULER, which has been used in over 2000 schools worldwide to teach about emotional intelligence. Without further ado, here are five skills you need to practice now to improve your EQ:

Recognize

The first step to control your emotions is to recognize them. Many people make the mistake of ignoring their feelings and burying them deeply. Little do they know that this is merely a temporary solution to keep your emotions at bay. Over time, the emotions you bury will haunt you, and it will have a greater impact on your mental health.

It is important to recognize your emotions so you can face them head-on. If you're sad, angry, or frustrated, don't shy away from the situation. Instead, let them out. Acknowledge that they exist even if you don't know the reason for it. This will help you understand what the problem is so you can solve it from the roots.

If you're confused about your emotions, you can use the mood meter as recommended by Brackett. The Mood Meter can help you assess what you're feeling in the moment to give you insight into your problem.

Understand

The next step to achieve emotional intelligence is to understand your emotions. Ask yourself why you're feeling that way. What happened prior to your feelings? Who was involved in the situation? What memories do you remember that may have aggravated your feelings?

Understanding these causes will give you clues on how to address them. For example, someone said that you're irresponsible. Normally, you would not get offended by it because you don't usually care about what other people think. But all of a sudden, you feel so affected by it now. The first step is to recognize that you're feeling frustrated. Now, understand why. Who said it to you? When was the last time you were told you're irresponsible? Did anything happen today that set you off in a bad mood? Consider all of these factors to determine the root of your feelings so you can tackle them.

Label

It's not enough to identify and understand an emotion; we can also benefit from finding the appropriate words to express it. There are thousands of words in the English dictionary. Use them to label what you're feeling. It's not enough to say you're feeling stressed or frustrated. It's best to be as specific as possible. Instead of saying, "I feel frustrated," you can say, "I'm angry at the person who said I'm irresponsible."

Saying "frustrated" alone could mean other things. If you don't specify it, it could derail you from assessing the real problem and creating a solution for it.

Express

After putting a label on your feelings, it is important to express them. Although there are times when you cannot convey them right away, never neglect to express your emotions in your own way. You can talk to a friend, a colleague, or a family member. You can write it in your journal or paint it out. You can even watch drama to help you bring your emotions out. But if you plan to convey your emotions directly to the person who has wronged you, make sure you do it proactively and respectfully so you don't say or do things you might regret.

Regulate

The final emotional ability is figuring out how to deal with our emotions. Regulating our emotions entails coping with them in a way that helps you calm down and work your feelings out. This does not imply suppressing our emotions. Rather, regulation entails learning to embrace and manage them effectively. There are many ways to regulate emotion. You can sleep or take a nap. You can listen to music or play games. Your goal now is to go back to your normal emotional state and move on with your life.

Many make the mistake of jumping from R to R. Meaning upon recognizing, they immediately move forward to regulation. While this seems to be the healthiest route, it could have a tremendous impact on your emotional well-being. This means that you were unable to express your emotions properly. It also means that you were unable to identify the problem and create a solution for it. If this happens, your emotions will haunt you one day and may cause more challenging circumstances.

Now that you have learned how you can increase your emotional intelligence, let's see what describes people with high EQ. This will help you monitor your behavior and identify points for improvement.

9 Signs That You Have High Emotional Intelligence

Sign 1: Accountable

People with low emotional intelligence are often prone to making excuses. They blame others and their environment for their mistakes. These people do not take accountability for their actions which can only lead to unproductivity and demotivation.

Conversely, people with high EQ are eager to hear feedback—positive or negative. They take this constructively and use it to improve themselves.

Sign 2: Open-minded

Emotionally intelligent people are always open to suggestions. They do not shut people off. Chances are that these people will still listen out of respect to the speaker. Also, they are willing to change their minds and assimilate information, especially when they hear better ideas from other people.

Sign 3: Active listeners

The third characteristic that describes people with high emotional intelligence is being active listeners. When these people listen, they do it intently. They focus on understanding what is being said and the emotion that comes with it. As active listeners, emotionally intelligent people also know how to separate their biases and prevent them from clouding their judgment. This is why emotionally intelligent people make outstanding therapists, counselors, leaders, teachers, and businessmen. They take into account all verbal and non-verbal cues of their clients to give the best service to them.

Sign 4: Demonstrate Empathy

Empathy, or the ability to acknowledge and comprehend others' thoughts and emotions, allows you to communicate with others on a deeper level. Rather than passing judgment or assigning labels to others, you strive to see things from their perspective. Empathy does not always imply agreement with another person's viewpoint. Instead, it's about attempting to comprehend, which helps you form deeper, and more fulfilling bonds.

Sign 5: They don't sugarcoat the truth

Emotionally intelligent people can tell people the truth while considering other people's feelings. They know how to read non-verbal cues which could indicate if a person is in a bad or good mood. They also pick up on hints easily which allows them to determine the right time to tell people good or bad news. This way, they don't aggravate people's feelings which could lead to impulsive behavior.

Sign 6: They apologize

To be willing to say "I'm sorry" requires bravery and courage. It also displays modesty which is evident among emotionally intelligent people.

When they know they're wrong, people with high emotional intelligence don't waste time trying to prove they're right. Rather than making excuses, they deliver a straightforward and sincere apology to the people they wronged. And after the situation, they will learn from the experience and change for the better.

Sign 7: Forgive and forget

Holding a grudge is another effect of holding your feelings in and not expressing them. It's like carrying a ton of cement on your chest. It's heavy and difficult to bear. Often, non-forgiveness makes people do inappropriate things that could aggravate their problems.

People with high emotional intelligence know better. Instead of grudges, they learn to forgive and move on even without an apology. It's not that the person who wronged them is off the hook. The reason why they choose to forgive is to set themselves free from the burden of anger and frustration. This allows them to heal and move forward with their lives.

Sign 8: Desire to help others succeed and succeed for themselves

Some people try to bring everyone down so they can rise to the top. Emotionally intelligent people are different. They're the complete opposite of condescending people. Instead of pulling people down, their security allows them to push people up to help them achieve their goals. Emotionally intelligent people will even act as a beacon to motivate others to achieve their goals. They do not think about the rewards of their actions because to them, the best reward is the joy of helping and seeing others succeed.

Sign 9: Showing authenticity

In this day and age, many people need to belong even if it means sacrificing their principles and giving up the people who truly believe them. Emotionally intelligent people are different. They are secure about themselves, their values, and principles. These people are strong enough to stand alone, especially if it means upholding their principles and values. Belonging to a group

214

does not mean much to them, especially if it means changing their personality and discarding what they believe. Knowing how secure they are, they already form a support system consisting of people as emotionally intelligent as them.

Can you imagine becoming emotionally intelligent? This means you no longer have to put up with other people's negativities because you are mature enough to ignore them. With emotional intelligence, there is peace and tranquility. Rather than focusing on hate, anxiety, and anger, you will learn to let these feelings go and just focus on your goals. If you come to think of it, building emotional intelligence is one of the most vital ways to break free from the chains of society and finally transcend.

Apart from these benefits, emotional intelligence also helps you avoid being victimized by manipulators, liars, and condescending people. How? Read on to the next chapter.

Chapter 9 – Protecting Yourself Against Dark Influence and Manipulation

While emotional intelligence helps ward off manipulation, it does not stop people from trying their best to get what they want from you. No matter how much you try to avoid liars, scams, or deceivers, someone will always come your way to challenge your emotions by breaking them to make you their little puppet. This is why it is important to protect yourself against dark influence and manipulation.

How Does Dark Influence and Manipulation Work?

Dark psychology encompasses dark influence and manipulation. It is the science and art of mind control. This shouldn't be confused with psychology, which is the study of human behavior and is central to a person's thoughts, actions, and interactions. Dark psychology is a phenomenon by which people use motivation, persuasion, manipulation, and coercion to get what they want.

People who use dark influence attack others' mental and emotional states to get what they want. They seek imbalance of power, and they take advantage of people's weaknesses to get control, benefits, and privileges. The worst part about dark influence is it often happens in close relationships. This is because the manipulator already knows what drives the victim. They already know their weaknesses, so it's easy for them to manipulate their thoughts and feelings.

However, manipulation can also happen in casual relationships. It could be in the form of blackmailing, feigning ignorance or innocence, lying, denying, blaming, gaslighting, withholding information, isolating people, implicit threatening, and many more.

This leaves the question, "Are people born to be manipulators, or are they conditioned? This is yet again another question of nurture vs. nature. While we all know that nurture has a large impact on one's behavior, we shouldn't discount genetics. Research has already proven that there are biological anomalies within people with antisocial behaviors. This means that a person could be predisposed to grow up with destructive behaviors. And if this is matched with a hostile environment where a person needs to survive your manipulation, their tendency to display antisocial behaviors will be increased.

Psychologists have come up with the "Dark Triad." This consists of factors that can help authorities and doctors predict if a person has manipulative properties. Here are some of the indicators:

a. **Narcissism**
   Clinically diagnosed narcissistic people have inflated self-worth. They need to be validated for being superior. They want to be worshipped and adored. Whatever they want, they feel they are entitled to it and that people should give it to them no matter the expense. These people have no problem using dark psychology to get what they want. The worst part is these people seem so sweet and charming in the beginning. But as you trust them, you'll see how fast they can drain the life and resources out of you.

b. Machiavellianism

In psychology, this refers to a personality trait in which a person is focused on their needs above all else. This is why they are prepared to manipulate, deceive, and exploit others to get what they want.

c. Psychopathy

This is defined as a mental disorder wherein an individual manifests immoral and antisocial behavior. These people express extreme egocentricity. They don't follow norms and laws, and they are unable to establish meaningful relationships.

Sociopathy, on the other hand, is commonly interchanged with psychopathy. It is a trait that defines someone who is without conscience. It is a description of people who are hateful or hate-worthy.

To differentiate the two, sociopaths make it clear that they don't care what you feel. They behave angrily and impulsively. And when they do something wrong, they recognize it, but they rationalize their behavior. Sociopaths also cannot maintain regular work and family life. They find it difficult to form deep connections with people.

Psychopaths, on the other hand, pretend to care. However, they display cold-hearted behavior. They cannot recognize other people's distress, and they are likely to build shallow and fake relationships. These people maintain a normal life so they can cover any criminal activity. They can love people in their own way, but they still prioritize what they need and continue committing crimes and other immoral behaviors.

If you think these are the only people who can use dark manipulation, think again. Almost everyone around you can do it, especially those who you might idolize or admire. Examples of this are attorneys whose only goal is to win their case. Often, they resort to dark persuasion and manipulation to get what they want. Politicians also use dark psychology to get people to believe in them and to vote for them. Other examples include salespeople and public speakers who want to use their persuasion skills to get you to buy their products or believe what they are saying. Many people might deny this. But if they look closely at the lengths they are willing to go to get what they want, there's no doubt that at some point, they used dark psychology. This leaves the question what is going through their head when they manipulate? Is it intentional or unintentional? Let's find out.

A Peek into the Head of These Malicious People

There's no doubt that each of us has encountered a manipulative experience. It could be from a family member, a friend, a romantic partner, a colleague, or even a stranger. When we figure out that we were just manipulated or coerced, we feel angry and frustrated. Sometimes we blame ourselves for putting up with their behavior and for letting it go on for so long. This anger could lead to depression and anxiety, which, over time, can cause dysfunction in your life. One way to help you cope with the anger you are feeling is to understand what's happening within the mind of the manipulator. What were they thinking, and how is their brain wired?

Thinking about these questions, the most common answers are:

"because they are bad people..."

"some people are just like that..."

"because they are evil psychopaths..."

But if you fully analyze the situation, don't you think that they are victims too? Are they really evil or are they made to be evil? Earlier, we discussed the dark triad and the people who are more likely to display manipulative acts. This includes people with Narcissism, Machiavellianism, and Antisocial Personality Disorders. Let's look at the main causes of these psychological disorders.

Narcissism

Narcissistic personality disorder is a mental condition in which people have an inflated sense of importance. When you encounter these people, chances are, you judge them, and you avoid them. And with good reason! Because of their ruthless personality, they can manipulate you or insult you, which can only ruin your day. But have you ever asked yourself the root of narcissism? It could change how you view others with the disorder.

In one school of thought, psychologists believe that narcissism is a result of insecurity as a child. It could be that their parents didn't give them enough attention, so they compensated for this when they grew older. It's also possible that they grew up having nothing. As a child, they could be jealous of other kids for having fancy objects they couldn't have. And so, as adults, they prey on others' resources to get what they want.

In another theory, psychologists believe that narcissism is a product of abuse. Because of this, narcissism has become their defense mechanism to block out what hurts or what terrifies them. Over time, this narcissistic personality got the best of them and they ended up embodying it fully.

Because of these experiences, people with narcissistic personalities find it difficult to grasp the concepts of healthy relationships. To them, having relationships could only hurt them. So, before people can, they do it first. It's also possible that all their lives, having relationships is the only way they get through life. And because of the rewards, they no longer focus on the connections, only the shallow and materialistic aspects of partnership.

Machiavellianism

As discussed, Machiavellianism is a trait that describes people who are so focused on their own interests. Some of the signs that one has a Machiavellian personality are as follows:

- Focused on getting what they want
- Prioritizes money and power over relationships
- Comes across as confident
- They lie and deceive to get what they want
- They come across as aloof and difficult to get to know
- Low levels of empathy
- Lack of warmth in social interactions

When people come across Machiavellians, the first word that comes to mind is heartless because the above statements are what they see. But they don't know that people who have a high Machiavellianism trait are also:

- Lonely
- Possibly depressed
- Anxious
- Confused
- Insecure

Sometimes, people use Machiavellianism as a defense mechanism. Because they have been beaten up by life, they forget all the good things about it, such as love, companionship, and intimacy. These people may have been victims of extreme poverty, to the point where they had to fight tooth and nail for a piece of grain. It's also possible that they are victims of abuse as children. They adapted the Machiavellian mindset to protect themselves from people who can hurt them and prevent themselves from experiencing the hardships they experienced before. It's probably why they prioritize power and money, so they feel secure that they will never go poor again.

It's sad, really. These people make you think that they are strong and capable on the outside. But on the inside, they are as confused and lonely as anybody else. They crave attention and intimacy. But they're afraid that if they let their guards down, it could derail them from their plan. This gives them fear and apprehension. That's why they prefer being alone and disconnected from other people.

Psychopathy

The third and last aspect in the triad is psychopaths. They are the rule breakers of society. Yet, behind that tough exterior is a beaten person. Psychologists have proven that people who develop psychopathy have been exposed to dysfunctional environments as early as childhood. They may have been abused, neglected, or separated from their parents at an early age. This is why they did not have any guidance about the dos and don'ts of life.

Poor bonding with parents is also a common factor of psychopathy. It's possible that their parents have mental health issues of their own, or they have substance abuse problems that cause a disconnect between them and their children. Lastly, it could be that these children have unresolved traumas which continue to haunt them even as adults.

These causes do not justify the fact that what they're doing is wrong. However, it gives you an idea about where they are coming from. It could help alleviate the anger and frustration you're feeling. And instead of resorting to self-blame, you will realize that life can be cruel, and some could not cope as well as they should. No one can avoid these people. So, the best way to deal with manipulators is to develop a discerning eye.

Developing a Discerning Eye

There are several red flags to watch out for that indicate whether a person tends to manipulate you. Here are some of the most common signs that a person belongs to the Dark Triad:

1. *They take pleasure in other people's misfortune.*
   These people like to stir the pot. And when it goes badly for one person, they enjoy it. They like to see the drama and the commotion of people fighting. Sometimes, you can even see them enjoying hearing terrible news.

2. *They make you uncomfortable*
   Although there is no solid proof that they are a part of the dark triad, they give off this creepy and uncomfortable vibe. Listen to your gut. It's probably telling you to run as far away as you can.

3. *Being mean to animals*
   Psychologists have proven that mean and cruel people to animals are likely to belong to the dark triad.

4. *Using humor as an insult*
   When you get offended by it, they eventually say, "Relax, it's just a joke."

5. *They lie all the time*
   They scam people to get what they want. Plus, they use deception to hide who they truly are.

6. *They belittle your fears*
   They joke about your fears despite your strong feelings toward it. Instead of giving comfort, they will give you ridicule, and they make you feel stupid for feeling terrified.

7. *They don't feel guilt*
   Even if they know they are at fault, they do not care. You won't hear an apology from them.

8. *Lacks empathy*
   They don't feel for others' emotions. They don't care if you're sad or grieving. All you wanted to do was give them what they want.

9. *Being racist or sexist*

They believe that some people are more superior to others. And when others are victims of racism or sexism, they would blame the minorities and ridicule them.

10. *They need to be in control*

These people like to be in control of things. If not, they tend to react harshly and impulsively.

11. *They have a reputation*

You may already be hearing negative stories about them. Even when you don't want to judge, consider the truthfulness behind the story and watch your back.

12. *They believe that everything is about them*

Even when an event does not concern them, they make it a habit to butt in and try to turn the whole scene towards them.

13. *They're inconsistent*

You can observe them changing their statements, perspectives, and attitudes in an instant, especially when it helps them get what they want.

14. *They want you to prove yourself to them*

Another red flag that you need to watch out for is they want you to prove your loyalty to them. You can observe that some of the requests are too difficult and unreasonable. This may include choosing between your family or them. Despite doing the things they want, they continuously seek negativity. Hence, they have a reason to ask for more assurance from you.

15. *They make you defend yourself*

The last but not the least red flag is making you defend yourself. Even when they're not interested in your point of view, they want you to continue defending yourself. These people will listen to every word you say to look for mistakes and question you for them.

5 Ways to Protect Yourself

Seeing how exhausting it is to deal with manipulators and toxic people, it is important to learn how to protect yourself from them. Here are some of the ways:

1. **Avoid giving them the attention they want**

   This is a common solution, when you're dealing with narcissists. If you don't give them the attention they want, chances are, they will leave you alone. As much as possible, do not instigate and do not confront them no matter how irritating they are. These people don't know that they have a problem. Their brains are hardwired to think grandiosity. If you confront them, you will not get a healthy response. They will turn the situation around to make you look stupid or to make you feel awful.

2. **Cut your ties**

   If you observe that the person you're dealing with belongs to the dark triad, cut your ties immediately, or at the very least, keep your distance. Do not pretend that what they're doing is OK. There's nothing OK with manipulation and deception. If you're starting to feel toxicity or you suspect it, it's best to keep your distance. You can make up some reason why you need to go to work or home. You could also go with other people so they don't try to victimize you.

3. **Never let your guard down**

   These people can "smell" your fear and your weakness. So, if you suspect manipulation, never let your guard down. Do not tell them important details about your life. Once they fish for enough information, they will use it to manipulate you.

4. **Don't let them lie.**

   One of the techniques that people use when dealing with manipulators is to play along with the deception. They make it fun. However, not everyone can banter playfully with manipulators, especially if they have anxiety or if they are under a lot of stress.

   When you play along with a manipulator, make sure you don't get attached. These people can get so charming. Even when you think you're playing them, it might be the other way around.

5. **Ignore insults and negativity**

   Some manipulators use insult to get your attention, especially if it means creating drama. During these situations, remember that it's not the people talking, it's the demons inside them. Try to stay calm as much as possible because if you show anger or frustration, they will fuel it up and cause you more trouble.

6. **Beware of false kindness**

   Some people get deceived because they believe in the slightest change of perspective or attitude from these people. You can't blame them. Some people are hay wired to look at the positive side and hope that a person can change. It's not the same story to people who belong to the dark triad. These people do not even know that they have personality disorders. They don't care about their reputation. It's safe to say that they are callous. Spending a day with them will not change who they are. They need psychological treatment, in fact, a series of them, to help them change their perceptions in life. So, if they show you some kindness such as honesty or protection, don't believe them. This could be their modus to get you to trust them.

Manipulation does not only come from strangers. The most painful form of manipulation comes from your friends and loved ones. It might be difficult to be with them, but it's also difficult to keep your distance. But you need to remember to respect yourself enough to walk away. Dealing with manipulators can take a toll on your mental health. So, before they cause permanent damage, you need to choose yourself first and move on. Remember what Karl Marx said, there comes a time when you need to let go of pointless drama, and the people who create it. The best way to have a fulfilling life is to surround yourself with the people who truly love you and gives you the support and care you need.

Chapter 10 – More on People with Dark Personality

Manipulators and liars are not the only people with dark personalities. There are more people you need to worry about who are far worse than these people—criminals. These people include rapists, arsonists, thieves, and murderers, among others. They can do far worse than manipulators and liars. This is why it is essential to tell them apart from others. Criminal behavior is one of the most difficult topics to discuss because various factors affect the situation. But generally, a criminal act occurs when there is a motive, a means, and an opportunity.

Know Who You are Facing Against

According to research, there are specific criminal behaviors that lead offenders to push through with a crime. These are called risk factors or criminogenic needs. One way to understand criminal behavior is to understand criminogenic needs. These needs are traits associated with criminal thinking. It is also dynamically defined as the crime-producing factors that increase the risk of criminality.

But before we delve into criminogenic needs, it is important to understand the deeper root of criminality. Apart from environmental or external factors, psychologists believe that criminality can start with biology and genetics.

Biological risk factors are defined as anything that "impinges on the child from conception to birth." Parents who possess criminogenic needs can pass these traits to their children. According to psychologists, these genetic predispositions also play a role in shaping the environment. Genes influence how parents raise their children. In turn, genes affect the responses that children evoke to their external environment. It has also been found that genetics can define an individual's ability to control temperament, confidence, empathy, and impulsivity.

Let's move forward to criminogenic needs. As discussed, these are traits that a person possesses that lead to criminal behavior. And according to psychology, there are six criminogenic needs:

1. Antisocial values
   This refers to one's criminal thinking. It includes criminal rationalization, which makes people believe that their criminal behavior is justified. People who possess this trait usually blame others for negative behavior. They see nothing wrong with how they think or act. Hence, they show no remorse.

2. Criminal peers
   Another factor that can lead to criminal behavior is having criminal peers. This is not a surprise due to the influence of other people. If they see others who think and act like them, they feel like they belong. These criminal peers act like their support system, and it makes it okay for them to commit criminal acts.

3. Antisocial personality
   These traits involve atypical behavior prior to the age of 15. Some of these behaviors include running away, getting into fights, skipping school, possessing weapons, lying, stealing, and causing property damage.

4. Dysfunctional family
   Psychologists have proven that criminality's most common risk factor is lack of family support, financially or emotionally. If a person's family cannot solve problems and communicate effectively, this could affect how one thinks. It could make someone callous to survive.

5. Low self-control
   This refers to one's inability to control their impairment or impulsivity. These people do not plan or think before acting. Their mindset lies on "now" rather than the consequences later.

6. Substance abuse
   The last but not the least criminogenic need is substance abuse. This includes the use of drugs and alcohol that significantly affects how one engages in a productive lifestyle. Because of continuous usage, they could develop tolerance to the substance which will make them need more to become intoxicated. This abuse drives people to commit further acts of criminal activity.

Despite these criminogenic needs, there are times when people do not qualify for most of them. Yet, they still turn out to be criminals. Take Ted Bundy, for example, the notorious criminal who confessed to killing 30 women in 7 states between 1973 to 1978. He was an exemplary law student who built a relationship with Carole Ann Boone, his wife. People did not see him abuse drugs or alcohol. He was even-tempered with his wife, and he didn't even display antisocial behavior. This is why people never knew he was the murderer for all those years. He was a college-educated and charismatic man. People even describe him as very likable with a good sense of humor.

The only risk factor people may have noticed in his adulthood is his dysfunctional family. His grandmother suffered from depression and agoraphobia, while his grandfather had a raging temper. Archives report that Bundy may have experienced physical or psychological abuse from his grandfather, despite insisting that the two had a good relationship. Because of this, genetics could have played a role in Ted Bundy's behaviors.

After further studies, many of his relatives started to speak about Ted as a kid. Possibly because of trauma and abuse, he started acting strangely around his family. His aunt said that on one occasion, he found Ted placing knives near her as she sleeps. Also, when his mother remarried Johnnie in 1951, Ted was jealous of his mom's new relationship, so he started acting out. As he grew older, he learned to hide these predispositions well to cover his need to kill innocent women.

All of us want criminals to change and adopt a more productive life. Unfortunately, because of their experiences, they may not even have control of their actions. Believe it or not, many people want to change for the better, but they don't know where to start. For us civilians, the best way to deal with these people is to avoid them. But for the system, it's best to innovate more and more ways to identify risk factors of criminal behaviors as early as possible to prevent them before they happen.

Before a Pickpocket Gets to You

You can predict some criminals before they act on their impulses. This gives you a chance to fight or flight. But what about criminals you cannot predict, such as pickpockets? These people swoop in, penetrating your belongings and taking what's yours. Often it will take time before you figure out you're missing something. By that time, the criminal would have already gone. In this segment, let's delve into the minds of pickpockets—one of the most common issues faced by society. Knowing how they think and how they move will help you protect yourself from being victimized. So, how do pickpockets move, and how do you protect yourself from them?

Pickpocketing is one of the most widespread crimes in the world. It is one of the most common because there is a lower risk of getting caught than armed robbers and murderers. Skilled pickpockets can vanish into thin air. You never know where they are or if they're already behind you. They're as slick as foxes, and they make no commotion when they're in action. Believe it or not, a pickpocket down the street can make as much money as those who attempt bank robbery even without putting in much effort. This is why criminals find this an effective and easy way to get money. These people can take your money, gadgets, credit cards, and identification cards in one swoop. And there's little hope of getting them back. This is bad news for the rest of us. That's why we need to understand more about them to know how to stop them.

According to researchers, there are different levels of pickpocketing in the world. The lowest level consists of simple opportunists. They don't have specific or special techniques in the field, leaving them at risk of getting caught. They target easy people such as those with open bags and those sleeping on benches. The pickpocket simply positions themselves nearby and slowly reaches into the victim's bag. This can only be effective when there's no one else in the scene. But in a crowd, it could be difficult to perform.

A higher level of pickpocketing is targeting wallets. Most people keep their wallets in their side or back pockets. These are more difficult to grab because the person could feel the act. One technique that pickpockets use to grab someone's wallet is to make benign contact. They pretend to bump into you accidentally, so you're focused on the upper side of your body. You neglect to see their hands sliding into your pocket to swipe your wallet. They can cover their hands with their bag or a newspaper to avoid getting caught.

The same method applies in less crowded areas where pickpockets intentionally sandwich you between them. The stalling partner suddenly stops in front of the victim while the "pick" pretends to accidentally bump behind the victim. The stall will apologize to divert the focus of the victim as the "pick" swipes the wallet out.

How does this work?

In the movie "Now You See Me," they reiterated, "The closer you get, the less you see." This means that "magic" happens when people are distracted by something else.

As humans, we tend to focus on one thing and disregard other stimuli in the environment. Little do we know that the real commotion is displayed outside the distracting stimulus. This is how pickpockets take our valuables. And voila! Your belongings are gone without you knowing it.

In the pickpocketing world, all of them are actors. Some pretend to fight in the middle of the crowd while the other "picks" take advantage of the inattentive people. Pickpockets also use children's charm. They instruct kids to show you their toys while they sneak up from behind. Another common trick is intentionally spilling water on the victim's shirt and offering to wipe it off to establish contact and distraction.

The next trick in the book is using sexually appealing people; usually, a woman, to attract others. She will pretend to be drunk and will show affection to other people. Distracted by her sex appeal, the victim is unknowing that the woman is already lifting his wallet or watch. Another trick is "accidentally" dropping coins or papers to get people to help them. While the victim kneels, other members will attempt to steal their wallet.

The last but not the least scheme that pickpockets use is playing the victim. In a crowd, someone might say, "Somebody stole my wallet!" This makes people check if they still have their belongings with them. When they check their bags and pat their pockets, people just showed where their expensive items are, which makes the job of the pickpockets easier.

Seeing how cunning these people are, you need to protect yourself from "picks." One way is to make your valuables difficult to reach. If you are often in a crowded place, wear pants with zippered pockets. When you have a purse or backpack, always secure your belongings in the deepest and most hidden compartment. Better yet, get a money belt so it's difficult for people to take your money.

Another technique you can use is to have a dummy wallet and show it. This way, pickpockets will focus on getting the dummy wallet rather than your actual wallet. It's also important to look confident and secure. Pickpockets can sense confusion and distraction. When they see that you're a tourist, they will most likely target you. So, even when you're new to a place, act as if you belong, like you know where you are going. When you suspect people following you, get inside a secure establishment like a restaurant or a bank, even a police station and wait for them to disappear. You can even report it to the authorities for better protection.

No matter how prepared you are against pickpockets, you still need to be careful. You never know how cunning they can be. So, you always need to be vigilant anywhere you go.

Spotting a Person with Condescending Attitude

Apart from manipulators and criminals, you might also want to avoid people with condescending attitudes. These people need to feel superior among others. Hence, they display arrogance, pride, and hatefulness to other people. Believe it or not, interacting with these people can affect your well-being. Because they tend to degrade people around them, you may start to question yourself, your decisions, and you may experience low self-esteem. In the long run, it could lead to psychological disorders. This is why you need to identify condescending people and protect yourself from them.

Here are signs that people are condescending:

1. Being constantly late
    Everyone values their time, especially busy bees who want to stay productive throughout the day. One of the most common pet peeves of professionals is constantly waiting for people. To them, this means that the person does not respect their time. They could have been more productive. Instead, they end up waiting for other people.

    This is why being constantly late is a sign of having a condescending attitude. These people like to enter the room dramatically to catch attention. In return, they end up wasting people's time.

2. Interrupting others a lot
    This is another manifestation of a condescending attitude. They like interrupting others either to correct their grammar or their pronunciation. Other times, they butt in just to give their opinions, even if others have already stated it.

3. Believing they are better than others
    A classic form of condescending behavior is believing they are better than others. This makes them question others' abilities to accomplish tasks. It makes them take on responsibilities because they believe that if they don't do it, it's not going to be perfect.

4. They cannot accept their mistakes
    Condescending people do not like being corrected. Even when they know they are at fault, they don't want anyone telling them what to do or what to change. To them, giving criticisms and negative feedback about their behavior means stepping on their toes.

5. Believing their status is more important
    These people believe that their life has greater importance. They usually exaggerate their contributions to society so people will think highly of them. And when people share their experiences and achievements, condescending people make it a habit to degrade others' stories to keep their place at the top.

6. They always believe they can
    You can observe condescending people at work when they always say they "can" do it, even if they can't. This results in unproductivity and work errors that can cause losses and back lags.

7. Despising weak people
    When people admit their inability to accomplish some tasks, condescending people show disgust towards these people. Instead of showing empathy and helping others in need, they will give remarks about how that person should have learned more or trained better.

8. Inability to reflect
    These people find it difficult to look in the mirror and see themselves for who they really are. They cloud their perceptions towards themselves and fail to recognize their failures and weaknesses.

9. Loves being the center of attention

   These people also love being the center of attention. They never fail to turn others' heads even if it means irritating others. Condescending people like to interrupt conversations even if they are not a part of it. They are always late and when they enter the room, they make a scene. And when people are not paying attention to them, they get dramatic to capture people's eyes.

10. Considering everyone as threats or enemies

    Condescending people see everything as a competition. So, even when you're just trying to do your job, these people will see you as a threat. Sometimes, these people even believe that everyone is against them. This is why they seek assurance from others, and they destroy others before it happens to them.

Seeing how draining it is to be with a condescending person, here are strategies you can use to protect yourself from their selfish and egotistical ways.

Don't take it personally. The best way to deal with condescending people is to ignore them and not to take their words personally. This will give you more security, plus they are likely to leave you alone because you are not giving them the position or attention they want.

Call them out. When you're offended by an arrogant person, try calling them out professionally, like "That comment sounds offensive. Do you mind dropping the attitude?" Sometimes, when condescending people get called out, they get surprised that people can stand up to them. And when you can, they may no longer repeat the same mistake.

Neutralize your body language. No matter how irritating they can get, always maintain a neutral body language. This means avoid showing hostility through your facial expressions or behavior. If you do, this will show that arrogant person that they're succeeding. Instead, stand straight and take up your space. And as much as possible, hold your ground and do not shrink back in offense.

Be tactful. When a condescending person starts to attack you for giving criticism or feedback, try clarifying both your goals. You can address the issue by saying, "I want to make sure we're on the same page in improving our efforts to achieve goals. Because how you are acting right now is uncalled for." You can also assure them that you understand how it feels to hear a bad comment. You can say, "I understand how awful it might feel to get a bad review. But that's how we learn." When you put things in a professional tone, that person is more likely to respect you.

Change the subject. As discussed, these people like to be the center of attention. They like to interrupt people while talking, even if the conversation does not involve them. If this happens and they ramble about 'me, me, me,' feel free to change the subject. Direct the spotlight to someone else. Ask them about their achievements or their activities. This will throw the condescending person off and will likely leave you alone.

Keep distance. Perhaps the best way to deal with a condescending person is to avoid them. If they're already in the same room or conversation as you, minimize interacting with them. When they talk to you, just nod and smile. And if it fails, politely excuse yourself from the situation.

Recognize the Body Language of Aggressive Behavior

Despite avoiding these people and changing the subject, some of them can display aggression, which could lead to fights and injuries. This is why it is important to recognize the body language and other nonverbal cues of aggressive behavior so you can predict danger before it happens. Here are some of the most common cues that indicate aggression:

1. Chin up forehead back. You can observe condescending people put their chin high and look down their nose to feel superior. Sometimes, this could be a red flag that someone is willing to resort to aggression.
2. Four degrees. Another red flag is when a person starts to raise their voice. It could mean that they're starting to lose their temper and are starting to get impulsive. If people keep on provoking, this could lead to a physical fight.
3. Chin thrust. Also known as the jaw clench, this is the act of gritting your teeth and shoving the jaw towards people. When someone does this to you, they are threatening you. It is a nonverbal way of saying back away or else I'll hurt you.
4. Flaring nostrils. This happens when people fan the outer lobes of their noses, so they are as wide as possible. Biologically, when people dilate their noses, it allows more oxygen to enter the lungs. If a person is agitated, they must be filling their lungs to have enough energy to fight.
5. Pursed lips. When people are in tension, you can observe them pursing their lips. But when they are agitated, and they purse their lips, it's a way of saying, "That's the last straw!"
6. Chest puff. When a person is angry, the body gets as wide as possible to assert dominance and strength. It is a way of scaring their opponent to back off before something bad happens.
7. Pupil dilation. Although this is a difficult body language to catch, you still need to know this when you need it. According to experts, the eyes dilate to capture as many details from the environment as possible. This happens when a person is preparing for a fight. Their eyes dilate to see every weapon, every form of attack, and possible defense strategies.
8. Lowered eyebrows. This is the most common body language that shows aggression. Often, you can even see heads tilted downward. When it's matched with a long, hard stare, it could mean that a person can't wait to lay their hands on you.
9. Teeth-licking. According to experts, human teeth are a primitive weapon we use when we feel threatened. This is why you can observe teeth licking from people who are about to fight. Sometimes, people lick their teeth when their mouth is closed. So, you might see movement on the jaw area or the side of the face that pushes the cheeks and widen it.
10. Blading. Observe boxers in the ring. They use a blading stance in which their bodies turn away to cover their most vulnerable areas. They pull their leg and shoulder back so their

attacker can only access the side of the body. Blading does not only happen in a boxing arena. You can also observe it in real life when people are so agitated, they want to fight.

11. Another common sign of aggression is clenched fists. This indicates anger or dismissal. If you see people clenching their fists, observe how hard they do it because it indicates the severity of their anger.

12. Ocular Orbital tension. When people are doubtful, suspicious, curious, or angry, they narrow their eyes. It could mean that the person heard something offensive, so they tighten their eye muscles as a way of saying, "You did not just say that" or "Watch what you're saying." If the person continues to provoke, it could lead to a fight.

If you observe any of this body language, de-escalate the situation. As much as possible, do not mirror the aggressive body language. Keep your body relaxed and take a step back to give them the emotional space they need. It also helps to show your hands to say to them that you mean no harm non-verbally.

So, you see, manipulators are not the only people you should be worried about. Criminals and condescending people can affect your physical and emotional wellbeing. Remember to review these concepts from time to time as a reminder to protect yourself at all times. If you need any help managing these people, don't hesitate to seek professional guidance. These people can help you decide what to do when people start to affect your life.

Chapter 11 – How the World Sees You

Do You Really See Yourself When You Look in the Mirror?

As we discussed in the previous chapters, body language plays an important role in reading people, understanding what drives them, and predicting their actions. Now that you have learned how to interpret others' non-verbal cues, it's time to focus on your own.

Reading the past chapters, you may have wondered what body language and facial expressions you evoke to the world. You may also ask what posture you do in front of an audience.

Before you learn how to develop your body language, record yourself speaking using your phone or your camera. You can choose a speech on the web which is about three to five minutes long. For this exercise, you don't need to rehearse because it defeats the purpose of seeing the actual body language you evoke in a normal conversation or in public speaking. It would also be best not to use mirrors or phone screens. You should not see yourself while speaking to the camera. This way, you will not control how you act. When positioning the camera, make sure you can see your whole body. Position it front and center to get the best view of yourself while speaking.

After the activity, watch the video once or twice and check the following body languages that apply to you:

- I have a fairly serious expression.
- My body looks pretty still and tense.
- I lean back sometimes.
- I have a reserved posture.
- I seldom smile.
- I smile too much.
- I turn my head away sometimes.
- I often look down.
- I don't spread my eye contact to the audience.
- My hands have minimal movements.
- My hands fidget when I'm nervous
- My hands are clenched.
- My hands are folded
- My hands are in my pocket.
- My hands are rested behind me.
- I keep touching my face.
- My legs are crossed sometimes.
- My legs fidget when I'm nervous.
- I use "uh," "uhm," often.
- My voice is too soft.
- I talk too fast or slow.
- I can't understand some words I'm saying.

- There is no variation in my tone.

If you use any of this body language, don't worry! You're not alone. I, too, didn't know that there was a proper way to interact with people using body language. But with experience and practice, you can improve your public speaking ability and become an effective conduit of motivation and information.

Develop Your Body Language

There is no specific advice on how you can improve your body language due to individual differences. Our minds and bodies are hardwired differently, which is why there is no particular solution for each of us. You already know effective body language. What I can offer you now is tips on how you can tailor-fit the solution to prevent negative body language.

As discussed in the previous chapters, the body and mind are a system. What you feel inside will show on the outside, and it reflects on your body language. When your mind emancipates fear, anxiety, and tension, you will show negative body language. But if your mind is happy, excited, and confident, you will show positive body language. In my years of experience, how you engage with other people depends on your mindset. So, in this chapter, I will be giving you strategies for battling the negativities in your mind and exuding confidence in various situations.

Here are some techniques you can employ:

1. Know your topic.
It is a fact that when you know your topic well, you can increase your chances of delivering your message effectively. With research, you feel more knowledgeable. And if you are knowledgeable, you feel more powerful.

2. Know your audience.
Another important way to feel confident when engaging with people is to know your audience. Professional public speakers always ask the culture and age bracket of their audience all the time. This way, they can tailor their speech to match the interest of their listeners. You can also prevent dead air which could be one of the causes of anxiety. When you know your audience, you can make them relate to your illustrations. Even if there's silence, you can start a topic that they can relate to gather attention. You can use trending apps, movies, and songs. With these, you will observe how they are willing to learn more which gives you success in delivering your message

3. Getting organized.
The next technique to manage your anxiety is to get organized. Carefully plan what you need to say and the sequence of your thoughts. Also, don't forget to prepare the props you need for the presentation. This may include pens and paper, a laptop and projector, and a mic.

To keep yourself on track, use digital tools to engage your audience, such as PowerPoint presentations. Design them strategically to keep it informative and entertaining. It could help if you add movies or clips that can help you get your point across.

4. Practice.
Remember the negative body language you embody. With practice, you can be aware of these non-verbal cues to catch yourself before you show them.

5. Challenge your worries.
When people engage an audience, they might feel that they're not good enough, that people might ridicule them after the speech. These are yet again brought by anxiety, and it will show in your speech. This is why you need to challenge your thoughts as they come. In your thinking about not being good enough, ask yourself, "What makes you say that? You practiced for how many nights for this event. You can do it."

If you fear that you may be ridiculed after your speech, think that these words are like water off a duck's back. It means that any remark from these people will not affect you unless they are communicated as constructive feedback. In that case, take it positively and act on it for your improvement.

6. Allow yourself to make mistakes.
When you engage an audience, don't be afraid to commit mistakes. Even professional speakers commit mistakes all the time. Sometimes, they never know that they're doing something wrong until after the speech. Because of this, they may receive negative feedback. It could be frustrating at first. But if you look at it proactively, these comments are important to improve your public speaking abilities.

If you catch yourself making a mistake in front of an audience, approach it with humor. You'll be surprised how forgiving and understanding your audience can be. Your audience knows that you're human and that nobody's perfect. So, even if you commit mistakes, it's usually not a big deal to your audience. So, just play with it. Ease your mind. And focus on what is important—that is, getting your message across.

7. Visualize success.
In public speaking, the law of attraction works wonders in the success of an event. If you visualize success, chances are, you will have a more fulfilling result. It makes you trust the process and feel more confident. And even when you feel nervous or terrified on stage, visualizing success will help you push through these barriers. As a result, you can deliver an inspiring and motivating speech.

8. Reward yourself for your successes
When you accomplish a goal, big or small, it is important to reward yourself. This motivates the brain to keep pushing forward despite the challenges. For example, after you completed the activity to identify your body language, reward yourself with rest or food. This will train the brain that there is a prize for every achievement. Instead of feeling demotivated or embarrassed, rewarding trains your brain to move forward and move to the next task to receive another prize.

It does not matter if your goal is to practice, write your speech, or deliver your speech. It would help if you rewarded your brain to fuel that drive towards success.

9. Deep breathing.

When you feel anxious or terrified, deep breathing is one of the best ways to lower stress in the body. When you inhale deeply, it sends a message to your brain, commanding it to calm down and relax. With practice, you can control your reactions to specific situations and exude confidence to mask the tension you're feeling.

10. Get support.

If you continue to doubt your skills in public speaking, one way to get better is by joining support groups. Some organizations offer public speaking classes and workshops that can help you improve verbal and non-verbal communication.

In these groups, you can see that you're not alone. You can share your fears and weaknesses to get assurance from people. You can learn better approaches to save yourself from blacking out when you make a mistake. Besides that, you will also learn how to deal with hecklers and establish rapport with your audience.

11. Get enough rest.

The last but not the least strategy to improve your confidence while engaging with people is to get enough rest. This is a proven and tested method to relax and energize the brain to prepare it for the event. If a person is well-rested, you can observe more confidence. You can feel them exude a lively and positive vibe. This is because sleeping normalizes the hormones in your body that affect how you act and react. These include the following:

Endorphins. These are hormones released by your glands that help relieve stress and pain.

Serotonin. Also known as the happy hormone, serotonin is the key to organize your mood and promote feelings of happiness It also enables brain cells and other nervous system cells to communicate with each other efficiently.

Cortisol. Sleep also normalizes cortisol in the body, also known as the stress hormone. With balance, you can reduce feelings of anxiety and apprehension which can help you achieve success when dealing with a crowd.

What if You Have an RBF?

I know what you might be thinking right now. What if I have a resting bitch face? Don't worry! I have some tricks to improve it. But first, let's discuss the psychology of RBF or resting Bitch face.

RBF is a cultural advent that describes a facial expression conveying a particular mix of judgment, boredom, and irritation. The worst part is people have no idea that they have the face. They don't even know that they are warding people off because of the ingrained expression on their faces. Because of this, others think they are unapproachable and mean. This can affect how one builds relationships and rapport with people.

Unfortunately, researchers still have no idea about the cause of RBF. Some say that it is just how their face is formed. Others, however, claim that it is a learned trait to ward off unwanted people. But because they do it often, they embodied the face and made it a habit. Whatever the case is, you need to learn how to manage your resting bitch face to look more approachable, especially when dealing with clients, customers, and listeners. Here are some techniques:

1. When looking at someone, look up at them. Raise your head, so your eyes look more open and less intimidating.
2. You can also use makeup to reshape downcast eyes. You can use eyeliner and eye shadow to draw more attention to your upper eyes and make them look welcoming.
3. Another technique is replacing that frown with a small smile. It would help if you exercise the muscles around your mouth. Smile in front of the mirror for 20 seconds when you wake in the morning and before you sleep at night. This accustoms your muscles to this behavior, so you can display it in public like it's your nature.
4. Use the eyebrow flash. When you arch your brows upward, it is a non-verbal way of saying, "Hi! I recognize you, and I'm friendly." This makes you exude a warmer and more welcoming vibe.
5. You can also try accessorizing and wearing brighter clothing. This can help counteract your unapproachable face and allows your body to exude liveliness

Once you apply the strategies, try re-recording yourself with the same speech. You should observe a major difference in how you hold yourself in front of the camera. Remember practice, practice, practice. Even when it feels difficult and challenging, break free from your limits and keep moving forward.

Don't Let Anything Give You Away

Aside from delivering speeches, you can also use the techniques above when interacting in other situations like debates, arguments, or meetings, professional or casual ones. During these times, you cannot avoid dealing with condescending people. Knowing how they act, expect to be ridiculed, provoked, agitated, and insulted. Despite this, you need to keep your composure and focus on what matters. Because if you let them get under your skin, they could turn the situation around and make you seem like the unprofessional one.

So how do you deal with condescending people in social interactions without losing your calm composure?

One technique you can use is putting up a poker face. This is an effective way to maintain an emotionless, apathetic demeanor, especially when dealing with arrogant and narcissistic people. Once you master the poker face, people cannot affect how you respond to the whole situation. You control what you say and what you do despite the agitation that people cause. This is important to maintain a neutral demeanor that shows people that you can be professional despite the challenges presented to you. This will also shed light on the real instigator so the head of the meeting can call them out.

So, how do you present a poker face? Here are some techniques.

1. Maintain neutral body language.
   This means avoiding any negative cues that may give you away. No matter how much you want to roll your eyes, don't do it. The instigator will notice it and add more flair to the situation. When you're being agitated in a meeting, relax your face. Don't give a snark, a smile, or a frown.

   You also need to watch your hands and legs. As usual, do not cross them and do not clench your fists. If there's a table, it's important to show your hands to make people feel that you can still trust them. If you have a pen, hold onto it. It could help control any hand twitches that could give you away.

2. Keep blinking.
   Often, when people hear surprising news, they neglect to blink. Don't make the same mistake. Catch yourself when you're not blinking and blink normally as if you heard nothing.

3. Look away.
   When difficult people face you, direct your eyes to another subject to allow your brain to process the situation and gather your composure. If the instigator requires to be looked eye to eye, focus your sight on their forehead. This way, you can hide any sudden movement of the eyes that can give you away.

4. Bite your tongue. Even if you feel like speaking up when it's not your turn, don't do it. If you have pent-up feelings or thoughts, there is a great tendency that you'll spill them like tea. There can be incoherence, and you may not deliver your message effectively, which can only confuse your audience. Instead, bite your tongue. It shouldn't be too hard, so it bleeds. But bite it strong enough to remind yourself to keep your cool.

5. Always stay the positive route.
   When everything gets too overwhelming or if you need to respond, always take the positive route. Even when you feel like you've been beaten down or when you feel agitated, always exude a level of positivity. Don't forget to smile, acknowledge others' opinions, and say 'thank you.'

   In the eyes of your bosses and other experts, this is a form of professionalism. It gives them the impression that you take criticism and feedback constructively. It also says a lot of things about your personality. Other people can infer that you have a high tolerance for condescending people, and you like taking the high road rather than stooping to their level. So, even if you feel hurt or degraded, you still win the battle because now, your boss trusts you and is confident about you. This means the plan of the instigator did not work.

There you have it! These are some of the most common techniques to alleviate anxiety and promote positive body language. With practice, you can exude positivity and confidence that can help you succeed in your presentations, meetings, promotions, debates, and many more. With these strategies, you can ignore hecklers and maintain a professional composure no matter how challenging the situation is. In time, you will observe that learning to control your body language works wonders. It can help you succeed in all the facets of your life.

Chapter 12 – Using Body Language to Become the Person You Want to Be

Body language is critical in communication. The right gestures and behavior during a conversation will help you get your message across more efficiently than words. Studies show that 60-90% of all communication is non-verbal.

The way you present yourself for the first few minutes is critical in making a lasting impression. Here are some techniques in mastering the art of body language to help you become the person you want to be.

The Best Kind of Handshake
Different countries have varying greeting customs. But a handshake is internationally recognized as the standard formal greeting gesture. Unbeknownst to some people, this practice has been around since the 5th Century BC in Greece. It was a gesture indicating peaceful intentions as it shows that both people do not carry weapons in their hands.

Much has changed over the years, but the handshake was passed down to this modern era. Today, most job interviews and business meetings start with a handshake. It has even become a gauge for initially assessing a person's character and personality. As well as a symbolic seal of a deal, promise, or commitment. Hence, the importance of having a good handshake.

These are the best handshakes that convey a positive personality:

Equality Handshake

Though some people mistakenly believe that a strong handshake conveys a strong personality, it does not. It only presents you as dominant and authoritative. Another form of the dominant handshake is a palm-down thrust with the other person's palm facing up. During job interviews and business negotiations, this is certainly not what you would want to project.

When shaking a person's hand, it's always good to express equality as it shows respect and encourages trust. In a proper handshake, both person's hands should be vertical. Modulate the pressure of your grip to match the other person's grip.

Double Handler Handshake

The double handler handshake is also known as the politician's handshake. It is a powerful handshake that conveys sincerity and a strong bond. This involves placing the left hand over the right and cupping the clasped hands.

This handshake can be used when you find yourself on the other end of a dominant handshake. When a person offers you a palm-down thrust, respond with a palm-up handshake. Then, use your other hand to clasp and straighten your palms vertically.

This also works for a bone breaker and lingering handshakes. By clasping your other hand over the handshake, you are signaling the other person to let go of your hand.

It is important to know that handshaking is more than just handshaking. The perfect handshake must be accompanied by these elements:

Eye Contact

Handshake extends to the eyes. Looking at the person in the eyes conveys passion, respect, and sincerity. Eye contact is said to activate the secretion of oxytocin or what is otherwise known as the love hormone. This hormone gives people the feeling of well-being and connection. Making eye contact during a handshake, lays out the foundation of rapport between two people.

Firm Grip

A firm grip shows confidence and strength. A firm grip involves moderate pressure and an unrushed clasp. A hasty handshake can appear disrespectful. Clasp the other person's hand with your fingers and lock your thumbs with theirs.

Moderate Shake

A good handshake can go up to three small pumps. Beyond that will make you look overly excited. Release the person's hand after the shake. A lingering handshake can be very awkward especially if it's with a person you are not close with. You also have to remember that shaking doesn't mean yanking. Do not pull or yank the person's hand. Shake it up and down by lifting your hands by the elbows.

Verbal Introduction

Use words in conjunction with the handshake. Introduce yourself and offer a greeting. This will further give the impression of confidence. You can say a few compliments but do not gush over the person so as not to make them uncomfortable. Remember the person's name and use it when addressing them. This shows that you care and projects a positive impression.

A good confident handshake can be achieved with constant practice. You can rehearse shaking hands with some friends and family and asking them what their impressions are based on the handshake.

Does Mirroring Work?

The human brain is hardwired to mirror the behavior of people we like in what is called limbic synchrony. As early as infancy, babies' heartbeats tend to synchronize with the person they are closest to—their mothers. This is why children often mimic the behavior of people around them and establish connections with body movements.

Mirroring was first discovered in the early 90s by a group of researchers in Italy. Oddly enough, they were studying macaque monkeys. According to accounts, one researcher was reaching for his food when he noticed that some neurons of the monkey fired up. The monkey's brain is unable to differentiate between doing it and seeing it be done. This is when they accidentally stumbled on what was later called the mirror neurons.

Most of the time we are unaware that we are mirroring people we like or are attracted to. And in the same way, we unconsciously gravitate towards someone that mirrors our behavior. Mirroring has proven to be a very effective tool when you want to influence someone. For the past decades, politicians and businessmen have recognized the value of mirroring behavior. This is also true in dating, men and women are likely to mirror the actions of a person they are interested in.

If done correctly, mirroring can be a powerful persuasive technique. Let's take a look at some tips to help you use the mirroring technique to your advantage.

Nonverbal Mirroring

The first thing to do is to establish a foundation for rapport by starting with what is called fronting. Face the other person squarely whether you are standing or sitting. Positioning your body towards them shows that you are giving them your full attention.

Next is eye contact. It's an effective technique in establishing a connection. This is backed up by science. According to one study, making eye contact releases oxytocin which is necessary for forming social bonds. But it can be very tricky; too much eye contact can make the other person feel awkward.

Another essential nonverbal element that is useful in the mirroring technique is the triple nod. Try slowly nodding three times and tilting your head when a person is speaking. People like to be listened to. This does not only show that you are agreeing with what they are saying but you are also conveying empathy towards their feelings. This makes them feel understood on a deeper level and more likely to feel warm towards you.

After establishing a connection, mirror their body language, gesture, and even facial expression. Cross your legs when the other person crosses their legs. Some people constantly raise their eyebrows or gesture with their hands when making a point. Copy their gestures but do not be too obvious otherwise it will backfire on you. You must also remember to steer away from mirroring negative body language like folding the arms and looking away. Reflect only actions that convey interest and positive energy toward the person you are talking to.

Vocal Mirroring

Mirroring is much more than just copying physical actions. It extends to mimicking all nonverbal aspects. Have you ever noticed two close friends who are talking to each other? The tone, pitch, speed, and volume of their voices gradually mimic each other. This phenomenon is called phonetic convergence.

Match the cadence of the person's speech. Vocal cadence is the rhythm or flow of a person's speech. A person's cadence is unique and can be affected by what they are feeling at that moment. They can speak slowly, monotonously, soothingly, excitedly, or animatedly. By mimicking a person's vocal pace and volume, you also mirror their emotions which makes you more likable.

Again, the mimicry should be subtle. Do not ever try to copy the person's accent. This can be very disastrous and appear insulting when done incorrectly.

Verbal Mirroring

Research shows that waitresses and salespeople who repeat the customer's words get a higher tip and close more deals. People have certain words and phrases that they use too often. When talking to a person try listening to slang and quotes that they like to repeat and integrate these into your speech. To avoid being obvious, you can rephrase.

You can test if a person has warmed up to your mirroring technique by checking if they mirror you back. Make an overt action that is unrelated to your conversation like scratching your nose and seeing if they copy you.

Mirroring is a function of the brain and has been proven to be an effective technique countless times. We are attracted to people who look and act like us. In the late '80s, one researcher suggested that couples who have been together for a long time tend to look alike over time. But an opposing theory has recently surfaced claiming that couple's faces do not gradually become similar. Instead, they have always been similar. The Similar/Attraction Theory posits a person will more likely be attracted to another person who has similar qualities than a person who does not.

7 Effective Ways to Show Your Confidence

Confidence is knowing and believing in yourself and your abilities. Confidence does not mean that you feel superior to other people. Instead, it's a feeling of security of knowing that you are capable of overcoming things and succeeding. It makes you feel ready for what life throws at you.

In work settings and relationship settings, confidence plays an important role. Confident people will stand out during job interviews and are more likely to land promotions. Confidence gives you more influence among your peers.

Some people grow up to be naturally timid and reserved, but it doesn't mean that they cannot learn to look and appear confident. Confidence is not a born trait. It is a skill that is learned over time through practice. Here are some ways to project confidence.

1. Assume a Confident Posture

Posture says a lot about a person. When a person sits slumped and hunched, it gives the perception of weakness, fear, and shame. But when a person stands tall and sits upright, they communicate a strong confident personality.

To assume a confident stance, align your legs with your shoulders. With both arms hanging loose on your sides or your hips. Relax your shoulders, lean back a little, and open up your chest. Slightly raise your chin. When sitting down, you can cross your legs and lean back on the backrest. Use the armrest if there are any or place both hands on your lap.

You should stand tall but not uncomfortably upright. Your posture should feel and look natural otherwise you will appear uptight and tense.

Face the person squarely and point your feet towards them. Doing this expresses interest which will make you feel rewarding to talk to. Refrain from actions that make other people think you have to go somewhere or wish that you are somewhere else.

2. Work on your Eye Contact

Eye contact goes a long way to show confidence and respect to the people you are interacting with. Avoiding eye contact can convey anxiety, shame, and doubt. For some people, making eye contact can be uncomfortable. To manage this, you can use the time-tested solution of focusing on the space between the person's eyebrows. Avoid focusing your gaze on a person's mouth, nose, or peculiar marks on their faces as this can be perceived as offensive.

3. Use Mirroring Technique

Mirroring can be key to connecting with people. Behaving and looking like them will increase the chances of acceptance and understanding between you. When the person is excited about something, it's good to match their energy and enthusiasm in the same subject. Copy their tone of voice and use similar words to what they use. Mirroring is an art that is accompanied by subtlety and if applied properly can greatly increase your influence over others.

4. Be conscious of Your Hands

The way you hold your hands can show the level of confidence you have. Wringing your hands makes you look nervous and anxious. Sticking them in your pockets shows you're reserved and doubtful. Crossing them over your chest or holding them over your belly projects defensiveness and discomfort.

To avoid negative perceptions, just let your arms hang naturally by your sides. If you are holding a phone or a bag, hold them at waist level. You can stick your thumbs in your pockets and let your other finger point downwards.

Hand gestures are also a critical part of body language. One of the most positively recognized hand gestures is the steeple hand gesture. Place your fingertips together to form a point. Spread your fingers and arch them to form the shape of a church steeple. It's a powerful gesture that shows commitment and sincerity to what you are saying.

Another hand gesture is the palms up or rogatory hand position. Here the person offers up their open palms as they speak. It gives people the impression of openness, compliance, humility, and cooperation. It is often used by politicians as a subtle way of saying, "My hands are clean" or "I am at your service".

When presenting, avoid pointing your index fingers. While this may show passion, it can often be offensive. Gesture and point with your palms instead. This way you appear more composed and poised.

5. Avoid Fidgeting

We all have that thing that we do when we're nervous. It can be tapping our fingers or feet, jingling coins in our pockets, or shifting our weight when seated and uncrossing and crossing our legs. These show a lack of confidence and can be very distracting to the person you are talking to.

For some people fidgeting has become a habit. To counter this, you must recognize your triggers and try to avoid them. Focus your mind on the conversation and task at hand.

6. Pay attention to your voice and facial expression

Study your facial expressions in the mirror. Look at what your normal face looks like and what it conveys. Some people have very stern faces that make them appear angry even if they aren't. Others have unsmiling faces that make them unapproachable. These make it hard for you to communicate your emotions effectively. Smiling and putting on a pleasant face will naturally make you sound pleasant, inviting, and confident.

The way you speak is as important as what you say. Avoid stammering and using fillers like "um" and "uh". Never use the question inflection. It makes you sound unsure. Speak with conviction and confidence. Let the words flow smoothly and look the person in the eyes while speaking.

7. Use Power poses

A decade ago, Amy Cuddy fueled the power pose craze. She claimed that assuming a superman or wonder woman pose for a few minutes increases your confidence. Her theory was that our body language affects what we think about ourselves and our abilities. Hence, by assuming a powerful stance we also feel more powerful.

Taking Full Control of Your Life

Life is so uncertain. No matter how much planning we do, it just doesn't go as planned. No matter how much work you put in, you just don't get to where you want to go. No matter how persistent we try to be, the world seems to just fling endless challenges in our direction. Like it doesn't want us to succeed—to be happy. This is when life becomes unfair and confusing. We start to lose a sense of what we are doing and where we are going.

Other times we feel like we make wrong decisions after wrong decisions and we lose confidence in our wisdom. So, we trust other people's opinions more than our own to be the right opinion. We start to believe that they know better than us because they made the right decisions with their lives.

We can see this in family settings where children are told that mothers always know what is best for their children. And while this may be true for some moms and younger kids, it's not always the case for everyone. Some of us grew up in a toxic family environment. We have family members who compete with us and do not want to see us succeed. The same goes for some friends and colleagues.

Accepting advice is a sign of maturity as we give recognition to the fact that we still have a lot to learn about life. But we should never entrust our lives with someone else. Though it might seem to be an easier option when we are faced with a dilemma, it also means relinquishing control of our lives. If we let this happen, our life is not ours but someone else's version of what our life should be. We are sacrificing our authenticity and individuality. We become drifters, alive but not living.

So how can we take back control?

Acceptance

First, you need to deal with the regret for the time that you lost. Come to peace with every wrong decision you made. Accept that not everything in life is predictable. Acceptance does not mean surrender. Resisting things that are out of your control will not change anything and will only hurt you more. Instead of trying to change the scenario, try changing how you deal with it. Change your attitude towards it and think of ways to make the best out of a bad situation.

Set your goals

Shift your focus to your needs by setting new goals. Visualize not just where you want your life to go but how it should be in the present. Prepare for the unexpected but focus on the things within your circle of influence. Your time is your most valuable asset. Use it for things that will benefit you and help you achieve your goals. Outlining your goals will enable you to direct your life where you want it to go, giving you a feeling of control.

Come Up with Alternative Plans

Planning should always include a contingency plan. And when possible, try to prevent situations that you don't want to happen. We have already established that not everything will go smoothly. Think of the worst-case scenario and deliberate all possible alternative actions. When you encounter a small failure, you usually decide and act on impulse and emotion. Having an alternative plan will help you deal with setbacks and help you get back on track.

Recognize your self-worth

We all need validation whether for our abilities or looks. When we fail to receive it from people we love and admire, it weakens our confidence and self-worth. People who truly care and love you will encourage your growth and self-esteem. Selfish and manipulative people will engage in withholding behavior. They will continually refuse to recognize your positive qualities.

To counter this, do not be reliant on others' validation. Recognize your self-worth. Believe in your abilities—in what you can do and what you can become. Encourage yourself. You are your own person. You are perfectly imperfect.

Create Your Moment

A lot of times, we feel trapped or out of control because of other people's actions or inaction. They can disagree with us and fail to see how we think certain things should be done. When you feel stuck in the same position for a long time, it's time to start thinking of ways to change the setting.

Take this work scenario for example. Penny has been working in a company for ten years and has applied for promotion many times, but her boss has appointed someone else every time. Penny begins to doubt her abilities which affects her self-esteem and self-worth.

Instead of being depressed. Penny can seek places where she will feel secure and appreciated. Penny can request a transfer to another department where there is a different boss and more opportunities. She can also start a small side business in which she feels passionate. Then she can quit her job, once the business is doing well.

Sometimes, we are not given the same opportunities as others. This is why we need to create and seize our moments.

Associate Selectively

It's important to remember that the people we associate with have a big influence on what we do and how we feel and act. Your life will become better and healthier if you surround yourself with positive and supportive people. Distance yourself from people who give you a negative feeling or make you act in opposition to your values. Disentangle yourself from toxic, one-sided, and limiting relationships.

Recent studies show that exposure to social media has a great impact on how we behave and view ourselves. People who interact on social media often reportedly feel more insecure, anxious, and jealous. Social media leads some people to feel depressed from comparing their lives with others. It lets people set an unachievable standard for how they should look and behave. Also, social media lets you project the best digital version of yourself. This can be good for expressing oneself, but it can foster negative feelings when a person realizes it's all just an illusion.

The bottom line is you should hang out with the right people and expose yourself to the right environment. This will greatly improve your mood, attitude, and outlook on life making you happier and more productive.

Conclusion

Dealing with narcissists, liars, manipulators, criminals, and condescending people is an inevitable part of life. So, if we cannot avoid them, the best thing to do is to protect ourselves from being victimized by them.

In this book, we discussed the effects of long-term manipulation and exposure to arrogant people. It can lead to self-doubt, anxiety, passivity, unproductivity, depression, shame, and guilt. Seeing how severe the consequences are, there is a need to learn how the body reacts and how it communicates. Understanding this will give you insight into interpreting one's body language. But then again, it is important to create your baseline before you start reading other people's non-verbal cues. This baseline will allow you to interpret body language more accurately. With this guide, you can identify the normal behavior and body language of people and spot sudden changes which could indicate lying or deception.

We also discussed how humans communicate verbally and non-verbally. In the past chapters, we tackled some of the strategies to improve verbal communication and nonverbal communication. Both of which are important to convey a message effectively to your audience. To give you a more detailed guide, we have discussed the types of non-verbal cues such as gestures, posture, proxemics, oculesics, and haptics. Studying these will help you interpret their meanings. Plus, it can help you understand what nonverbal cues are appropriate in specific situations. We also discussed how to avoid miscommunication. A huge factor of it is considering one's culture. Remember that body language which is common in your country may not be appropriate to others. This is why it is crucial to become culturally sensitive. It promotes respect and understanding among people despite their race and beliefs.

We also learned the different body languages and their specific indications. While ascribing meaning to individual body language can give you a hint about one's intentions, it would help if you read body language as a whole. This is why it is important to remember the concepts about posture and its impact. In this book, we also discussed open and closed posture which can tell you a lot about a person's intentions and personality.

Aside from posture, considering proxemics is also necessary to show respect to other people. As discussed, there are four main levels of distance that depend on the relationship of people. The closest distance is intimate distance which is shared by couples and spouses. The second level is personal distance shared by close friends and family. This is about 1.5 feet to 4 feet. The third level is social distance shared by acquaintances. And lastly, public distance is used in public speaking. Always remember to identify the relationship so you can determine the proper distance you need to maintain with the people you're interacting with.

After these topics, we also talked about liars, the types of liars, and their reasons for lying. Seeing how detrimental it is to be victimized by liars, it is important to remember the most common ways to spot a liar. Watch out when a person moves their head quickly and when their breathing starts to change. You can also observe that they blink more often, or they don't blink at all. These are only some of the signs that you may be dealing with a liar. Review these concepts from time to time to protect yourself from deception in your daily interactions.

Another important topic we discussed in this book is liars who hide behind their computer screens. Without knowledge about these people, you may become a victim of a scam, identity theft, and many more. Always remember how you can determine when a person is lying over the web or over the phone. This will help you ignore or take action against people who attempt to scam you.

The next enticing topic we discussed was speed-reading people. This is the process of gathering as much information about a person's intentions at first glance. Speed-reading is important to remember, especially when people try to take advantage of your feelings and hectic schedules. By learning how to speed-read people, you can already think about your reaction so you can act before you get victimized.

Since part of speed-reading is considering people's emotions, it's also important to become emotionally intelligent. This is one's ability to recognize and manage one's emotions. Many people discount the importance of EQ. Little do they know that this plays a role in the achievement of success. Aside from this, it also helps people achieve peace and true happiness in life. It also grants protection against people who try to instigate or cause any trouble.

We also discussed manipulation, its risk factors, and its determinants. These factors help you identify manipulators and manage them as soon as possible. Unfortunately, these are not the only people you need to deal with in your daily life. Some are criminals who can do far worse than manipulators while others are condescending people who try to demean you to feel more superior. Emotional intelligence, matched with the ability to discern warning signs, can help you avoid the damaging and detrimental actions these people may commit against you.

After you have learned how to read people's actions and predict their behavior before it happens, you also learned how to focus on your own body language and how to improve it. In this book, we discussed positive and negative body language that can affect your presentation and interaction with other people. In the latter part, we tackled how to monitor the body language you evoke to the world and how you improve it to make communication more effective. With practice and determination, you will observe that body language matched with high emotional intelligence can grant success in various aspects of life.

If you've been a victim of manipulation and you feel doubt, shame, and guilt, you now have an opportunity to do something with your life. Don't let yourself succumb to the toxicity of your relationships. Apply what you have learned and slowly break free from the chains that have been holding you back. Use this book as your weapon, as your guide to cutting ties from toxic people in building relationships with healthier ones. Let this be a beacon that gives you direction to the help you need so you can heal and slowly rise from the ashes. In no time, I guarantee you will become a more empowered individual. Now that you know what to do, it's time to make a move.

www.ingramcontent.com/pod-product-compliance
Lightning Source LLC
Chambersburg PA
CBHW052110020426
42335CB00021B/2706

* 9 7 8 1 9 7 0 1 8 2 5 7 6 *